E S T A T E   P U B L

G000139294

HAMPS

TOWN CENTRE MAPS

Street maps with index
Administrative Districts
Road Map with index
Postcodes

Scale of street plans: 4 Inches to 1 Mile (unless otherwise stated)

Motorway 'A' Road / Dual 'B' Road / Dual Minor Road / Dual Track Pedestrianized Railway / Station Footpath	Every effort has been made to verify the accuracy of information in this book but the publishers cannot accept responsibility for expense or loss caused by an error or omission. Information that will be of assistance to the user of the maps will be welcomed. The representation on these maps of a road, track or path is no evidence of the existence of a right of way.	Stream / River Lock Canal One-way Street Car Park Public Convenience Tourist Information Place of Worship Post Office

prepared and published by ESTATE PUBLICATIONS, Bridewell House, TENTERDEN, KENT.
The Publishers acknowledge the co-operation of the local authorities of towns represented in this atlas.

ISBN 1 84192 196 3

OTHER ATLASES IN THIS COUNTY

COUNTY RED BOOKS contain street maps for each town centre. The street atlases listed below are SUPER & LOCAL RED BOOKS, with comprehensive local covergae.

BASINGSTOKE & ANDOVER

including: Alton, Heath End, Kingsclere, Oakley, Overton, Tadley, Whitchurch etc.

FAREHAM & GOSPORT

including: Lee-on-the-Solent, Portchester, Sarisbury, Stubbington, Titchfield, Warsash etc.

PORTSMOUTH

including: Clanfield, Denmead, Emsworth, Havant, Hayling Island, Petersfield, Southbourne, Southsea etc.

SOUTHAMPTON & EASTLEIGH

including: Bishopstoke, Cadham, Chandlers Ford, Hamble, Holbury, Hythe, Romsey, Wickham etc.

WINCHESTER

including: Kings Worthy, New Alresford, Twyford etc.

For a complete title listing please visit our website
www.estate-publications.co.uk

CONTENTS

ADMINISTRATIVE DISTRICTS: pages 4-5

GAZETTEER INDEX TO ROAD MAP: pages 6-7

COUNTY ROAD MAP: pages 8-11

TOWN CENTRE STREET MAPS:

Aldershot	page 13
Alton	12
Andover	14
Ashurst	15
Basingstoke (Enlarged Centre)	16
Bishops Waltham	15
Bordon	18
Brockenhurst	17
Cosham	20
Cowplain	21
Denmead	36
Eastleigh	22
Emsworth	31
Fareham (Enlarged Centre)	23
Farnborough	25
Fawley	24
Fleet	26
Fordingbridge	27
Gosport	28-29
Hartley Wintney	32
Havant	30
Headley	33
Headley Down	33
Heath End	34
Hook	32
Hordle	36
Hythe	35
Kingsclere	37
Lee-on-the-Solent	38
Lindford	19
Liphook	39
Liss	40
Lymington	41
Lyndhurst	37
Milford on Sea	42
New Alresford	43
New Milton	44
North Baddesley	45
Oakley	45
Petersfield	46
Portsmouth	47
Ringwood	48
Romsey	49
South Hayling	52
Southampton (Enlarged Centre)	50-51
Totton	53
Waterlooville	54
Whitchurch	55
Wickham	54
Winchester (Enlarged Centre)	56
Yateley	57

INDEX TO STREETS: page 58

Scale of street plans: 4 Inches to 1 Mile (unless otherwise stated)

COUNTY RED BOOKS

This atlas is intended for those requiring street maps of the historical and commercial centres of towns within the county. Each locality is normally presented on one or two pages and although, with many small towns, this space is sufficient to portray the whole urban area, the maps of large towns and cities are for centres only and are not intended to be comprehensive. Such coverage is offered in the Super and Local Red Book (see Page 2).

ADMINISTRATIVE DISTRICTS

East Kennett
Lockeridge
Clench Common
Cadley
Chisbury
Little Bedwyn
Kintbury
Enborne
Newbury
Thatcham
Greenham
Bagshot
Inkpen
Hamstead Marshall
Roundway
Bishops Cannings
Allington
Stanton St Bernard
Huish
West Stowell
Oare
Wootton Rivers
Durley
Gt. Bedwyn
Shalbourne
Lower Green
Upper Green
West Woodhay
North End
Ball Hill
Broad Layings
Newtown
Headley
Crook
Coate
All Cannings
Alton Barnes
Wilcot
Devizes
Milton Lilbourne
Burbage
Wilton
Rivar
Ham
East Woodhay
East End
Woolton Hill
Burghclere
Plastow Green
Etchilhampton
Woodborough
Beechingstoke
Manningford Bruce
Pewsey
Easton Royal
West Grafton
East Grafton
Marten
Buttermere
Combe
Highclere
Ecchinswell
Potterne
Stert
Patney
North Newnton
Wexcombe
Oxenwood
Faccombe
Old Burghclere
Kingsclere
Marden
Manningford Bohune
Tidcombe
Fosbury
Linkenholt
Ashmansworth
Sydmonton
Potterne Wick
Wedhampton
Urchfont
Wilsford
Rushall
Collingbourne Kingston
Vernham Street
Vernham Dean
Upton
Crux Easton
Hannington
Littleton Panell
Eastcott
Easterton
Charlton
Upavon
Market Lavington
Everleigh
Collingbourne Ducis
Upper Chute
Lower Chute
Ibthorpe
BASIN[GSTOKE]
& D[EANE]
Hurstbourne Tarrant
Binley
Litchfield
North Oakley
West Lavington
East Chisenbury
Compton
Enford
Ludgershall
Tangley
Wildhern
Hatherden
Little London
Stoke
St. Mary Bourne
Quidhampton
Dean
Fittleton
Netheravon
Tidworth
Appleshaw
Clanville
Enham Alamein
Overton
Tilshead
Figheldean
Kimpton
Fyfield
Weyhill
Penton Mewsey
Charlton
Picket Piece
Whitchurch
Laverstoke
Steventon
Hurstbourne Priors
Orcheston
Durrington
Milston
Shipton Bellinger
Thruxton
Monxton
Anna Valley
Andover
Andover Down
Longparish
Chitterne
Shrewton
Larkhill
Bulford Camp
Bulford
Amport
Upper Clatford
Middleton
Quarley
Abbotts Ann
Amesbury
Boscombe Down
Cholderton
Grateley
Goodworth Clatford
Wherwell
Newton Stacey
Barton Stacey
Sutton Scotney
East Stratton
Winterbourne Stoke
Wilsford
Newton Tony
Palestine
TEST
Chilbolton
Wonston
Stoke Charity
Micheldever
Deptford
Berwick St. James
Lake
Allington
Boscombe
Fullerton
Steeple Langford
Gt. Durnford
Over Wallop
Middle Wallop
Longstock
Leckford
Wylye
Stapleford
Upper Woodford
Idmiston
Hanging Langford
Little Langford
Stoford
Porton
Nether Wallop
South Wonston
Great Wishford
Middle Woodford
Lower Woodford
Winterbourne Dauntsey
Gomeldon
Lopcombe Corner
Winterbourne Gunner
Stockbridge
Kings Worthy
South Newton
Winterbourne Earls
Middle Winterslow
VALLEY
Itchen Abbas
Teffont Magna
Firsdown
Broughton
Houghton
Dinton
Baverstock
Wilton
Bemerton Heath
West Winterslow
The Common
Up Somborne
Littleton
Barford St. Martin
Quidhampton
Laverstock
Pitton
West Tytherley
King's Somborne
Ashley
Sparsholt
Headbourne Worthy
Easton
Burcombe
Salisbury
Horsebridge
Fovant
Compton Chamberlayne
Netherhampton
Farley
East Tytherley
Brook
Winchester
Harnham
East Grimstead
Chilcomb
Coombe Bissett
Britford
Alderbury
East Dean
Mottisfont
Standon
Oliver's Battery
WINC[HESTER]
Stratford Tony
Odstock
Whaddon
West Grimstead
West Dean
Lockerley
Michelmersh
Compton
Morestead
Broad Chalke
Bishopstone
Homington
Nunton
Bodenham
Braishfield
Ebbesbourne Wake
Carter's Clay
Kent's Oak
Timsbury
Hursley
Shawford
Twyford
Charlton-All-Saints
Whiteparish
Abbottswood
Newtown
Otterbourne
Colden Common
Owslebury
Bowerchalke
Sherfield English
Awbridge
Ampfield
Chandler's Ford
Woodminton
Downton
Romsey
Fisher's Pond
Martin Drove End
Wick
Morgan's Vale
Redlynch
Landford Manor
East Wellow
North Baddesley
Eastleigh
Bishopstoke
Fair Oak
Lower Upham
Woodfalls
Lover
Whitsbury
Woodyates
Martin
Tidpit
Upper Street
Nth. Charford
Landford
West Wellow
Plaitford
Toothill
Wintershill
Hale
Chilworth
EASTLEIGH
Pentridge
Rockbourne
Breamore
Nomansland
Lee
Rownhams
Horton Heath
Canada
Ower
Upton
Woodgreen
Nursling
Durley
Damerham
Bassett
CITY OF
Swaythling
West End
Bramshaw
Newbridge
Calmore
Testwood
Sandleheath
Fordingbridge
Godshill
Copythorne
Portswood
Long Common
Monkton Up Wimborne
SOUTHAMPTON
Cranborne
Stuckton
Blissford
Fritham
Brook
Cadnam
Totton
Millbrook
Shirley
Botley
Curdridge
Bitterne
Northam
Hedge End
Thornhill
Wimborne St Giles
Edmondsham
Alderholt
Bickton
Hyde
Bartley
Netley Marsh
Eling
SOUTHAMPTON
Gussage All Saints
North Gorley
Stoney Cross
Minstead
Sholing
Woodlands
Ashurst
Pooksgreen
Woolston
Burridge
South Gorley
Newtown
Marchwood
Bursledon
Lower Swanwick
Swanwick
Verwood
Ibsley
Mockbeggar
Linwood
Emery Down
Woodlands
Horton
Netley
Sarisbury
Park Gate
Wigbeth
Lyndhurst
Dibden
Hythe
Locks Heath
Chalbury Common
Three Legged Cross
Blashford
Linford
Bank
Hamble-le-Rice
Warsash
Hinton Martell
Mannington
Picket Post
Dibden Purlieu
Titchfield
Gaunt's Common
Ashley Heath
St Ives
Ringwood
NEW FOREST
Holt
Burley Street
Hardley
Fawley
Holbury
St Leonards
Avon Castle
Balmerlawn
Broom Hill
West Moors
Hill Top
Blackfield
Stubbington
Burley
Bisterne Close
Brockenhurst
Kingston
Beaulieu
Clapgate
Trickett's Cross
Stapehill
Calshot
Exbury
Langley
Colehill
Setley
Ferndown
Thorney Hill
East Boldre
Bucklers Hard
Lee-on-the-Solent
Hampreston
West Parley
Avon
Ripley
Sway
Merley
Longham
Parley Cross
Wootton
Battramsley
Boldre
Norleywood
Bransgore
Lepe
East End
Bashley
Sopley
Neacroft
Portmore
Cowes
Broadstone
Bearwood
Ensbury
Hurn
Lymington
East Cowes
Hinton
Gurnard
Waterloo
Moordown
Burton
New Milton
Hordle
Newtown
Winton
Highcliffe
Downton
Everton
Lower Pennington
Whippingham
Branksome
Boscombe
Christchurch
Barton on Sea
Lymore
Northwood
Parkstone
Westbourne
Southbourne
Mudeford
Keyhaven
Porchfield
Wootton Bridge
Poole
Branksome Park
Bournemouth
Milford on Sea
Yarmouth
Norton
Hamstead
Cranmore
Newtown
Shalfleet
Parkhurst
Staplers

HART
RUSHMOOR
EAST HAMPSHIRE
HAVANT
CITY OF PORTSMOUTH
GOSPORT
BASINGSTOKE
WINCHESTER

Ufton Nervet
Burghfield Common
Grazeley
Arborfield
Barkham
Easthampstead
Sunninghill
Sunningdale
Shepperton
Padworth
Wokefield Park
Spencers Wood
Arborfield Cross
Arborfield Garrison
Lyne
Chertsey
Aldermaston
Mortimer
Beech Hill
Swallowfield
Farley Hill
Finchampstead
Crowthorne
Windlesham
Addlestone
Wasing
Mortimer West End
Stratfield Mortimer
Riseley
Ottershaw
Weybridge
Hersham
Heath End
Pamber Heath
Silchester
Stratfield Saye
Bramshill
Eversley
Sandhurst
Bagshot
Lightwater
Chobham
Woodham
West End Green
Stratfield Turgis
Eversley Cross
Camberley
West End
Sheerwater
West Byfleet
Byfleet
Cobham
Tadley
Pamber Green
Little London
Bramley
Turgis Green
Heckfield
Yateley
Donkey Town
Bisley
Horsell
Pyrford
Wisley
Stoke D'Abernon
Charter Alley
Pamber End
Sherfield on Loddon
Hound Green
Hazeley
Hartley Wintney
Hartfordbridge
Blackwater
Frimley
Knaphill
Woking
Hartley Wespall
Mattingley
Hawley
Deepcut
Brookwood
Ripley
Ockham
Monk Sherborne
Sherborne St. John
Church End
Rotherwick
West Green
Phoenix Grn.
West Heath
Cove
Mayford
Chineham
Newnham
Winchfield
Fleet
Mytchett
Pirbright
Send
Send Marsh
Farnborough
Wootton St. Lawrence
Old Basing
Up Nately
Hook
Dogmersfield
Church Crookham
Pitch Place
Worplesdon
West Horsley
East Horsley
Effingham
Henley Park
West Clandon
North Warnborough
Crookham Village
Ash
Fairlands
Oakley
Mapledurwell
Greywell
Odiham
Aldershot
Normandy
Wood Street
East Clandon
Mill Lane
Ewshot
Weybourne
Guildford
Tongham
Flexford
Onslow Village
Cliddesden
Tunworth
Upton Grey
South Warnborough
Crondall
Hale
Seale
Shere
Gomshall
Winslade
Broadmere
Weston Patrick
Long Sutton
Well
Runfold
Puttenham
Compton
Chilworth
Albury
Abinger Hammer
Farleigh Wallop
Ellisfield
Herriard
Farnham
Shalford
Dummer
Southrope
Shackleford
Wonersh
Farley Green
Sutton Abinger
Bentley
Peper Harow
Farncombe
Bramley
Peaslake
Nutley
Lower Froyle
Rowledge
Popham
Axford
Lasham
Golden Pot
Upper Froyle
Bucks Horn Oak
Tilford
Elstead
Godalming
Shamley Green
Holmbury St. Mary
Preston Candover
Bradley
Spreakley
Millbridge
Milford
Busbridge
Thorncombe Street
Shalden
Chilton Candover
Lower Wield
Holybourne
Binsted
Blacknest
Wheelerstreet
Hydestile
Rowly
Frensham
Rushmoor
Upper Wield
Bentworth
Alton
Wheatley
Thursley
Witley
Hascombe
Ewhurst
Brown Candover
Wyck
East Worldham
Kingsley
Churt
Bowlhead Grn.
Brook
Wormley
Hambledon
Loxhill
Cranleigh
Walliswood
Hattingley
Beech
Medstead
Sleaford
Headley Down
Northington
South Town
Chawton
West Worldham
Lindford
Hindhead
Chiddingfold
Dunsfold
Oakwood
Old Alresford
Bighton
Soldridge
Upper Farringdon
Oakhanger
Bordon
Headley
Alfold Crossways
Ellen's Green
Four Marks
Selborne
Whitehill
Standford
Grayshott
Grayswood
Alfold
Bucks Green
Rudgwick
New Alresford
Gundleton
North Street
Kitwood
Newton Valence
Blackmoor
Shottermill
Haslemere
Bramshott
Tisman's Common
Bishop's Sutton
Ropley
Ropley Dean
East Tisted
Empshott
Greatham
Longmoor Camp
Liphook
Camelsdale
Linchmere
Fisherstreet
Ifold
Loxwood
Plaistow
Slinfold
Itchingfield
Cheriton
Monkwood
Kingsley Green
Hawkley
Liss Forest
Langley
Roundstreet Common
Five Oaks
West Tisted
Hinton Ampner
Bramdean
Fernhurst
Northchapel
Kirdford
Newpound Common
High Cross
East Liss
Liss
Rake
Privett
Hill Brow
Milland
Lurgashall
Billingshurst
Kilmeston
Brockwood Park
Froxfield Green
Steep
Henley
Lickfold
Balls Cross
Wisborough Green
Brooks Green
Sheet
Rogate
Stroud
Langrish
Lodsworth
Coneyhurst
Warnford
West Meon
Ramsdean
Petersfield
Chithurst
Iping
Woolbeding
Stedham
Easebourne
Upperton
Coolham
Trotton
Tillington
Petworth
North Heath
Weston
Exton
East Meon
Nursted
Nyewood
Midhurst
Selham
Byworth
Gay Street
Broomer's Corner
Corhampton
Buriton
East Harting
West Lavington
South Ambersham
Meonstoke
Elsted
Stopham
Fittleworth
Pulborough
Nutbourne
West Chiltington
Brockbridge
South Harting
Treyford
Didling
Heyshott
Hardham
Thakeham
Bishop's Waltham
Droxford
Chidden
North Marden
Bepton
Cocking
Graffham
Duncton
Coldwaltham
West Chiltington Common
Soberton
Clanfield
East Lavington
Barlavington
Wiggonholt
Ashington
Swanmore
Hambledon
Chalton
Watersfield
Greatham
Shirrell Heath
Soberton Heath
Catherington
Compton
Chilgrove
Sutton
Storrington
Shedfield
Hoe Gate
Anthill Common
Horndean
Blendworth
East Marden
West Marden
Singleton
East Dean
Upwaltham
Bignor
Bury
West Burton
Rackham
Washington
Newtown
Finchdean
West Dean
Charlton
Amberley
Sullington
Hundred Acres
Denmead
Rowland's Castle
Forestside
Houghton
North Stoke
Wickham
Cowplain
Stoughton
Madehurst
North Boarhunt
Waterlooville
Walderton
Eartham
South Stoke
North End
Southwick
Woodend
West Stoke
Lavant
Halnaker
Slindon
Burpham
Boarhunt
Purbrook
Havant
Bedhampton
Westbourne
Funtington
East Ashling
Strettington
Boxgrove
Fontwell
Emsworth
Woodmancote
West Ashling
Westhampnett
Norton
Arundel
Clapham
Wallington
Wymering
Drayton
Hambrook
Nyton
Walberton
Patching
Langstone
Broadbridge
Chichester
Tangmere
Aldingbourne
Eastergate
Lyminster
Poling
Sompting
Durrington
Portchester
Cosham
Southbourne
Fishbourne
Oving
Westergate
Tortington
Barnham
Angmering
Bridgemary
Hilsea
North Hayling
Chidham
Bosham
Apuldram
Merston
Woodgate
Ford
Wick
Ferring
North End
Stoke
West Thorney
Donnington
Colworth
Shripney
Yapton
Rustington
East Preston
Hardway
Runcton
Climping
Goring-by-Sea
Gosport
Portsea
Fratton
West Itchenor
Birdham
Hunston
Flansham
Bersted
Littlehampton
Alverstoke
Southsea
South Hayling
Shipton Green
South Mundham
Felpham
Middleton-on-Sea
Eastney
Street End
Aldwick
West Wittering
Somerley
Sidlesham
Bognor Regis
Highleigh
Earnley
Pagham
East Wittering
Bracklesham
Church Norton
Ryde
Selsey
Fishbourne
Binstead
Seaview
Nettlestone
Havenstreet
St. Helens

INDEX TO ROAD MAP

Abbotts Ann 8 B4
Abbottswood 8 B6
Aldershot 9 H3
Alton 9 G4
Alverstoke 11 F3
Ampfield 8 C6
Amport 8 B3
Andover 8 B3
Andover Down 8 C3
Anna Valley 8 B3
Anthill Common 11 G2
Appleshaw 8 B3
Ashford Hill 9 E1
Ashley 8 C5
Ashmansworth 8 C2
Ashurst 10 C2
Avon 10 A3
Avon Castle 10 A3
Awbridge 8 B6
Axford 9 E4

Ball Hill 8 C1
Balmerlawn 10 C3
Bank 10 C2
Bartley 10 C2
Barton on Sea 10 B4
Barton Stacey 8 C4
Bashley 10 B3
Basingstoke 9 E2
Bassett 10 D1
Battramsley 10 C3
Baughurst 9 E1
Beaulieu 10 D3
Beauworth 9 E6
Bedhampton 11 H2
Beech 9 F4
Bentley 9 G3
Bentworth 9 F4
Bickton 10 A2
Bighton 9 E5
Binley 8 C2
Binsted 9 G4
Bishop's Sutton 9 E5
Bishop's Waltham 11 F1
Bishopstoke 11 E1
Bisterne Close 10 B3
Bitterne 11 E1
Blackfield 10 D3
Blackmoor 9 G5
Blacknest 9 G4
Blackwater 9 H1
Blashford 10 A2
Blendworth 11 H1
Blissford 10 B1
Boarhunt 11 F2
Boldre 10 C3
Bordon 9 G5
Botley 11 E1
Bradley 9 F4
Braishfield 8 C6
Bramdean 9 E5
Bramley 9 F1
Bramshaw 10 B1
Bramshill 9 G1
Bramshott 9 H5
Bransgore 10 B3
Breamore 10 A1
Bridgemary 11 F3
Broad Layings 8 C1
Broadmere 9 E3
Brockbridge 11 G1
Brockenhurst 10 B3
Brockwood Park 9 E6
Brook 8 B5
Brook 10 C1
Broughton 8 B5
Brown Candover 9 E4
Bucklers Hard 10 D3
Bucks Horn Oak 9 H4
Burghclere 8 D1
Buriton 9 G6
Burley 10 B3
Burley Street 10 B3
Burridge 11 E2
Bursledon 11 E2

Cadnam 10 C1
Calmore 10 C1
Calshot 11 E3
Canada 10 C1
Carter's Clay 8 B6
Catherington 11 G1
Chalton 11 H1
Chandler's Ford 8 C6
Charlton 8 B3
Charter Alley 9 E2
Chawton 9 F4
Cheriton 9 E5
Chidden 11 G1
Chilbolton 8 C4
Chilcomb 8 D5
Chilton Candover 9 E4
Chilworth 10 D1
Chineham 9 F2
Church Crookham 9 H2
Church End 9 F2
Clanfield 11 G1
Clanville 8 B3
Cliddesden 9 E3
Colden Common 8 D6
Compton 8 C6
Copythorne 10 C1
Corhampton 9 E6
Cosham 11 G2
Cove 9 H2
Cowplain 11 G2
Crawley 8 C5
Crondall 9 G3
Crookham Village 9 G2
Crux Easton 8 C2
Curbridge 11 F2
Curdridge 11 F1

Damerham 10 A1
Dean 11 F1
Deane 8 D3
Denmead 11 G2
Dibden 10 D2
Dibden Purlieu 10 D2
Dogmersfield 9 G2
Downton 10 C4
Drayton 11 G2
Droxford 11 G1
Dummer 9 E3
Durley 11 F1

East Boldre 10 D3
East Dean 8 A6
East End 8 C1
East End 10 D4
East Liss 9 G5
East Meon 9 F6
East Stratton 9 E4
East Tisted 9 F5
East Tytherley 8 B5
East Wellow 8 B6
East Woodhay 8 C1
East Worldham 9 G4
Eastleigh 8 C6
Eastney 11 G3
Easton 8 D5
Ecchinswell 8 D1
Eling 10 D2
Ellisfield 9 F3
Emery Down 10 C2
Empshott 9 G5
Emsworth 11 H2
Enham Alamein 8 B3
Eversley 9 G1
Eversley Cross 9 G1
Everton 10 C4
Ewshot 9 H3
Exbury 10 D3
Exton 9 E6

Faccombe 8 C2
Fair Oak 11 E1
Fareham 11 F2
Farleigh Wallop 9 E3
Fawley 11 E3
Finchdean 11 H2
Fisher's Pond 8 D6
Fleet 9 G2
Fordingbridge 10 A1
Four Marks 9 F5
Fratton 11 G3
Fritham 10 B1
Froxfield Green 9 F6
Fullerton 8 B4
Funtley 11 F2
Fyfield 8 B3

Godshill 10 B1
Golden Pot 9 F3
Goodworth Clatford 8 B4
Gosport 11 F3
Grateley 8 A4
Grayshott 9 H5
Greatham 9 G5
Greywell 9 G3
Gundleton 9 E5

Hale 10 B1
Hambledon 11 G1
Hamble-le-Rice 11 E2
Hannington 9 E2
Hardley 10 D3
Hardway 11 F3
Hartfordbridge 9 G2
Hartley Wespall 9 F2
Hartley Wintney 9 G2
Hatherden 8 B3
Hattingley 9 E4
Havant 11 H2
Hawkley 9 G5
Hawley 9 H2
Hazeley 9 G2
Headbourne Worthy 8 D5
Headley 8 D1
Headley 9 H5
Headley Down 9 H5
Heath End 9 E1
Heckfield 9 G1
Hedge End 11 E2
Herriard 9 F3
High Cross 9 F6
Highclere 8 C1
Hill Head 11 F3
Hill Top 10 D3
Hilsea 11 G3
Hinton 10 B4
Hinton Ampner 9 E6
Hoe Gate 11 G1
Holbury 10 D3
Holybourne 9 F4
Hook 9 F2
Hordle 10 C4
Horndean 11 G1
Horsebridge 8 B5
Horton Heath 11 E1
Houghton 8 B5
Hound Green 9 G2
Hundred Acres 11 F2
Hursley 8 C6
Hurstbourne Priors 8 C3
Hurstbourne Tarrant 8 C2
Hyde 10 B2
Hythe 10 D2

Ibsley 10 A2
Ibthorpe 8 B2
Ibworth 9 E2
Itchen Abbas 8 D5
Itchen Stoke 9 E5

Kent's Oak 8 B6
Keyhaven 10 C4
Kilmeston 9 E6
Kimpton 8 A3
King's Somborne 8 B5
Kings Worthy 8 D5
Kingsclere 8 D2
Kingsley 9 G4
Kingston 10 A3
Kitwood 9 F5

Langley 11 E3
Langrish 9 F6
Langstone 11 H3
Lasham 9 F4
Laverstoke 8 D3
Leckford 8 C4
Lee 10 D1
Lee-on-the-Solent 11 F3

Lepe 11 E3
Lindford 9 H4
Linford 10 A2
Linkenholt 8 B2
Linwood 10 B2
Liphook 9 H5
Liss 9 G5
Liss Forest 9 G5
Litchfield 8 D2
Little London 8 C3
Little London 9 E1
Littleton 8 C5
Lockerley 8 A6
Locks Heath 11 E2
Long Common 11 E1
Long Sutton 9 G3
Longmoor Camp 9 G5
Longparish 8 C3
Longstock 8 B4
Lower Froyle 9 G3
Lower Pennington 10 C4
Lower Swanwick 11 E2
Lower Upham 11 F1
Lower Wield 9 E4
Lymington 10 C4
Lymore 10 C4
Lyndhurst 10 C2

Mapledurwell 9 F3
Marchwood 10 D2
Mattingley 9 G2
Medstead 9 F4
Meonstoke 11 G1
Micheldever 8 D4
Michelmersh 8 B6
Middle Wallop 8 B4
Middleton 8 C3
Milford on Sea 10 C4
Mill Lane 9 G3
Millbrook 10 D1
Minstead 10 C2
Mockbeggar 10 A2
Monk Sherborne 9 E2
Monkwood 9 F5
Monxton 8 B3
Morestead 8 D6
Mortimer West End 9 F1
Mottisfont 8 B6

Neacroft 10 A4
Nether Wallop 8 B4
Netley 11 E2
Netley Marsh 10 C2
New Alresford 9 E5
New Cheriton 9 E5
New Milton 10 B4
Newbridge 10 C1
Newnham 9 F2
Newton Stacey 8 C4
Newton Valence 9 F5
Newtown 8 B6
Newtown 8 D1
Newtown 10 C2
Newtown 11 G2
Norleywood 10 D3
North Baddesley 10 D1
North Boarhunt 11 G2
North End 8 C1
North End 11 G3
North Gorley 10 A2
North Hayling 11 H3
North Oakley 8 D2
North Street 9 F5
North Waltham 9 E3
North Warnborough 9 G2
Northam 10 D2
Northington 9 E4
Nth. Charford 10 A1
Nursling 10 D1
Nutley 9 E3

Oakhanger 9 G5
Oakley 9 E3
Odiham 9 G3
Old Alresford 9 E5
Old Basing 9 F2
Old Burghclere 8 D2
Oliver's Battery 8 C6
Otterbourne 8 D6
Over Wallop 8 A4
Overton 8 D3
Ovington 9 E5
Ower 10 C1
Owslebury 8 D6

Palestine 8 A4
Pamber End 9 E2
Pamber Green 9 E1
Pamber Heath 9 E1
Park Gate 11 F2
Penton Mewsey 8 B3
Petersfield 9 G6
Phoenix Green 9 G2
Picket Piece 8 C3
Picket Post 10 B2
Plaitford 10 C1
Plastow Green 8 D1
Pooksgreen 10 D2
Popham 9 E3
Portchester 11 F3
Portmore 10 C4
Portsea 11 G3
Portsmouth 11 G4
Portswood 10 D1
Preston Candover 9 E4
Privett 9 F6
Purbrook 11 G2

Quarley 8 A4
Quidhampton 8 D3

Ramsdean 9 F6
Ramsdell 9 E2
Ringwood 10 A3
Ripley 10 A3
Rockbourne 10 A1
Romsey 8 C6
Ropley 9 F5
Ropley Dean 9 E5
Rotherwick 9 F2
Rowland's Castle 11 H2
Rownhams 10 D1

Saint Mary Bourne 8 C2
Sandleheath 10 A1
Sarisbury 11 E2
Selborne 9 G5
Setley 10 C3
Shalden 9 F4
Shawford 8 D6
Shedfield 11 F1
Sheet 9 G6
Sherborne Saint John 9 E2
Sherfield English 8 A6
Sherfield on Loddon 9 F2
Shipton Bellinger 8 A3
Shirley 10 D1
Shirrell Heath 11 F1
Sholing 11 E2
Silchester 9 F1
Sleaford 9 H4
Soberton 11 G1
Soberton Heath 11 G1
Soldridge 9 F5
Sopley 10 A3
South Gorley 10 A2
South Hayling 11 H3
South Town 9 F4
South Warnborough 9 F3
South Wonston 8 D4
Southampton 10 D1
Southrope 9 F3
Southsea 11 G3
Southwick 11 G2
Sparsholt 8 C5
Standford 9 H5
Standon 8 C6
Steep 9 G6
Steventon 9 E3
Stockbridge 8 B5
Stoke 8 C2
Stoke 11 H3
Stoke Charity 8 D4
Stoney Cross 10 B2
Stratfield Saye 9 F1
Stratfield Turgis 9 F1
Stroud 9 G6
Stubbington 11 F3
Stuckton 10 A1
Sutton Scotney 8 D4
Swanmore 11 F1
Swanwick 11 F2
Sway 10 C3
Swaythling 11 E1
Sydmonton 8 D2

Tadley 9 E1
Tangley 8 B2
Testwood 10 D1
Thorney Hill 10 B3
Thornhill 11 E2
Thruxton 8 A3
Tichborne 9 E5
Timsbury 8 B6
Titchfield 11 E3
Toothill 10 D1
Totton 10 C1
Tunworth 9 F3
Turgis Green 9 F1
Twyford 8 D6

Up Nately 9 F2
Up Somborne 8 C5
Upham 9 E6
Upper Clatford 8 B4
Upper Farringdon 9 G4
Upper Froyle 9 G4
Upper Street 10 A1
Upper Wield 9 E4
Upton 8 B2
Upton 10 D1
Upton Grey 9 F3

Vernham Dean 8 B2
Vernham Street 8 B2

Wallington 11 F2
Waltham Chase 11 F1
Warnford 9 E6
Warsash 11 E2
Waterlooville 11 G2
Well 9 G3
West Dean 8 A6
West End 11 E1
West End Green 9 F1
West Green 9 G2
West Heath 9 H2
West Meon 9 F6
West Tisted 9 F5
West Tytherley 8 A5
West Wellow 10 C1
West Worldham 9 G4
Weston 9 G6
Weston Patrick 9 F3
Weyhill 8 B3
Wheatley 9 G4
Wherwell 8 C4
Whitchurch 8 D3
Whitehill 9 G5
Whitsbury 10 A1
Wickham 11 F2
Wildhern 8 B2
Winchester 8 C5
Winchfield 9 G2
Winslade 9 F3
Wintershill 11 F1
Wolverton 9 E2
Wonston 8 D4
Woodgreen 10 B1
Woodlands 10 C2
Woodmancott 9 E4
Woolston 11 E2
Woolton Hill 8 C1
Wootton 10 B3
Wootton Saint Lawrence 9 E2
Wyck 9 G4
Wymering 11 G2

Yateley 9 G1

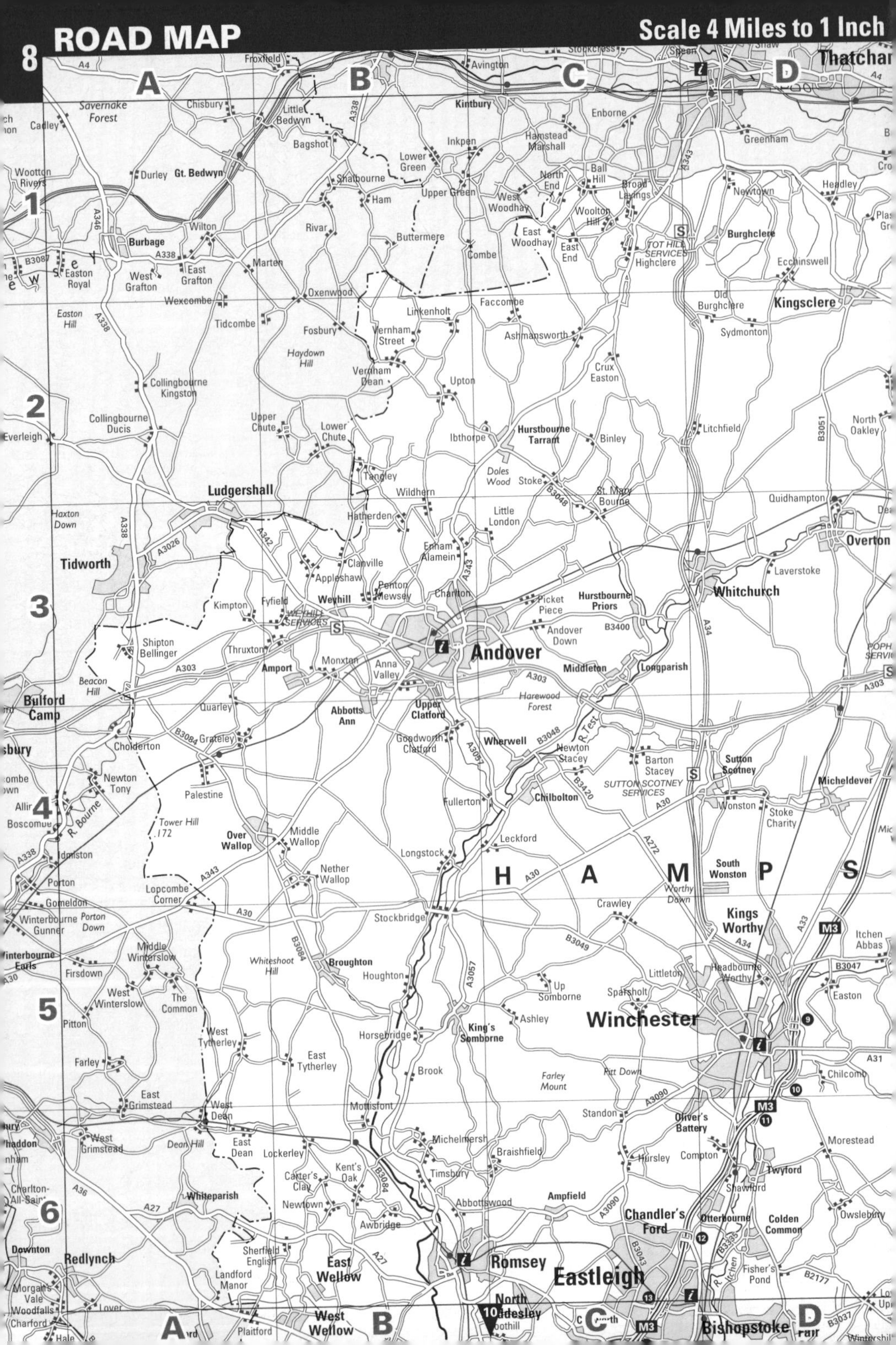
A
B
C
D
1
2
3
4
5
6
Thatcham
Froxfield
Avington
Stockcross
Speen
Shaw
A4
Savernake Forest
Cadley
Chisbury
Little Bedwyn
Kintbury
Enborne
Greenham
Bagshot
Inkpen
Hamstead Marshall
Lower Green
Wootton Rivers
Durley
Gt. Bedwyn
Shalbourne
Upper Green
North End
Ball Hill
Broad Layings
Newtown
Headley
Ham
West Woodhay
Woolton Hill
A346
Burbage
Wilton
Rivar
Buttermere
East Woodhay
East End
TOT HILL SERVICES
Highclere
Burghclere
A338
B3087
Easton Royal
West Grafton
East Grafton
Marten
Combe
Ecchinswell
Wexcombe
Oxenwood
Faccombe
Old Burghclere
Kingsclere
Easton Hill
Tidcombe
Linkenholt
Sydmonton
Fosbury
Vernham Street
Ashmansworth
Haydown Hill
Vernham Dean
Crux Easton
Collingbourne Kingston
Upton
Collingbourne Ducis
Upper Chute
Lower Chute
Ibthorpe
Hurstbourne Tarrant
Binley
Litchfield
B3051
North Oakley
Everleigh
Tangley
Doles Wood
Stoke
B3048
St. Mary Bourne
Wildhern
Ludgershall
Quidhampton
Haxton Down
Little London
Hatherden
A342
Enham Alamein
Overton
A3026
Clanville
A343
Tidworth
Appleshaw
Laverstoke
Penton Mewsey
Charlton
Whitchurch
Kimpton
Fyfield
Weyhill
WEYHILL SERVICES
Picket Piece
Hurstbourne Priors
Andover Down
B3400
Shipton Bellinger
Thruxton
Andover
A34
A303
Amport
Monxton
Anna Valley
Middleton
Longparish
Beacon Hill
Harewood Forest
Bulford Camp
Quarley
Abbotts Ann
Upper Clatford
Goodworth Clatford
Wherwell
Newton Stacey
Barton Stacey
Sutton Scotney
B3084
Grateley
Cholderton
A3057
R. Test
B3420
SUTTON SCOTNEY SERVICES
Micheldever
Newton Tony
Palestine
Fullerton
Chilbolton
Wonston
Stoke Charity
R. Bourne
Tower Hill 172
Over Wallop
Middle Wallop
Leckford
A272
Boscombe
Idmiston
Longstock
A30
Nether Wallop
H
A
M
P
S
South Wonston
Porton
Lopcombe Corner
Worthy Down
Gomeldon
Crawley
Winterbourne Gunner
Porton Down
Stockbridge
Kings Worthy
Middle Winterslow
Itchen Abbas
B3049
M3
A33
Winterbourne Earls
Firsdown
Whiteshoot Hill
Broughton
Houghton
B3047
Littleton
Headbourne Worthy
West Winterslow
The Common
Up Somborne
Sparsholt
Easton
Pitton
King's Somborne
Ashley
Winchester
West Tytherley
Horsebridge
Farley
East Tytherley
Brook
Farley Mount
Pitt Down
Chilcomb
A31
East Grimstead
West Dean
Mottisfont
Standon
A3090
Oliver's Battery
West Grimstead
Dean Hill
East Dean
Lockerley
Michelmersh
Braishfield
Morestead
Hursley
Compton
Carter's Clay
Kent's Oak
Timsbury
Twyford
Whiteparish
Shawford
A36
Charlton-All-Saints
A27
Newtown
Awbridge
Abbottswood
Ampfield
Owslebury
Chandler's Ford
Otterbourne
Colden Common
Downton
Sherfield English
Redlynch
Romsey
B3043
B3335
East Wellow
Eastleigh
Fisher's Pond
R. Itchen
B2177
Landford Manor
Morgan's Vale
Woodfalls
Lover
North Baddesley
Nursling
Charford
Plaitford
West Wellow
Rownhams
Bishopstoke
Fair Oak
B3037
Hale
10
9
11
12
13

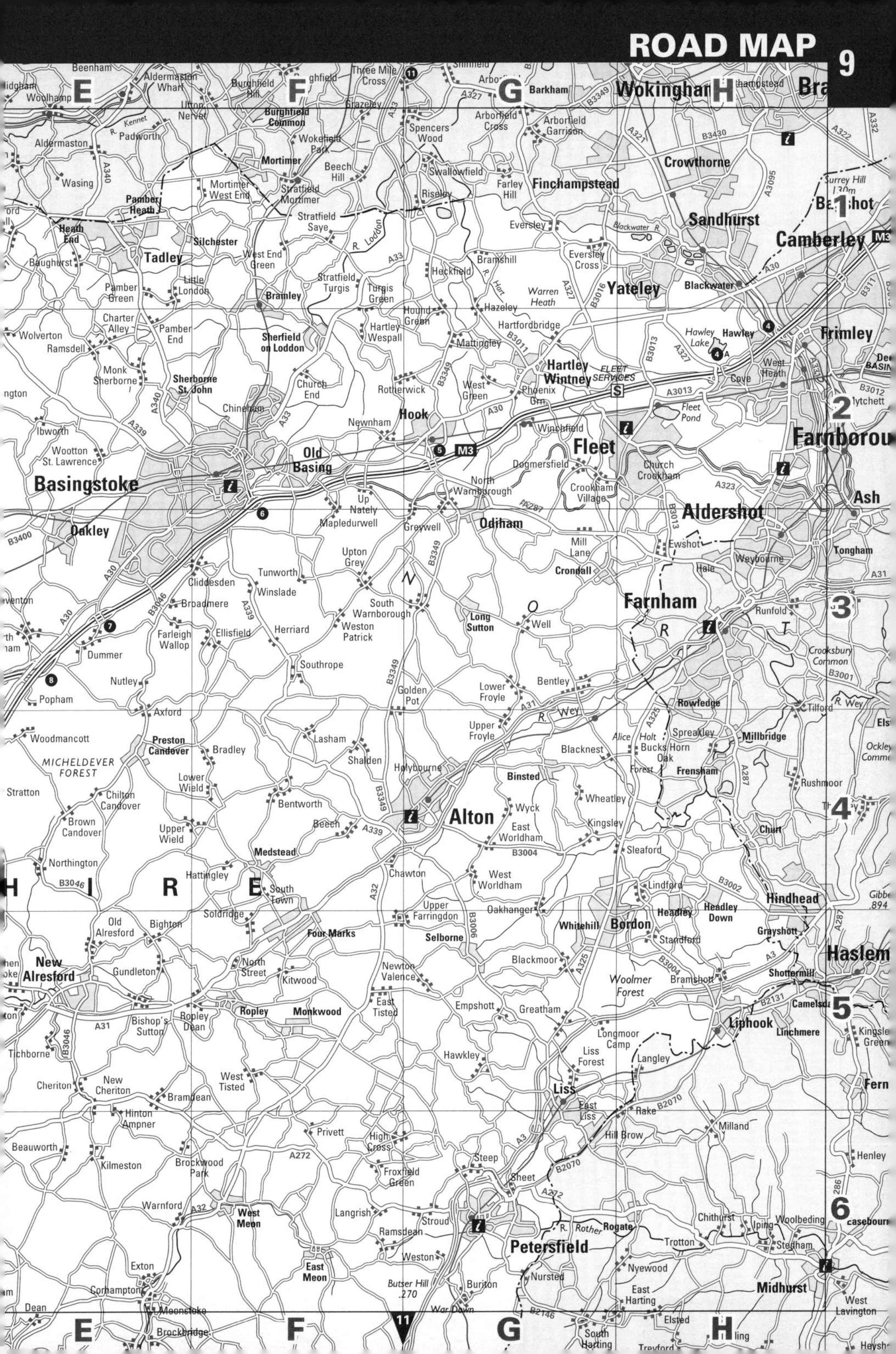
E
F
G
H
1
2
3
4
5
6
11
Beenham
Woolhampton
Aldermaston Wharf
Burghfield Hill
Three Mile Cross
Shinfield
Arborfield
Barkham
Wokingham
Ufton Nervet
Burghfield Common
Grazeley
Spencers Wood
Arborfield Cross
Arborfield Garrison
Aldermaston
R. Kennet
Padworth
Wokefield Park
Crowthorne
Wasing
Mortimer
Beech Hill
Swallowfield
Farley Hill
Finchampstead
Mortimer West End
Stratfield Mortimer
Riseley
Sandhurst
Camberley
Pamber Heath
Heath End
Stratfield Saye
R. Loddon
Eversley
Blackwater R.
Tadley
Silchester
West End Green
Bramshill
Eversley Cross
Yateley
Blackwater
Baughurst
Little London
Stratfield Turgis
Turgis Green
Heckfield
R. Hart
Warren Heath
Pamber Green
Bramley
Hazeley
Hawley Lake
Hawley
Frimley
Charter Alley
Pamber End
Hound Green
Hartfordbridge
Wolverton
Ramsdell
Sherfield on Loddon
Hartley Wespall
Mattingley
Monk Sherborne
Sherborne St. John
Church End
Rotherwick
West Green
Hartley Wintney
FLEET SERVICES
Phoenix Grn
Cove
West Heath
Chineham
Fleet Pond
Ibworth
Newnham
Hook
Winchfield
Farnborough
Wootton St. Lawrence
Old Basing
M3
Fleet
Basingstoke
Dogmersfield
Church Crookham
North Warnborough
Crookham Village
Up Nately
Mapledurwell
Aldershot
Ash
Greywell
Odiham
Oakley
Ewshot
Mill Lane
Upton Grey
Tongham
Weybourne
Crondall
Hale
Tunworth
Cliddesden
Winslade
Broadmere
South Warnborough
Long Sutton
Farnham
Runfold
Weston Patrick
Well
Farleigh Wallop
Ellisfield
Herriard
Crooksbury Common
Dummer
Southrope
Nutley
Popham
Golden Pot
Lower Froyle
Bentley
Axford
Upper Froyle
R. Wey
Rowledge
Tilford
Woodmancott
Lasham
Alice Holt Forest
Spreakley
Bucks Horn Oak
Millbridge
Preston Candover
Bradley
Shalden
Blacknest
MICHELDEVER FOREST
Holybourne
Binsted
Frensham
Stratton
Lower Wield
Chilton Candover
Wheatley
Rushmoor
Bentworth
Wyck
Brown Candover
Upper Wield
Beech
Alton
East Worldham
Kingsley
Churt
Medstead
Sleaford
Northington
Hattingley
West Worldham
Chawton
Lindford
South Town
Hindhead
Old Alresford
Bighton
Soldridge
Upper Farringdon
Oakhanger
Headley
Headley Down
Four Marks
Selborne
Whitehill
Bordon
Grayshott
Standford
New Alresford
North Street
Gundleton
Blackmoor
Newton Valence
Haslemere
Kitwood
Woolmer Forest
Bramshott
Shottermill
East Tisted
Ropley
Monkwood
Empshott
Greatham
Bishop's Sutton
Ropley Dean
Liphook
Linchmere
Tichborne
Longmoor Camp
Hawkley
Liss Forest
Langley
West Tisted
Cheriton
New Cheriton
Liss
Bramdean
East Liss
Rake
Hinton Ampner
Privett
High Cross
Milland
Hill Brow
Beauworth
Kilmeston
Brockwood Park
Steep
Froxfield Green
Henley
Sheet
Warnford
West Meon
Langrish
Stroud
Chithurst
Iping
Woolbeding
Ramsdean
R. Rother
Rogate
Petersfield
Trotton
Stedham
Weston
Nyewood
Nursted
Exton
East Meon
Butser Hill 270
Buriton
East Harting
Midhurst
Corhampton
West Lavington
Meonstoke
War Down
Elsted
Dean
Brockbridge
South Harting
Trefford
H I R E
N O R T
A33
A327
B3349
A321
B3430
A3095
A322
A332
A340
A30
B3016
B3011
B3013
A3013
A339
B3400
B3046
A323
A287
A31
B3001
A325
B3004
B3002
B3006
A32
A3
B2131
B2070
A272
B2146
A339
Surrey Hill 130m

Scale 4 Miles to 1 Inch

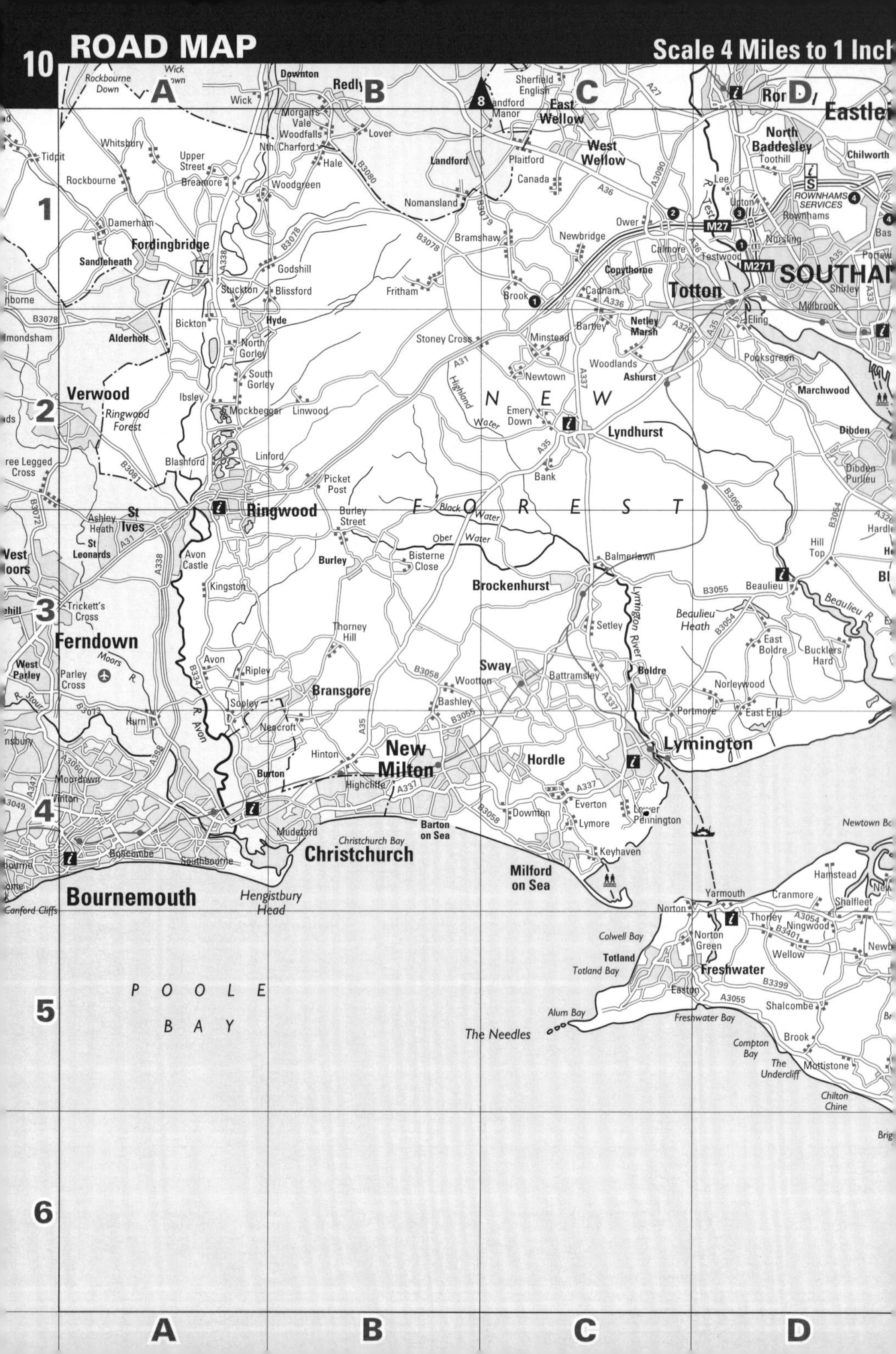

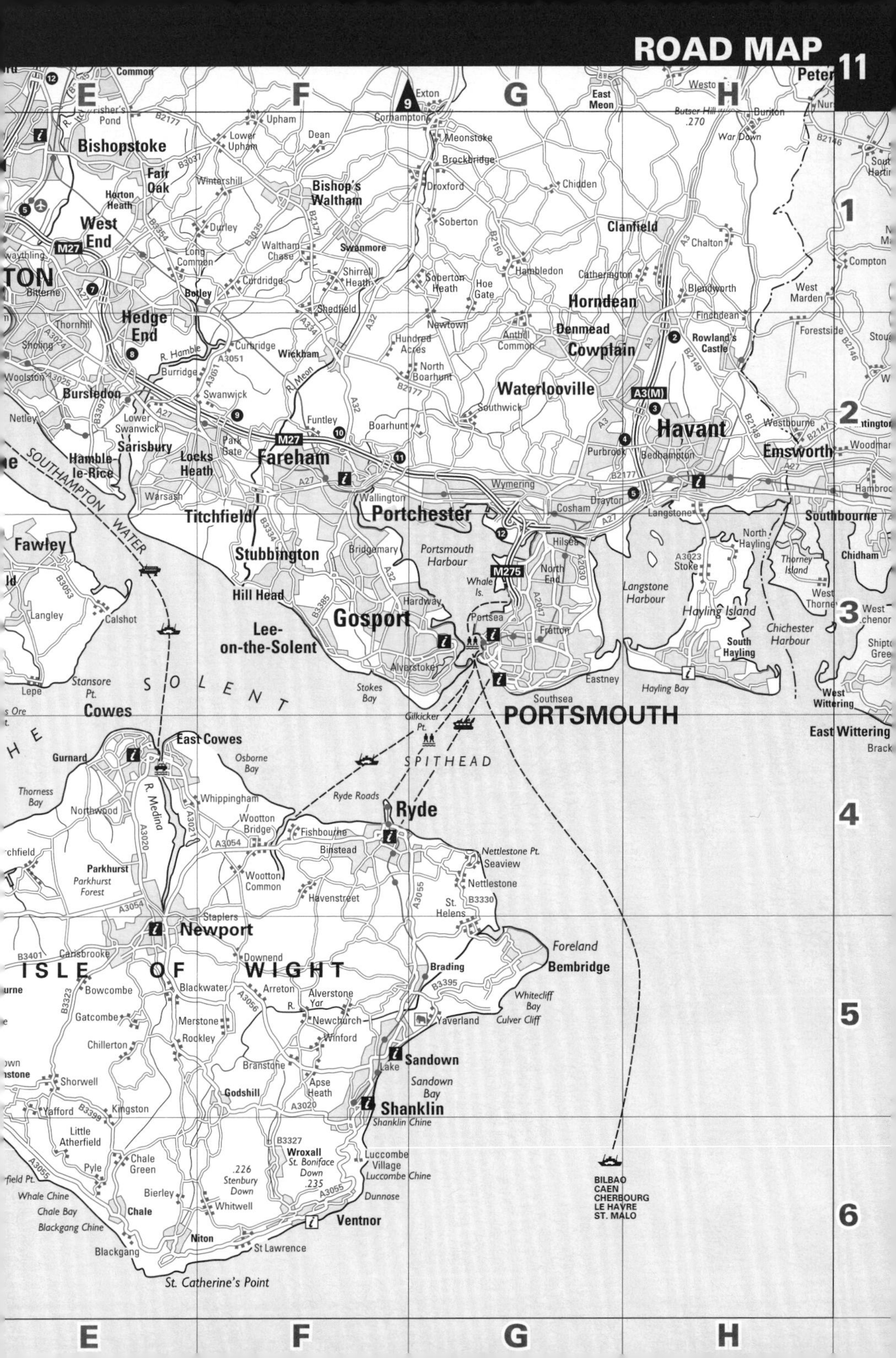
Bishopstoke
Fair Oak
Horton Heath
West End
Bitterne
Hedge End
Bursledon
Netley
Hamble-le-Rice
Sarisbury
Locks Heath
Warsash
Titchfield
Fareham
Wickham
Bishop's Waltham
Swanmore
Shirrell Heath
Shedfield
Botley
Curdridge
Durley
Upham
Lower Upham
Dean
Exton
Corhampton
Meonstoke
Droxford
Soberton
Soberton Heath
Hoe Gate
Hambledon
Chidden
Clanfield
Chalton
Catherington
Horndean
Blendworth
Finchdean
Rowland's Castle
Denmead
Cowplain
Waterlooville
Southwick
Havant
Bedhampton
Purbrook
Emsworth
Westbourne
West Marden
Compton
Forestside
East Meon
Butser Hill .270
War Down
Buriton
Portchester
Wallington
Wymering
Cosham
Drayton
Langstone
Southbourne
Chidham
North Hayling
Thorney Island
Stoke
Hayling Island
South Hayling
Langstone Harbour
Chichester Harbour
Hayling Bay
Hilsea
North End
Fratton
Eastney
Southsea
PORTSMOUTH
Portsmouth Harbour
Whale Is.
Portsea
Gosport
Hardway
Bridgemary
Stubbington
Hill Head
Lee-on-the-Solent
Alverstoke
Stokes Bay
Gilkicker Pt.
SPITHEAD
Ryde Roads
SOUTHAMPTON WATER
Fawley
Langley
Calshot
Lepe
Stansore Pt.
SOLENT
Cowes
East Cowes
Gurnard
Osborne Bay
Thorness Bay
Northwood
Whippingham
Wootton Bridge
Fishbourne
Binstead
Ryde
Nettlestone Pt.
Seaview
Nettlestone
St. Helens
Havenstreet
Wootton Common
Parkhurst
Parkhurst Forest
R. Medina
Staplers
Newport
Carisbrooke
Downend
ISLE OF WIGHT
Bowcombe
Blackwater
Arreton
Alverstone
Yar
Brading
Foreland
Bembridge
Whitecliff Bay
Culver Cliff
Yaverland
Newchurch
Winford
Gatcombe
Merstone
Rockley
Chillerton
Branstone
Sandown
Lake
Sandown Bay
Shorwell
Godshill
Apse Heath
Shanklin
Shanklin Chine
Yafford
Kingston
Little Atherfield
Pyle
Chale Green
Wroxall
St. Boniface Down .235
.226 Stenbury Down
Luccombe Village
Luccombe Chine
Dunnose
Bierley
Whitwell
Ventnor
Niton
St Lawrence
Blackgang
Chale
Whale Chine
Chale Bay
Blackgang Chine
St. Catherine's Point
BILBAO
CAEN
CHERBOURG
LE HAVRE
ST. MALO
West Wittering
East Wittering
M27
M275
A3(M)
E
F
G
H
1
2
3
4
5
6

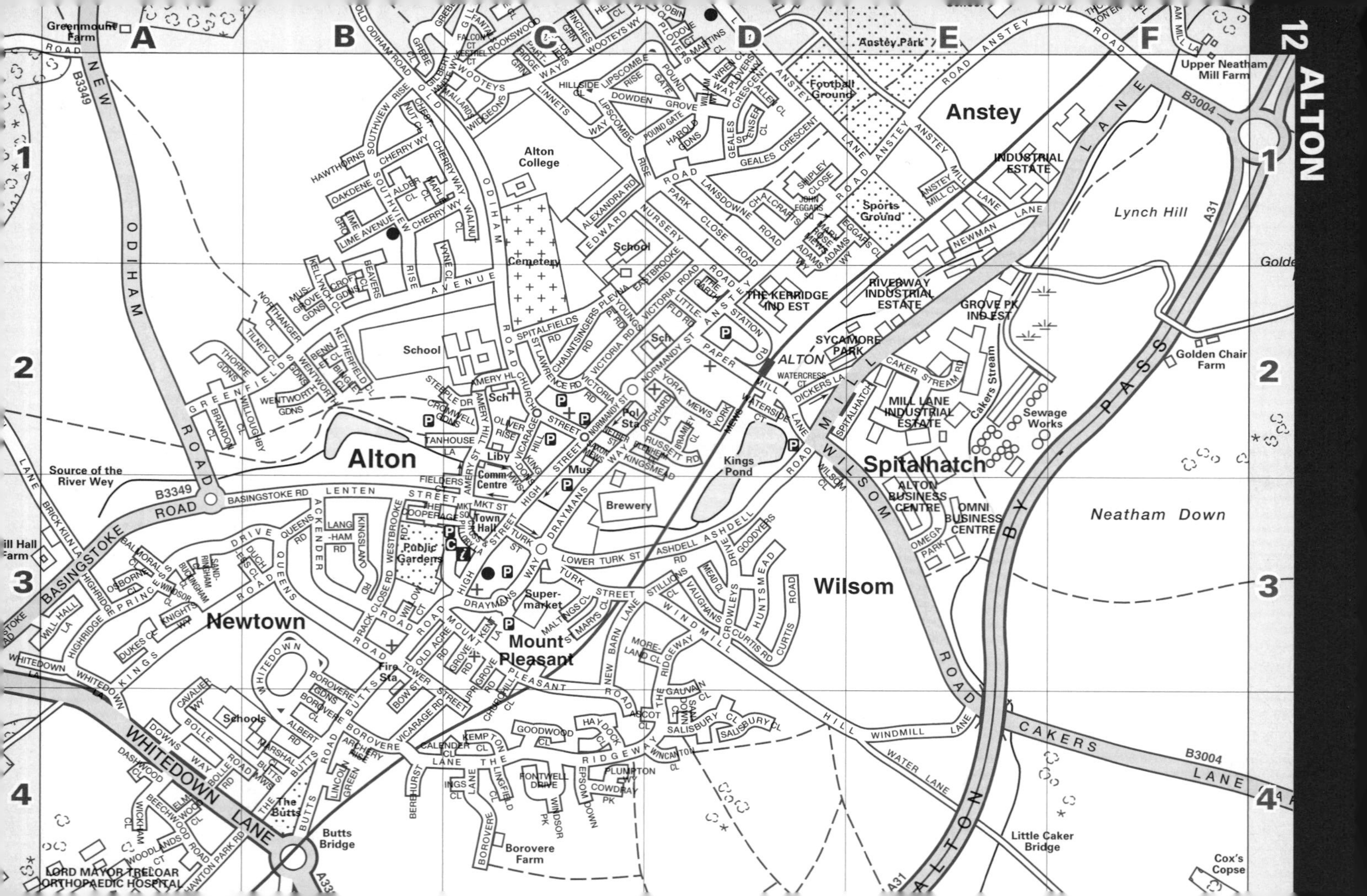
Anstey
Spitalhatch
Wilsom
Mount Pleasant
Alton
Newtown
Lynch Hill
Neatham Down
Upper Neatham Mill Farm
Golden Chair Farm
Cox's Copse
Little Caker Bridge
Sewage Works
Cakers Stream
INDUSTRIAL ESTATE
GROVE PK IND EST
RIVERWAY INDUSTRIAL ESTATE
MILL LANE INDUSTRIAL ESTATE
ALTON BUSINESS CENTRE
OMNI BUSINESS CENTRE
SYCAMORE PARK
THE KERRIDGE IND EST
Anstey Park
Football Ground
Sports Ground
Kings Pond
Brewery
Alton College
Cemetery
School
Public Gardens
Supermarket
Fire Sta
Schools
The Butts
Butts Bridge
Borovere Farm
Source of the River Wey
Greenmount Farm
LORD MAYOR TRELOAR ORTHOPAEDIC HOSPITAL
ALTON BY PASS
A31
B3004
B3349
ANSTEY ROAD
ANSTEY LANE
MILL LANE
WILSOM ROAD
CAKERS LANE
WINDMILL HILL
WINDMILL LANE
WATER LANE
NEW BARN LANE
ODIHAM ROAD
OLD ODIHAM ROAD
NEW ODIHAM ROAD
BASINGSTOKE ROAD
LENTEN STREET
HIGH STREET
TURK STREET
LOWER TURK ST
DRAYMANS WAY
BUTTS ROAD
WHITEDOWN LANE
KINGS ROAD
QUEENS ROAD
ACKENDER RD
ALBERT RD
VICTORIA RD
NORMANDY ST
CHURCH STREET
AMERY HILL
AMERY ST
MOUNT PLEASANT RD
THE RIDGEWAY
VICARAGE HILL
PAPER MILL LANE
STATION RD
NURSERY ROAD
PARK CLOSE ROAD
LANSDOWNE ROAD
EDWARD RD
ALEXANDRA RD
LIPSCOMBE RISE
SOUTHVIEW RISE
CHERRY WAY
WALNUT CL
VYNE CL
NETHERFIELD CL
WENTWORTH GDNS
WILLOUGHBY CL
BRANDON CL
HIGHRIDGE
BRICK KILN LA
WICKHAM CL
BEECHWOOD ROAD
DASHWOOD CL
CURTIS ROAD
HUNTSMEAD
ASHDELL RD
CROWLEYS
SALISBURY CL
WINDSOR PK
LINGFIELD CL
BOROVERE LANE
BEREHURST
1
2
3
4
A
B
C
D
E
F

ALDERSHOT
Round Hill
Superstore
Police Sta & Court
School
Gdns
Liby
Redan Hill
Recreation Ground
Wellington Ctr
Town Hall
Park
Schs
Rec Grd
Bus Station
ALDERSHOT
BEECHNUT IND EST
MANOR PK IND EST
Playing Field
Aldershot Manor Park
Sch
Ayling Hill
Rowhill Copse (Nature Reserve)
Playing Field
Sports Ground
Blackwater River
PREYMEAD IND EST
Pea Bridge
Weybourne
Playing Field
Recreation Ground
Badshot Lea
Rec Grnd
Sewage Works
FARNBOROUGH ROAD
WELLINGTON AVENUE
HIGH STREET
VICTORIA ROAD
QUEEN'S ROAD
GROSVENOR ROAD
CRANMORE LANE
YORK ROAD
EGGAR'S HILL
CHURCH LANE WEST
EAST CHURCH LANE
HILLSIDE ROAD
BRIDGE ROAD
PARK ROAD
LOWER FARNHAM ROAD
WEYBOURNE ROAD
LOWER WEYBOURNE LANE
BADSHOT LEA ROAD
GREEN LANE
LOW LANE
ST GEORGES ROAD
MONKTON LA
A325
A323
B3208
B3367
A31

14
ANDOVER
MERIDIAN INDUSTRIAL PARK
Engineering Works
WESTMARCH BUSINESS CENTRE
Superstore
Supermarket
CHURCHILL WAY
NORTHERN AVENUE
REDON WAY
WESTERN AVENUE
NEW ST
EAST ST
Cemetery
Cricklade College
Law Court
Sports Centre
Council Offices
THE CHANTRY CENTRE
Bus Sta
Liby
Guildhall
Pol Sta
Recreation Ground
Common Acre
Sports Ground
Schools
Playing Field
School
Sch
Fire Sta
WEYHILL ROAD
B3402
SALISBURY ROAD
ANTON TRADING ESTATE
River Anton
Works
Mill Lake
Barlows Lake
Club House
Golf Course
WINCHESTER ROAD
ANDOVER BY-PASS
A303
Bere Hill
Bere Hill Farm
Ladies Walk
Subway
Iron Bridge (FB)
Andover
Long Bridge
LONDON ROAD
VIGO ROAD
MICHELDEVER ROAD
A B C D
1 2 3 4 5 6

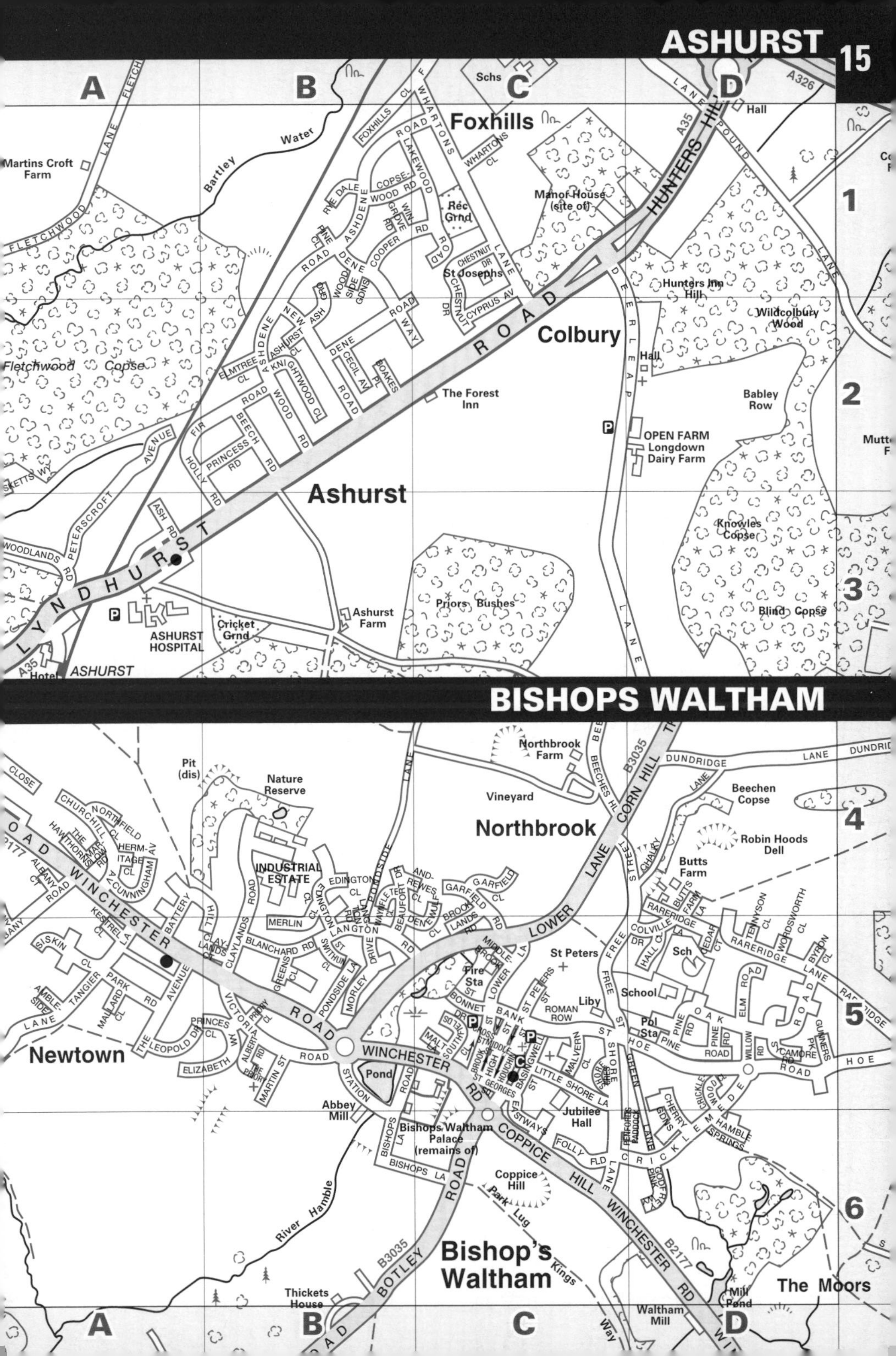
ASHURST
Foxhills
Colbury
Ashurst
ASHURST HOSPITAL
The Forest Inn
OPEN FARM Longdown Dairy Farm
Fletchwood Copse
Priors Bushes
Knowles Copse
Blind Copse
Babley Row
Wildcolbury Wood
Hunters Inn Hill
Manor House (site of)
BISHOPS WALTHAM
Northbrook
Newtown
INDUSTRIAL ESTATE
Nature Reserve
Vineyard
Beechen Copse
Robin Hoods Dell
Butts Farm
Bishops Waltham Palace (remains of)
Jubilee Hall
Coppice Hill
Bishop's Waltham
The Moors
Thickets House
Waltham Mill
Abbey Mill

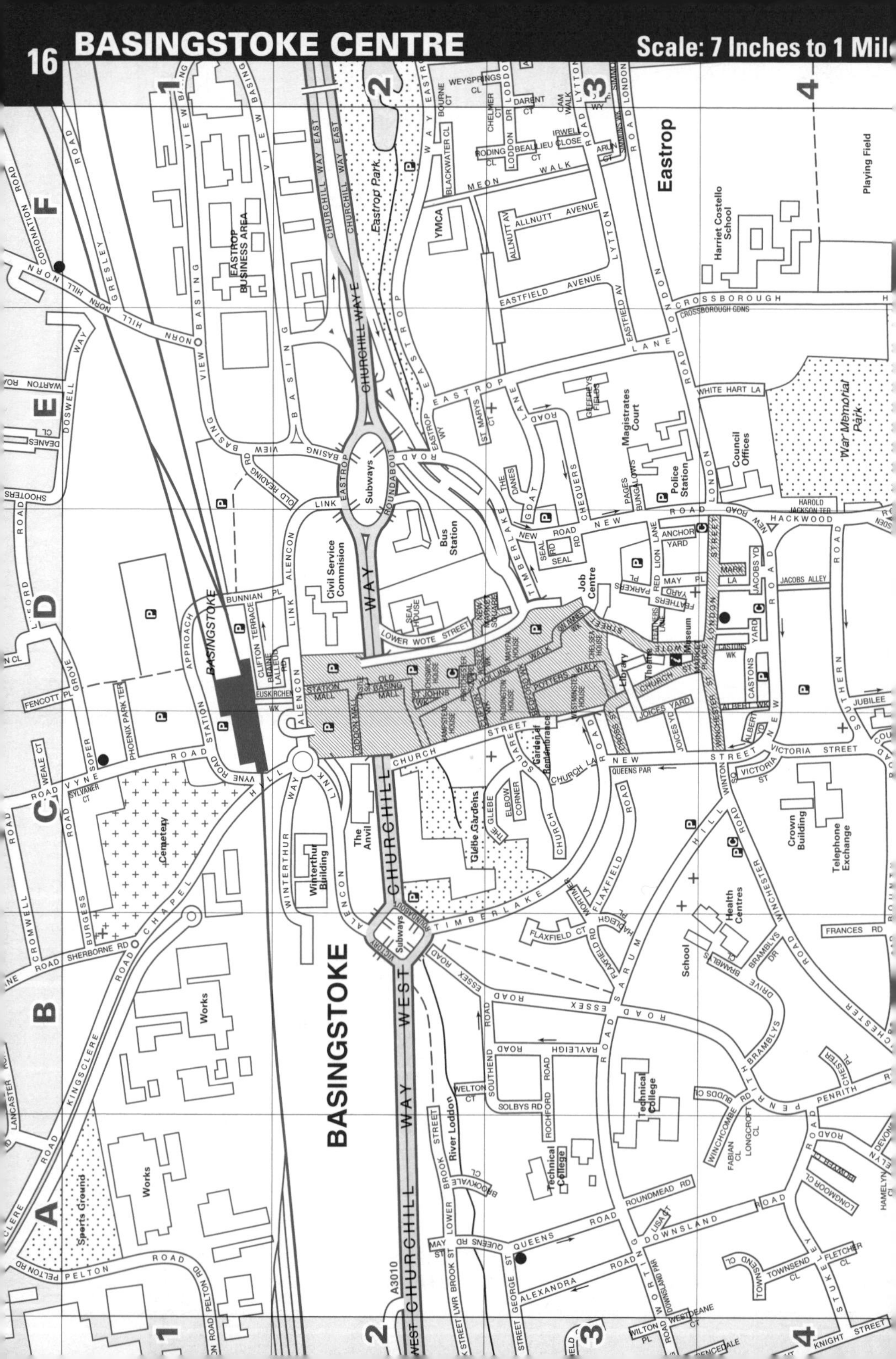
BASINGSTOKE
Eastrop
Eastrop Park
EASTROP BUSINESS AREA
Harriet Costello School
Playing Field
War Memorial Park
Council Offices
Magistrates Court
Police Station
YMCA
Bus Station
Civil Service Commision
Subways
Job Centre
Library
Theatre
Museum
Garden of Remembrance
Glebe Gardens
The Anvil
Winterthur Building
Cemetery
Works
Sports Ground
River Loddon
Technical College
School
Health Centres
Crown Building
Telephone Exchange
SEAL HOUSE
NEW MARKET SQUARE
STATION MALL
OLD BASING MALL
CHURCHILL WAY
CHURCHILL WAY EAST
CHURCHILL WAY WEST
A3010
EASTROP ROUNDABOUT
VICTORY ROUNDABOUT
ALENCON LINK
BASINGSTOKE STATION
STATION APPROACH
VIEW BASING
NORN HILL
CORONATION ROAD
GRESLEY ROAD
DOSWELL WAY
WARTON ROAD
DEANES CL
SHOOTERS ROAD
FENCOTT PL
PHOENIX PARK TER
SOPER GROVE
WEALE CT
VYNE ROAD
SYLVANER CT
BURGESS ROAD
CROMWELL ROAD
SHERBORNE RD
CHAPEL HILL
KINGSCLERE ROAD
LANCASTER RD
PELTON ROAD
PELTON RD
BUNNIAN PL
CLIFTON TERRACE
EUSKIRCHEN WK
OLD READING RD
LOWER WOTE STREET
WOTE STREET
CHURCH STREET
CHURCH SQUARE
ELBOW CORNER
THE GLEBE
CHURCH LA
NEW STREET
QUEENS PAR
CROSS ST
JOICES YARD
WINCHESTER ST
LONDON STREET
MARKET PLACE
VICTORIA STREET
ALBERT YD
CASTONS YARD
JACOBS YD
JACOBS ALLEY
MAY PL
RED LION LANE
ANCHOR YARD
FEATHERS YARD
PARKERS PL
NEW ROAD
SEAL RD
GOAT LANE
CHEQUERS ROAD
PAGES BUNGALOWS
THE DANES
ST MARYS CT
TIMBERLAKE ROAD
EASTROP LANE
EASTROP WY
EASTROP WAY
GEFFERYS FIELDS
WHITE HART LA
HAROLD JACKSON TER
HACKWOOD ROAD
SOUTHERN ROAD
JUBILEE
CROSSBOROUGH HILL
CROSSBOROUGH GDNS
LONDON ROAD
EASTFIELD AVENUE
EASTFIELD AV
ALLNUTT AVENUE
ALLNUTT AV
LYTTON ROAD
MEON WALK
BLACKWATER CL
BOURNE CT
WEYSPRINGS CL
CHELMER CT
LODDON DR
LODDON CT
RODING CL
BEAULIEU CT
DARENT CT
IRWELL CLOSE
CAM WALK
ARUN CT
SIMMONS WK
WINTON SQ
HILL ROAD
FRANCES RD
BRAMBLYS CL
BRAMBLYS DR
BRAMBLYS DRIVE
SARUM HILL
FLAXFIELD CT
FLAXFIELD RD
HAGLEIGH PL
MORTIMER LA
ESSEX ROAD
RAYLEIGH ROAD
SOUTHEND ROAD
ROCHFORD ROAD
SOLBYS RD
WELTON CT
BUDDS CL
PENRITH ROAD
CHESTER PL
WINCHCOMBE RD
LONGCROFT CL
FABIAN CL
ROUNDMEAD RD
DOWNSLAND ROAD
DOWNSLAND PAR
LISA CT
WORTING ROAD
ALEXANDRA ROAD
QUEENS ROAD
QUEENS RD
GEORGE STREET
BROOKVALE CL
LOWER BROOK STREET
LWR BROOK ST
MAY ST
WESTDEANE CT
WILTON PL
TOWNSEND CL
FLETCHER CL
STUKELEY ROAD
KNIGHT STREET
LONGMOOR CL
HAMELYN RD
DEVON

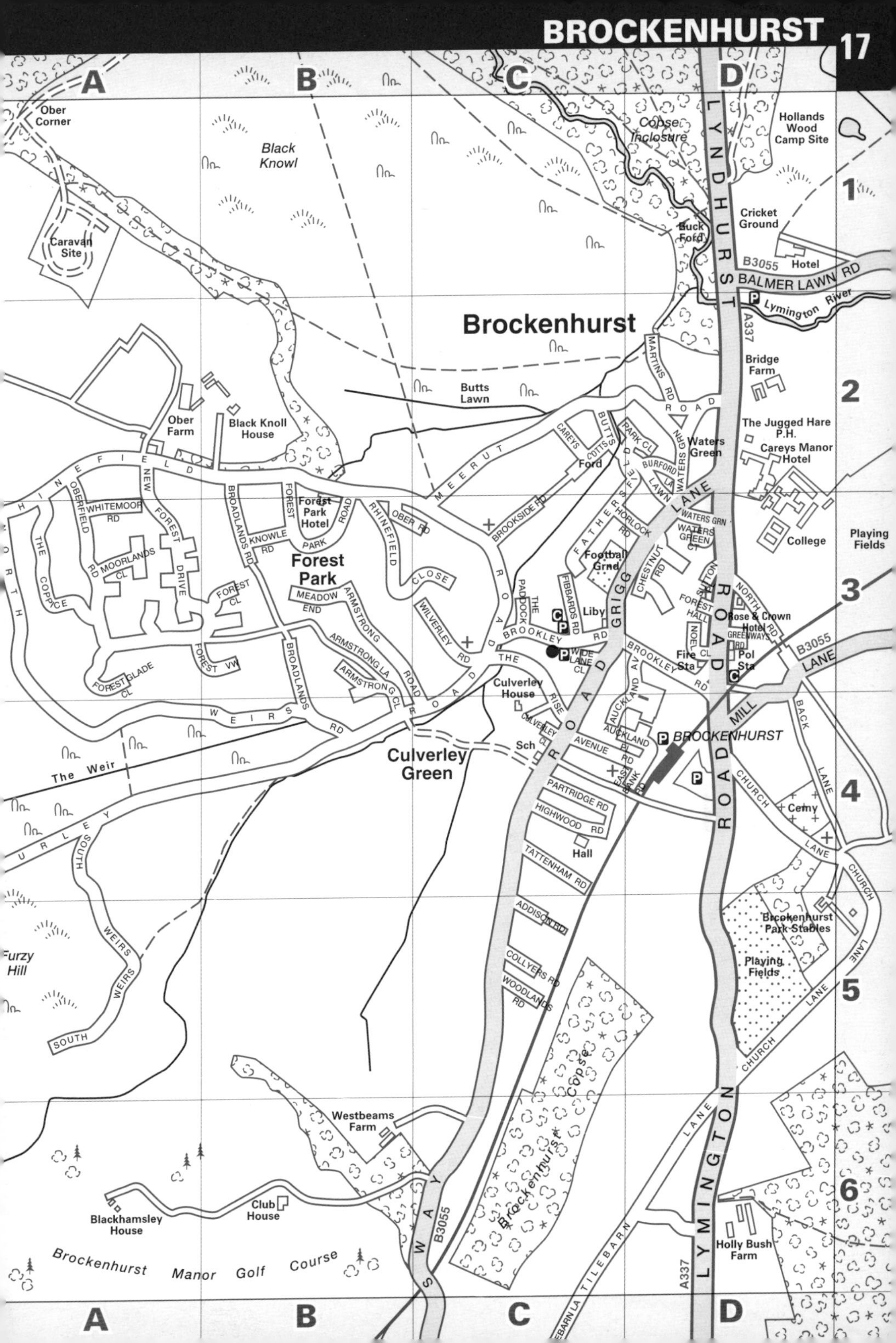
Brockenhurst
Forest Park
Culverley Green
Black Knowl
Ober Corner
Caravan Site
Ober Farm
Black Knoll House
Butts Lawn
Copse Inclosure
Buck Ford
Hollands Wood Camp Site
Cricket Ground
Hotel
B3055
BALMER LAWN RD
Lymington River
A337
Bridge Farm
The Jugged Hare P.H.
Careys Manor Hotel
College
Playing Fields
Waters Green
Ford
Football Grnd
Liby
Rose & Crown Hotel
Fire Sta
Pol Sta
BROCKENHURST
Culverley House
Sch
Hall
Cemy
Brockenhurst Park Stables
Playing Fields
Brockenhurst Copse
Westbeams Farm
Club House
Blackhamsley House
Brockenhurst Manor Golf Course
Holly Bush Farm
Furzy Hill
The Weir
LYNDHURST RD
LYMINGTON ROAD
GRIGG LANE
SWAY RD
RHINEFIELD RD
MEERUT RD
BROOKLEY RD
WEIRS RD
SOUTH WEIRS
CHURCH LANE
BACK LANE
MILL LANE
TILEBARN LA
FOREST PARK ROAD
NEW FOREST DRIVE
BROADLANDS RD
WHITEMOOR RD
OBERFIELD RD
KNOWLE RD
MOORLANDS CL
THE COPPICE
FOREST CL
FOREST VW
FOREST GLADE CL
MEADOW END
ARMSTRONG RD
ARMSTRONG LA
ARMSTRONG CL
OBER RD
RHINEFIELD CLOSE
WILVERLEY RD
BROOKSIDE RD
CAREYS COTTS
BUTTS LAWN
MARTINS RD
PARK CL
BURFORD LA
WATERS GRN
FATHERSFIELD
HORLOCK RD
WATERS GREEN CT
CHESTNUT RD
THE PADDOCK
FIBBARDS RD
WIDE LANE CL
SUTTON RD
NORTH RD
FOREST HALL
NOEL CL
GREENWAYS RD
AUCKLAND AV
AUCKLAND PL
AUCKLAND RD
AVENUE RD
EAST BANK RD
THE RISE
CULVERLEY CL
PARTRIDGE RD
HIGHWOOD RD
TATTENHAM RD
ADDISON RD
COLLYERS RD
WOODLANDS RD
A B C D
1 2 3 4 5 6

A
B
C
D
1
2
3
4
5
6
LOUISBURG RD
AMHERST ROAD
CENTRAL
EASTERN ROAD
PARADE
NORTH ROAD
STABLE ROAD
WESTERN ROAD
SOUTHERN
LOUISBURG BARBADOS BARRACKS
Oxney Moss
FARNHAM RD
A325
LINDFORD ROAD
STATION ROAD
BOLLEY AVENUE
BOLLEY AV
BORDON TRADING ESTATE
STATION WAY
OLD STATION
Cemy
OAKHANGER ROAD
BUDDS LANE
Bordon Camp
LADYSMITH PL
CONISTON
DERWENT CL
THIRLMERE RD
WINDERMERE RD
GRASMERE CL
BUTTERMERE CL
LOWESWATER GDNS
Fire Sta
OAKLEY RD
BEAUFORT RD
ULLSWATER CL
BASSENTHWAITE GDNS
ENNERDALE ROAD
RYDAL CL
HAWESWATER CL
HAMPSHIRE RD
KILDARE RD
Schools
SCHOOL RD
LAMERTON CL
LAMERTON RD
HAMPSHIRE CL
ESSEX RD
ESSEX CL
ESSEX ROAD
GARTH CL
CANADA WY
MAPLE LEAF DR
PRINCE PHILIP BARRACKS
CAMP ROAD
SAINT LUCIA PARK
Bordon Inclosure
Sewage Works
TRENCHARD PARK
Chase Farm
JUBILEE HO
Alexandra Park
BRANSON ROAD
HOLLYBROOK
SAVILE CRESCENT
HALE ROAD
ASHMEAD
PARK STREET
HIGH STREET
LYNTON ROAD
SOMERSET AVENUE
TILBURYS CL
CRES
ALEXANDRA CT
BLACKTHORN CL
VARNA RD
WILLOW CL
SYDNEY RD
SUNBURY CL
ALMA RD
ELM CL
DEVON RD
WOODSIDE
WOODSIDE PK
WOODSIDE CL
MANICA CL
FERNCOTE
LAKE
WOOLMER WAY
WOOLMER TRADING ESTATE
HEATHCOTE RD
Liby
THE FOREST SHOP CENTRE
BIRCH CL
LAVENDER GDNS
LILAC CL
PINEHILL ROAD
APOLLO
ROBINSON WY
JACARANDA RD
WISTERIA DR
OAK LODGE
FOREST ROAD
CHESTNUT CT
FOXGLOVE DR
HIBISCUS GRO
DUCKLANDS
Bordon
Caravan Site
MOOR CL
HOGMOOR ROAD
SPRUCE AV
CYPRESS RD
MORNINGTON ROAD
JUNIPER CL
WARREN CLOSE
SELBORNE WY
BRAMLEY WK
THE SANDS
WOODPECKER CL
SHAFTESBURY CT
COOPER HO
JOHN POUNDS HO
HENDON RD
CONNAUGHT CL
DENE CL
BLUE TIMBERS CL
JASMINE WY
KNOWLES CL
CONDE WY
CHASE COMM HOSP
ASHBURY RD
NUTLEY CL
MELROSE CL
AMBER CL
GARNET RD
Fire Sta
KINGFISHER CL
NIGHTINGALE
Hogmoor Inclosure
WELLINGTON AV
CONDE WAY
MALMSBURY
YORK CL
ARGYLE RD
ROXBURGHE CLOSE
ATHOLL RD
GRAFTON CL
Golf Course
ST ANDREWS RD
LYTHAM CL
BROOMFIELD RD
GOLF LANE
FERNLEA
GORSEDOWN
KENT RD
RICHMOND CL
DUDLEY CL
CORNWALL RD
NORTHUMBERLAND RD
SUTHERLAND CL
MONTROSE
THE LINKS
TWOWAYS CT
STUBBINGTON AV
SOUTH
OVERDALE WK
HURST
ALPINE RD
ASPEN CL
MONUMENT CHASE
Forest Lodge
NEW ROAD
Club House
Eveley Lane
THE FAIRWAY
SUTTON FIELD
HOGMOOR RD
WEST VIEW
FIR GROVE
HEATHER CL
CHAMPNEY CL
Police Station
LEMON GROVE
WITTCOMB TER
SPENCERS CT
OAKTREE RD
CONIFER CL
PRINCES
Whitehill
Sch
PLANTATION WAY
NORRIS CL
FIRGROVE ROAD
EVELEY CL
MAYFLOWER RD
BIRCH GROVE
PELHAM CL
THE WOODLANDS
PETERSFIELD ROAD
LIPHOOK ROAD
WALLDOWN ROAD
DRIFT ROAD
BRACKEN
WHITEHILL PARK

E
F
G
H
1
2
3
4
5
6
Lindford
Arford
Headley
Deadwater
Standford
Passfield
Hollywater
Curtis's Hill
BROXHEAD IND EST
Lindford Bridge
Huntingford Farm
Curtis Farm
Hatch House Farm
Headley Mill Farm
Headley Mill
Weydown Farm
Wey Valley Farm
Hatch Farm
Passfield House Farm
Passfield Farm
Hollywater Farm
Sewage Works
PASSFIELD MILL BUSINESS PARK
Sports Centre
School
Sch
Cemy
Ford
Eveley Wood
Passfield Common
FRENSHAM LANE
CURTIS LANE
LINDFORD ROAD
LIPHOOK ROAD
HEADLEY ROAD
STANDFORD ROAD
STANDFORD LANE
MILL LANE
CRABTREE LANE
LONG CROSS HILL
HIGH STREET
HEADLEY FIELDS
LIPHOOK ROAD
TULLS LANE
RIVERSIDE ROAD
PASSFIELD ROAD
STANDFORD HILL
HOUSE HILL
WHITEHILL ROAD
HOLLYWATER ROAD
CHASE ROAD
MILL CHASE ROAD
CANES LANE
TAYLORS LANE
WINDSOR ROAD
B3004
33

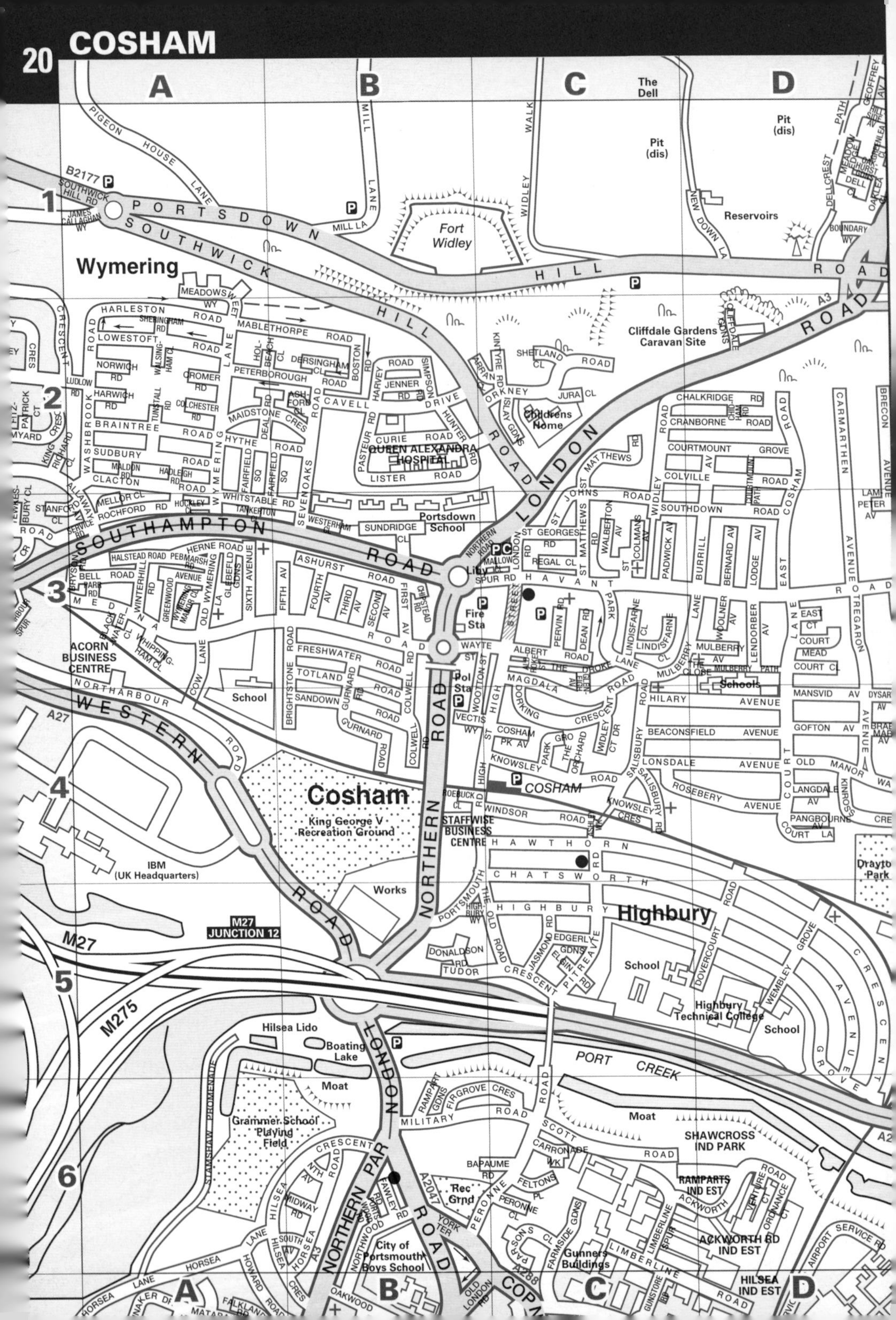
A
B
C
D
1
2
3
4
5
6
The Dell
Pit (dis)
Reservoirs
Fort Widley
Wymering
PORTSDOWN HILL ROAD
SOUTHWICK HILL ROAD
PIGEON HOUSE LANE
MILL LANE
WIDLEY WALK
NEW DOWN LA
B2177
Cliffdale Gardens Caravan Site
QUEEN ALEXANDRA HOSPITAL
Childrens Home
Portsdown School
SOUTHAMPTON ROAD
LONDON ROAD
HAVANT ROAD
NORTHERN ROAD
WESTERN ROAD
NORTHARBOUR
A27
A3
ACORN BUSINESS CENTRE
IBM (UK Headquarters)
School
Schools
Fire Sta
Pol Sta
PC
Cosham
King George V Recreation Ground
Works
STAFFWISE BUSINESS CENTRE
HAWTHORN
CHATSWORTH
HIGHBURY
Highbury
Highbury Technical College
M27 JUNCTION 12
M27
M275
Hilsea Lido
Boating Lake
Moat
PORT CREEK
Grammer School Playing Field
MILITARY ROAD
SHAWCROSS IND PARK
RAMPARTS IND EST
ACKWORTH RD IND EST
HILSEA IND EST
Gunners Buildings
City of Portsmouth Boys School
Rec Grnd
NORTHERN PAR
A2047
A288
HORSEA LANE
AIRPORT SERVICE RD
Drayton Park
CRESCENT
AVENUE

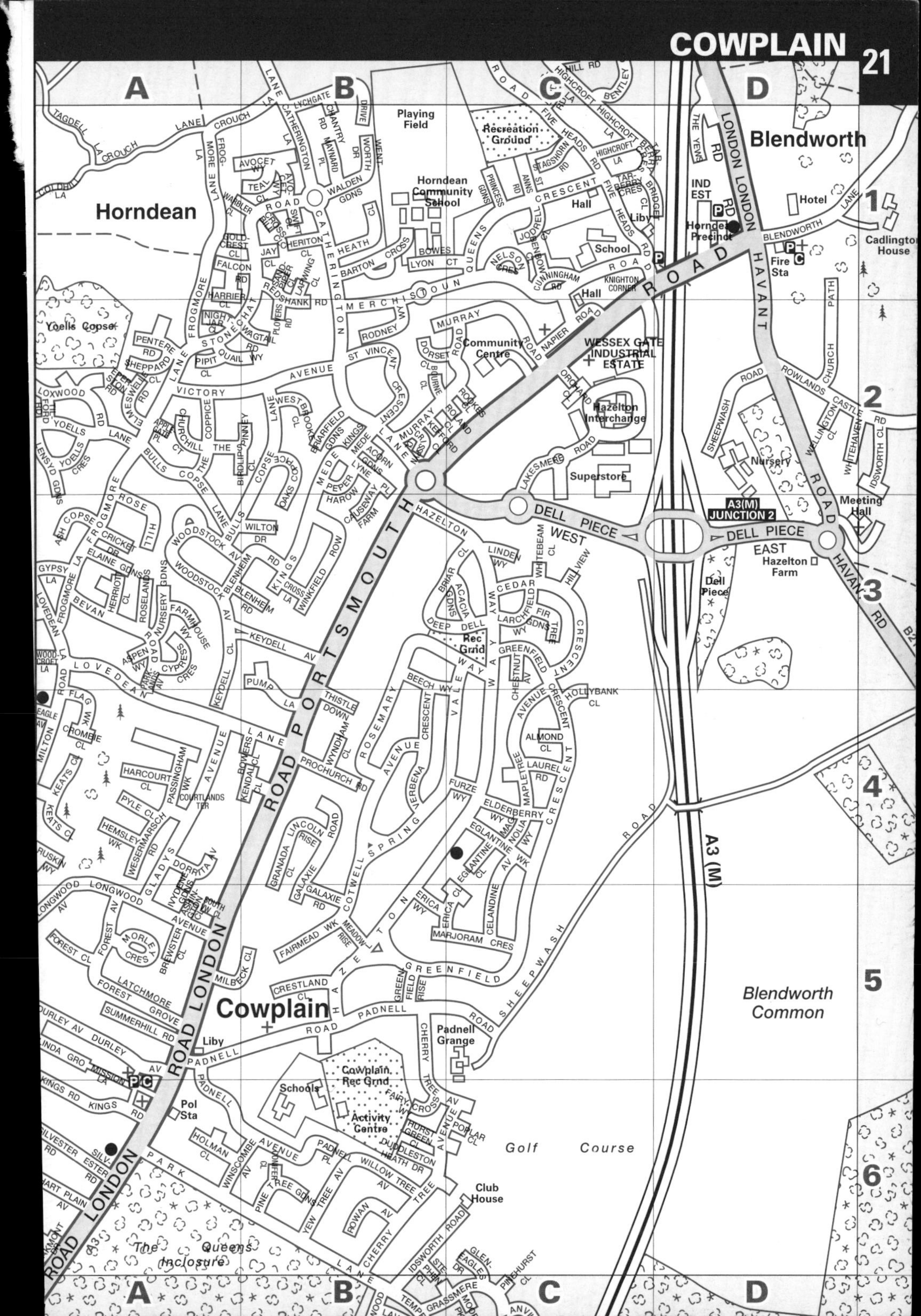
A
B
C
D
1
2
3
4
5
6
Horndean
Blendworth
Cowplain
Blendworth Common
Golf Course
The Queens Inclosure
Yoells Copse
Playing Field
Recreation Ground
Horndean Community School
Hall
School
Liby
IND EST
Horndean Precinct
Hotel
Cadlington House
Fire Sta
WESSEX GATE INDUSTRIAL ESTATE
Community Centre
Hazelton Interchange
Superstore
Nursery
Meeting Hall
A3(M) JUNCTION 2
Hazelton Farm
Dell Piece
Rec Grnd
Pol Sta
Padnell Grange
Cowplain Rec Grnd
Schools
Activity Centre
Club House
A3 (M)
PORTSMOUTH ROAD
LONDON ROAD
HAVANT ROAD
DELL PIECE WEST
DELL PIECE EAST
MERCHISTOUN ROAD
VICTORY AVENUE
PADNELL ROAD
HAZELTON WAY
SHEEPWASH LANE
LOVEDEAN LANE
FROGMORE LANE
CATHERINGTON LANE
PARK LANE
CHERRY TREE AVENUE
GREENFIELD CRESCENT
SPRING VALE
QUEENS CRESCENT
FIVE HEADS ROAD
BLENDWORTH LANE

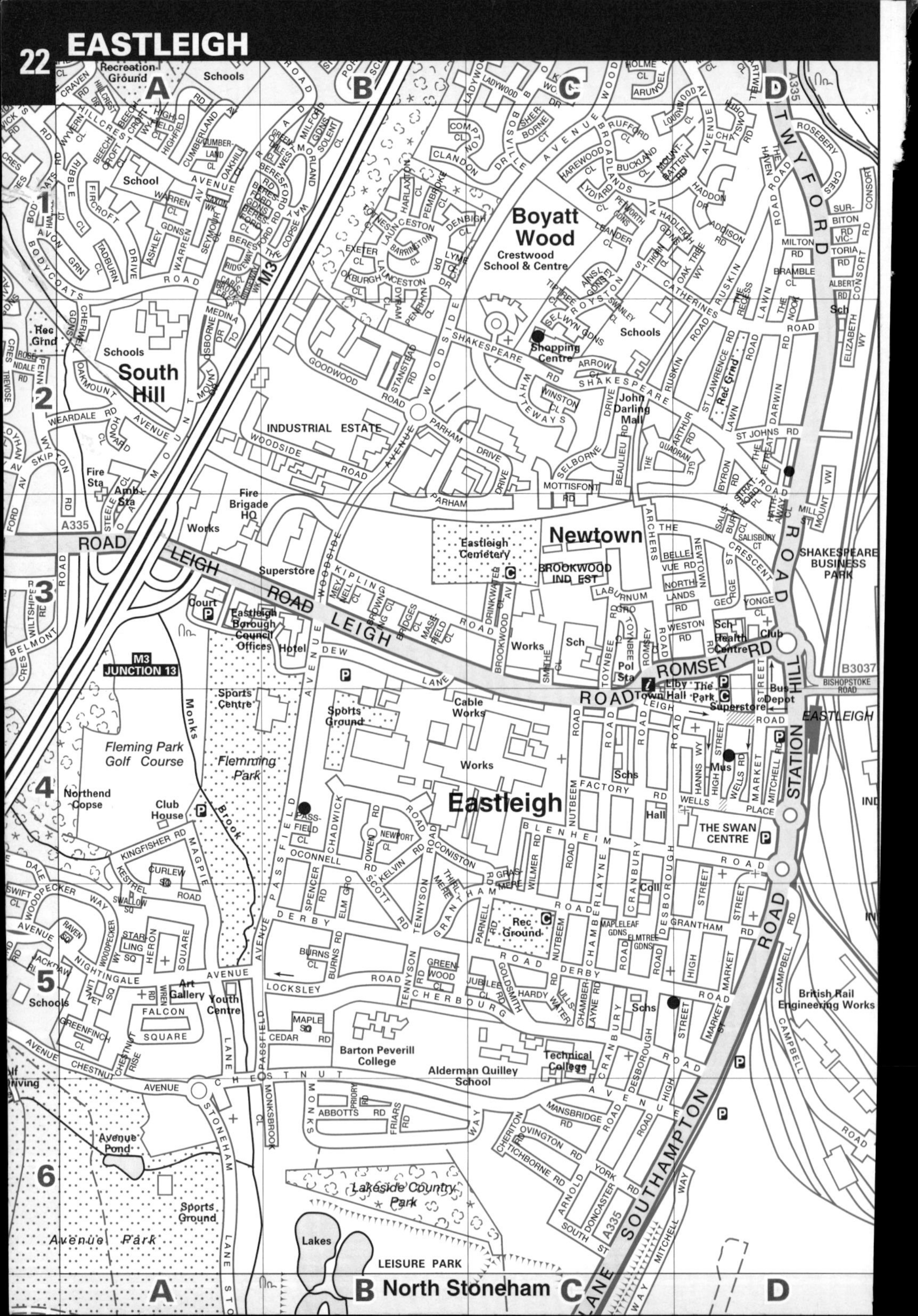

Recreation Ground
Schools
School
Boyatt Wood
Crestwood School & Centre
Shopping Centre
South Hill
INDUSTRIAL ESTATE
John Darling Mall
Fire Sta
Amb Sta
Fire Brigade HQ
Works
Superstore
Eastleigh Cemetery
Newtown
BROOKWOOD IND EST
SHAKESPEARE BUSINESS PARK
Court
Eastleigh Borough Council Offices
Hotel
M3 JUNCTION 13
Sports Centre
Sports Ground
Cable Works
Pol Sta
Liby
Town Hall
The Park
Superstore
Bus Depot
EASTLEIGH
Health Centre
Club
Fleming Park Golf Course
Flemming Park
Monks Brook
Northend Copse
Club House
Eastleigh
Mus
THE SWAN CENTRE
Hall
Schs
Coll
Rec Ground
Art Gallery
Youth Centre
Schools
British Rail Engineering Works
Barton Peverill College
Alderman Quilley School
Technical College
Avenue Pond
Sports Ground
Avenue Park
Lakeside Country Park
Lakes
LEISURE PARK
North Stoneham
TWYFORD ROAD
SOUTHAMPTON ROAD
STATION HILL
ROMSEY ROAD
LEIGH ROAD
PASSFIELD AVENUE
CHESTNUT AVENUE
STONEHAM LANE
A335
B3037
M3

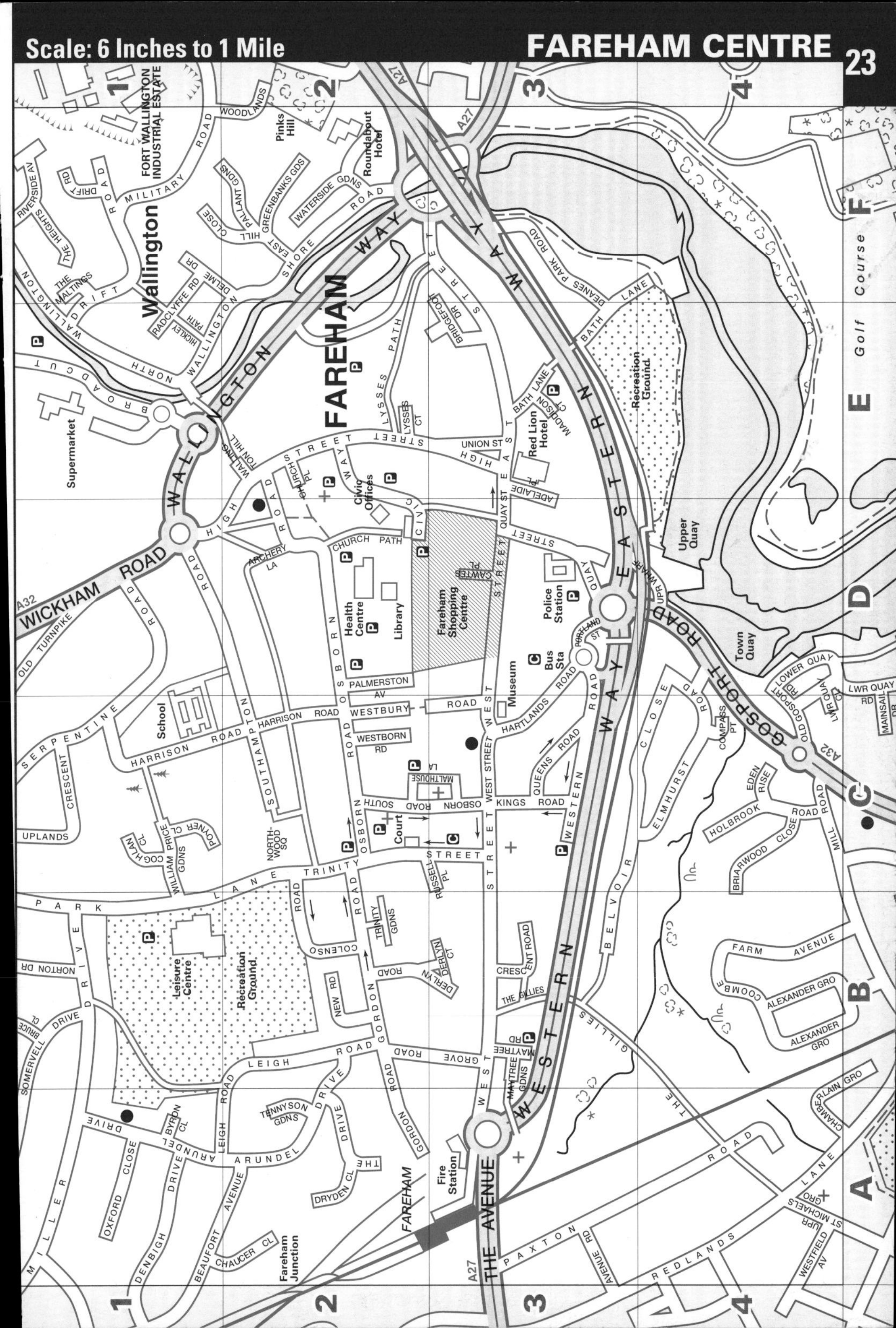
FORT WALLINGTON INDUSTRIAL ESTATE
Wallington
FAREHAM
Pinks Hill
Roundabout Hotel
MILITARY ROAD
WOODLANDS
SHORE ROAD
WATERSIDE GDNS
GREENBANKS GDS
PALLANT GDNS
EAST HILL CLOSE
RIVERSIDE AV
DRIFT RD
THE HEIGHTS
THE MALTINGS
DRIFT ROAD
DEIME DR
RADCLYFFE RD
HICKLEY PATH
WALLINGTON
NORTH WALLINGTON
BROADCUT
Supermarket
WALLINGTON WAY
WALLINGTON ROAD
WICKHAM ROAD
A32
A27
EASTERN WAY
WESTERN WAY
DEANES PARK ROAD
BATH LANE
Recreation Ground
MADDISON CT
Red Lion Hotel
UNION ST
HIGH STREET
EAST STREET
ADELAIDE PL
QUAY ST
LYSSES PATH
LYSSES CT
BRIDGEFOOT DR
Civic Offices
CIVIC WAY
CHURCH PL
CHURCH PATH
ARCHERY LA
WALLINGTON HILL
HIGH ROAD
Health Centre
Library
Fareham Shopping Centre
CAWTES PL
Police Station
QUAY
UPR WHARF
PORTLAND ST
Bus Sta
Museum
Upper Quay
Town Quay
GOSPORT ROAD
LOWER QUAY
LWR QUAY RD
MAINSAIL DR
OLD GOSPORT RD
Golf Course
OLD TURNPIKE
SERPENTINE ROAD
School
HARRISON ROAD
SOUTHAMPTON ROAD
OSBORN ROAD
PALMERSTON AV
WESTBURY ROAD
WESTBORN RD
HARTLANDS ROAD
QUEENS ROAD
MALTHOUSE LA
OSBORN ROAD SOUTH
KINGS ROAD
WEST STREET
Court
TRINITY STREET
RUSSELL PL
SERPENTINE CRESCENT
UPLANDS
COGHLAN CL
WILLIAM PRICE GDNS
POYNER CL
NORTH-WOOD SQ
PARK LANE
Leisure Centre
Recreation Ground
TRINITY GDNS
COLENSO ROAD
DERLYN CT
CRESCENT ROAD
THE GILLIES
GILLIES
NEW RD
GORDON ROAD
GROVE ROAD
MAYTREE RD
MAYTREE GDNS
ELMHURST CLOSE
BELVOIR
COMPASS PT
EDEN RISE
HOLBROOK ROAD
BRIARWOOD CLOSE
MILL ROAD
FARM AVENUE
COOMBE
ALEXANDER GRO
NORTON DR
BRUCE CL
SOMERVELL DRIVE
MILLER DRIVE
LEIGH ROAD
TENNYSON GDNS
BYRON CL
ARUNDEL DRIVE
OXFORD CLOSE
DENBIGH DRIVE
BEAUFORT AVENUE
CHAUCER CL
DRYDEN CL
THE DRIVE
Fareham Junction
FAREHAM
Fire Station
THE AVENUE
PAXTON RD
AVENUE RD
REDLANDS
THE ROAD
CHAMBERLAIN GRO
ST MICHAELS GRO
UPR
LANE
WESTFIELD AV
1
2
3
4
A
B
C
D
E
F

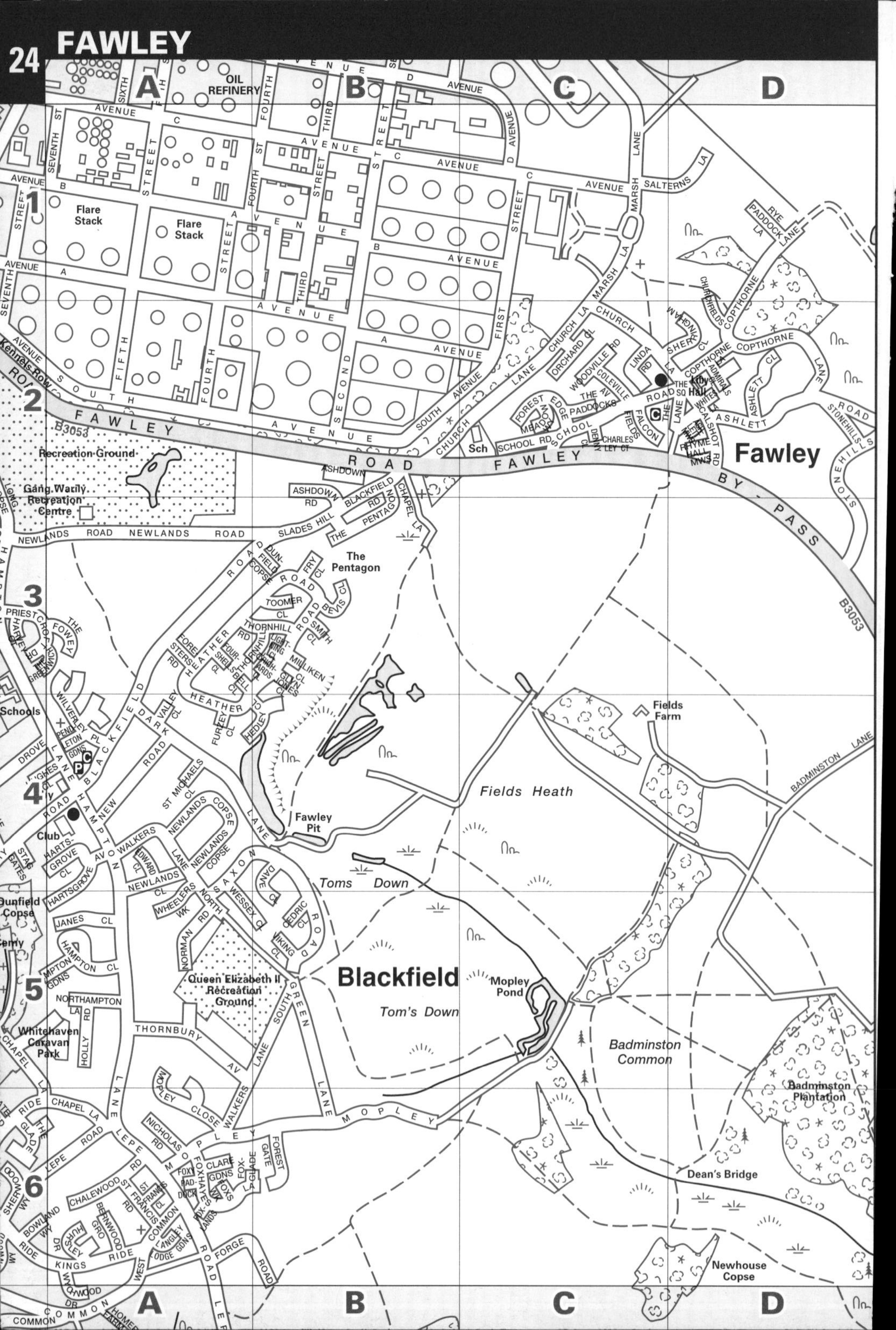
A
B
C
D
1
2
3
4
5
6
OIL REFINERY
Flare Stack
Flare Stack
FAWLEY ROAD
B3053
Recreation Ground
Gang Warily Recreation Centre
NEWLANDS ROAD
The Pentagon
Fawley Pit
Toms Down
Blackfield
Tom's Down
Mopley Pond
Fields Heath
Fields Farm
Badminston Common
Badminston Plantation
Dean's Bridge
Newhouse Copse
Fawley
FAWLEY BY-PASS
BADMINSTON LANE
Queen Elizabeth II Recreation Ground
Whitehaven Caravan Park
Schools
Club
Dunfield Copse
Sch
SCHOOL RD
CHURCH LANE
MARSH LANE
SALTERNS
COPTHORNE LANE
ASHLETT ROAD
STONEHILLS
BLACKFIELD ROAD
HAMPTON LANE
LEPE ROAD
MOPLEY
FORGE ROAD
CHAPEL LA
THORNBURY AV
NORTHAMPTON LA
SOUTH AVENUE

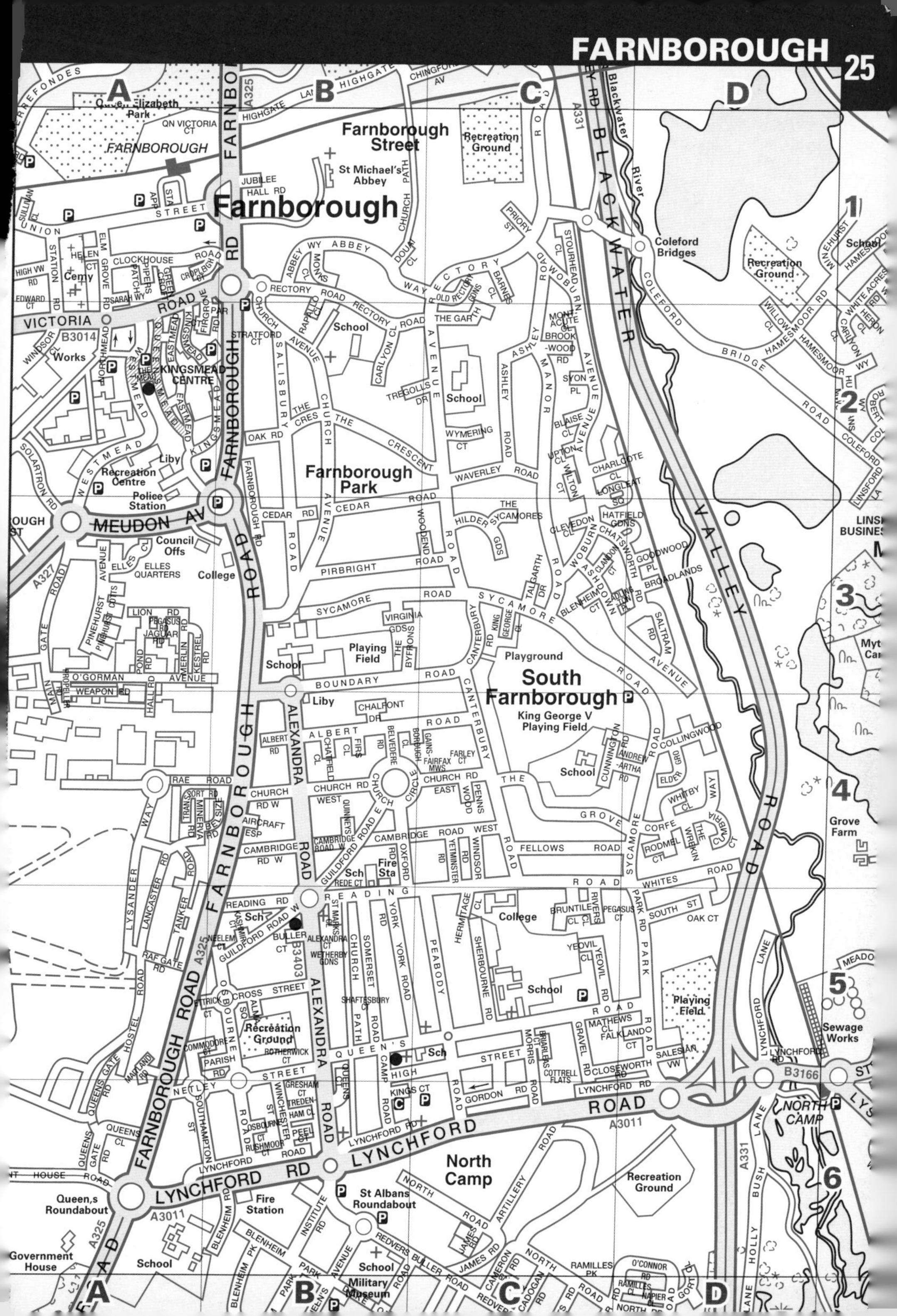

A
B
C
D
1
2
3
4
5
6
Queen Elizabeth Park
QN VICTORIA CT
FARNBOROUGH
HIGHGATE
HIGHGATE LA
CHINGFORD AV
Farnborough Street
Recreation Ground
St Michael's Abbey
JUBILEE HALL RD
Farnborough
A325
A331
BLACKWATER
Blackwater River
Coleford Bridges
School
Recreation Ground
COLEFORD BRIDGE ROAD
HAMESMOOR RD
HAMESMOOR WY
WILLOW CL
UNION
STATION RD
ELM GROVE RD
HELEN CT
Cemy
CLOCKHOUSE
HIGH VW RD
EDWARD CT
VICTORIA ROAD
B3014
Works
KINGSMEAD CENTRE
WESTMEAD
KINGSMEAD
Liby
Recreation Centre
Police Station
MEUDON AV
A327
Council Offs
ELLES QUARTERS
College
O'GORMAN AVENUE
WEAPON RD
RECTORY ROAD
ABBEY WY
CHURCH AVENUE
SALISBURY ROAD
School
CARLYON CL
TREGOLLS DR
School
OAK RD
THE CRESCENT
Farnborough Park
CEDAR ROAD
WAVERLEY ROAD
THE SYCAMORES
HILDER GDS
ASHLEY ROAD
MANOR ROAD
WOBURN AVENUE
STOURHEAD CL
PRIORY ST
CHARLOTTE CL
LONGLEAT SQ
HATFIELD GDNS
GOODWOOD PL
BROADLANDS
PIRBRIGHT ROAD
SYCAMORE ROAD
Playing Field
School
BOUNDARY ROAD
Playground
South Farnborough
King George V Playing Field
CANTERBURY RD
Liby
CHALFONT DR
ALBERT ROAD
ALEXANDRA ROAD
School
COLLINGWOOD
CHURCH RD W
CHURCH CIRCLE
THE GROVE
FELLOWS ROAD
CAMBRIDGE ROAD
WHITES ROAD
RAE ROAD
Fire Sta
READING ROAD
Sch
SOUTH ST
OAK CT
College
School
Playing Field
Sewage Works
LYNCHFORD RD
LYSANDER
LANCASTER
RAF GATE RD
CROSS STREET
Recreation Ground
PARISH RD
QUEEN'S STREET
HIGH STREET
Sch
GORDON RD
LYNCHFORD ROAD
A3011
B3166
NORTH CAMP
B3403
FARNBOROUGH ROAD
VALLEY ROAD
Grove Farm
North Camp
Recreation Ground
ARTILLERY ROAD
HOLLY BUSH LANE
Queen's Roundabout
Fire Station
St Albans Roundabout
Government House
School
School
Military Museum
BLENHEIM RD
REDVERS BULLER ROAD
JAMES RD
CAMERON RD
RAMILLES PK
O'CONNOR RD

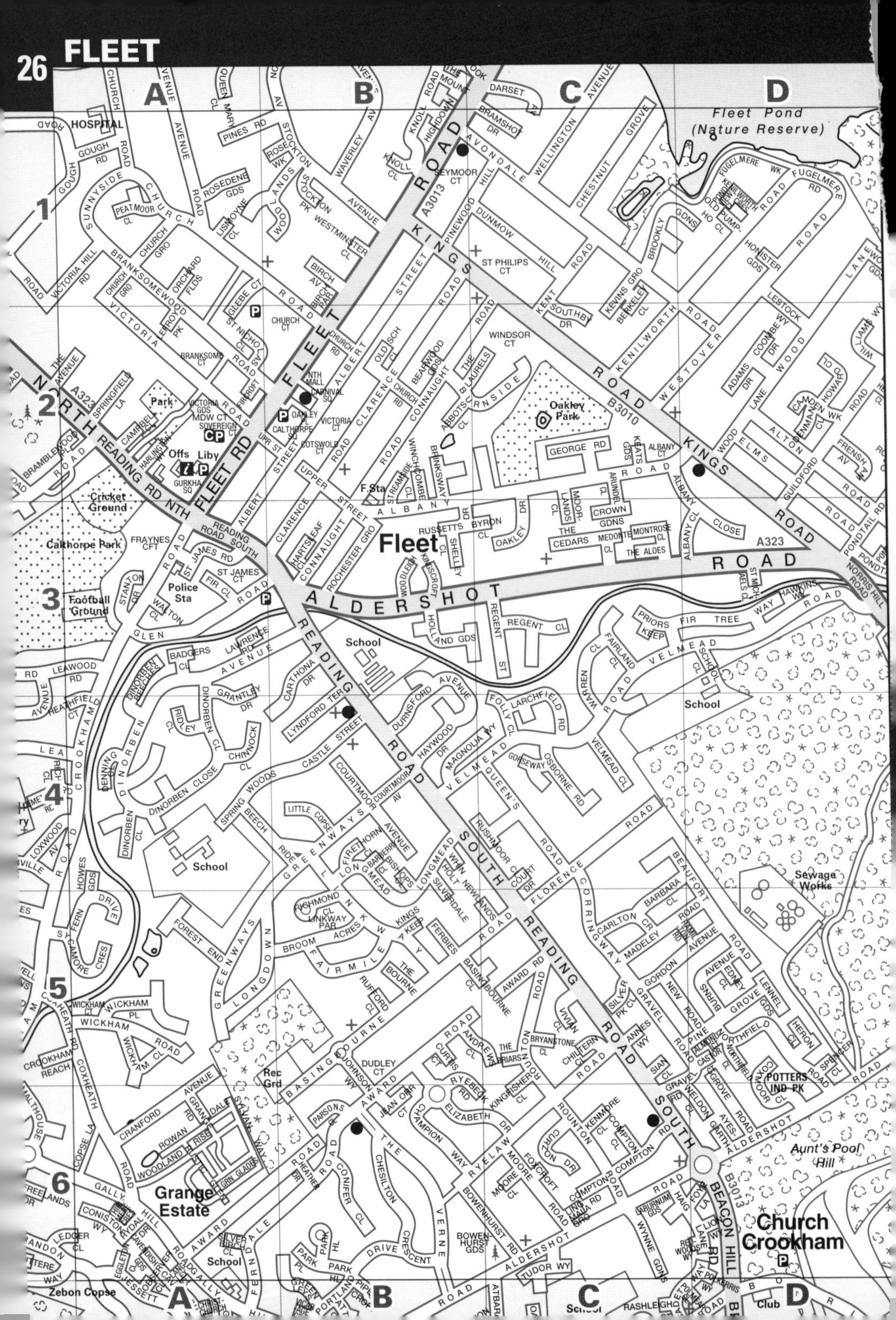
A
B
C
D
1
2
3
4
5
6
Fleet Pond
(Nature Reserve)
Fleet
HOSPITAL
Park
Offs
Liby
Cricket Ground
Calthorpe Park
Football Ground
Police Sta
F.Sta
Oakley Park
School
Sewage Works
Rec Grd
Grange Estate
Church Crookham
Aunt's Pool Hill
Zebon Copse
POTTERS IND PK
Club
FLEET RD
FLEET ROAD
A3013
KINGS ROAD
B3010
ALDERSHOT ROAD
A323
READING RD NTH
NORTH
READING ROAD SOUTH
BEACON HILL RD
B3013
CHURCH ROAD
AVONDALE
WELLINGTON AVENUE
CHESTNUT GROVE
FUGELMERE RD
FUGELMERE WK
VICTORIA ROAD
VICTORIA HILL RD
SUNNYSIDE
GOUGH RD
BRANKSOMEWOOD
CONNAUGHT ROAD
CLARENCE ROAD
ALBERT STREET
UPPER STREET
ALBANY ROAD
WESTOVER ROAD
KENILWORTH ROAD
ELMS ROAD
GUILDFORD ROAD
VELMEAD ROAD
FIR TREE WAY
HAWKINS WAY
AVENUE ROAD
LAWRENCE RD
DINORBEN AVENUE
DINORBEN CLOSE
CROOKHAM ROAD
GREENWAYS
LONGDOWN
BASINGBOURNE RD
FAIRMILE
ALDERSHOT RD
WICKHAM RD
GALLY HILL RD
COXHEATH RD
FERNDALE ROAD
CHESILTON CRESCENT
VERNE
CORRINGWAY
BEAUFORT ROAD
SILVER PK CL
GRAVEL ROAD
COMPTON RD
BOWENHURST RD
RYELAW RD
CHAMPION WAY
KENT RD
CASTLE STREET
COURTMOOR AVENUE
DURNSFORD AVENUE
HAYWOOD DR
FLORENCE ROAD
QUEEN'S ROAD
OSBORNE RD
GEORGE RD
CROWN GDNS
THE CEDARS
THE ALOES
MONTROSE CL
REGENT ST
REGENT CL
HOLLAND GDS

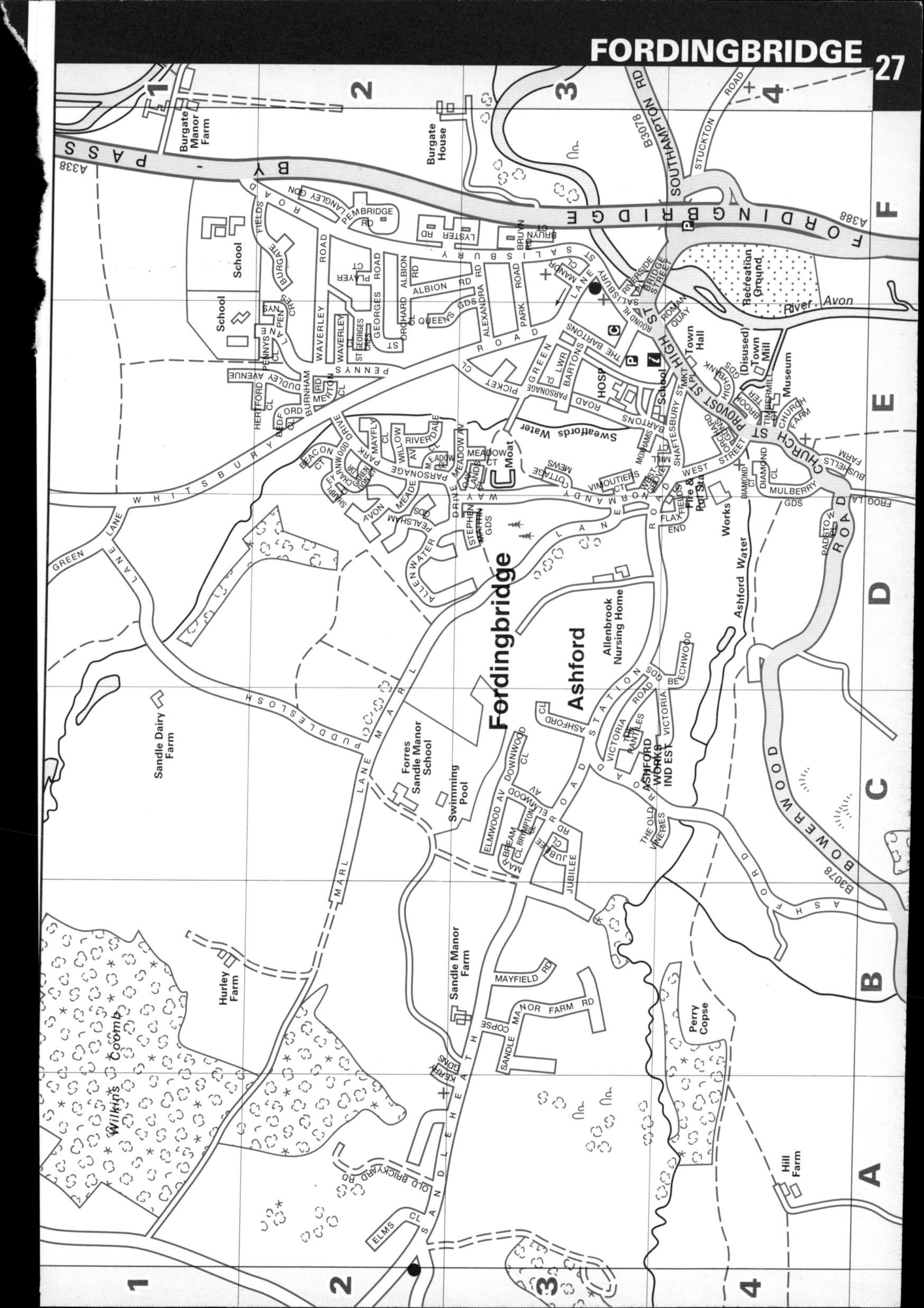

Burgate Manor Farm
Burgate House
B3078
SOUTHAMPTON RD
STUCKTON ROAD
A338
FORDINGBRIDGE BY-PASS
A388
School
School
School
Recreation Ground
River Avon
Town Hall
(Disused) Town Mill
Museum
HOSP
Sweatfords Water
Moat
Fordingbridge
Ashford
Allenbrook Nursing Home
Works
Ashford Water
ASHFORD WORKS IND EST
THE OLD VINERIES
Fire & Pol Sta
Forres Sandle Manor School
Swimming Pool
Sandle Dairy Farm
Hurley Farm
Sandle Manor Farm
Wilkins Coomb
Perry Copse
Hill Farm
WHITSBURY ROAD
GREEN LANE
PUDDLESLOSH
MARL LANE
SANDLEHEATH
OLD BRICKYARD RD
ELMS CL
KERRY GDNS
COPSE
SANDLE MANOR FARM RD
MAYFIELD RD
JUBILEE
STATION ROAD
ASHFORD ROAD
BOWERWOOD ROAD
CHURCH ST
PROVOST ST
HIGH ST
BRIDGE STREET
SALISBURY ST
SHAFTESBURY ST
WEST STREET
NORMANDY WAY
PARSONAGE PARK DRIVE
PENNYS
ALLENWATER
FROG LA
MULBERRY GDS
DIAMOND CL
BUSHELLS FARM
1
2
3
4
A
B
C
D
E
F

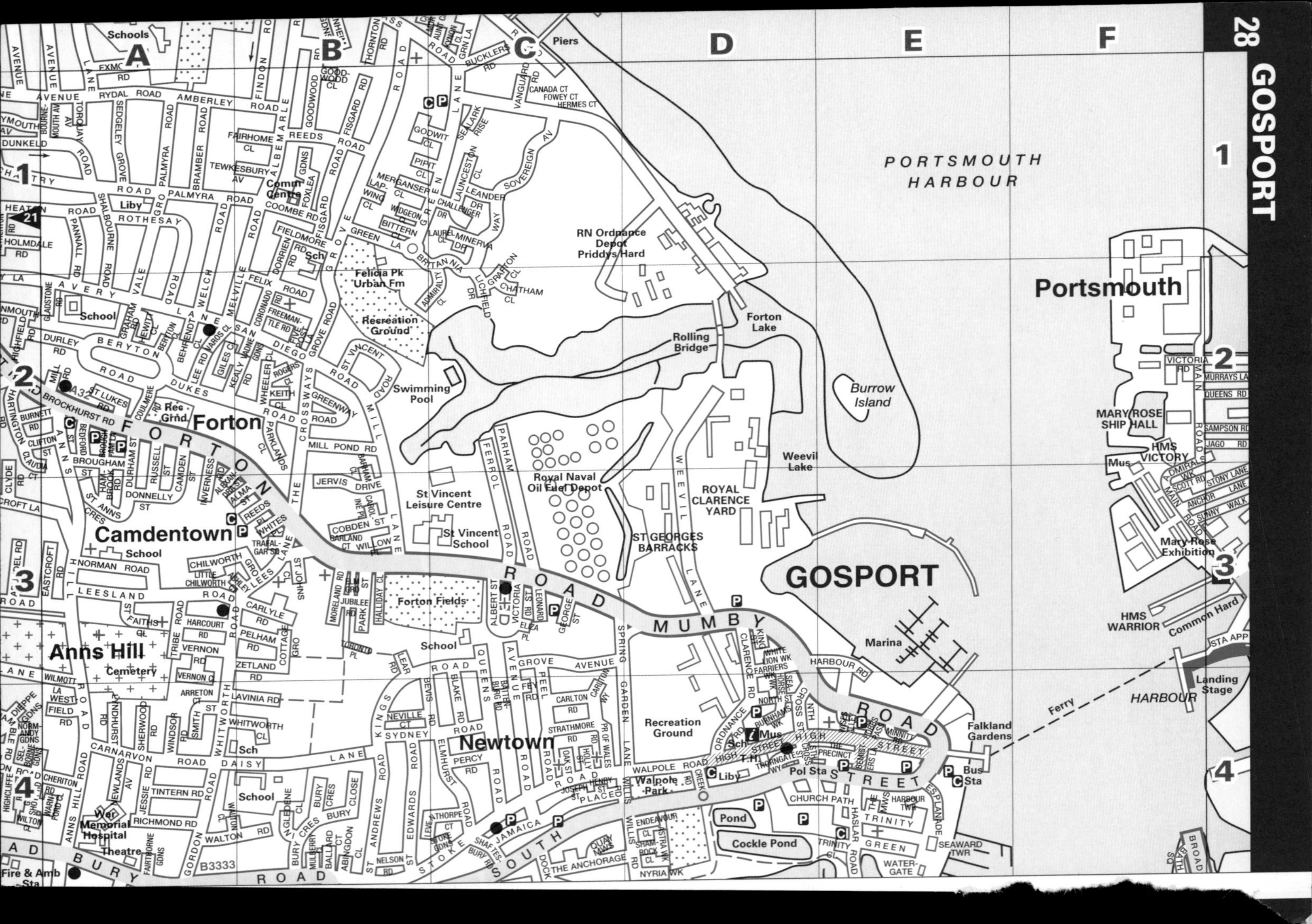
PORTSMOUTH HARBOUR
Portsmouth
GOSPORT
Burrow Island
Forton Lake
Weevil Lake
Rolling Bridge
ROYAL CLARENCE YARD
ST GEORGES BARRACKS
Royal Naval Oil Fuel Depot
RN Ordnance Depot Priddys Hard
Marina
Falkland Gardens
HMS WARRIOR
HMS VICTORY
MARY ROSE SHIP HALL
Mary Rose Exhibition
Landing Stage
Ferry
Recreation Ground
Walpole Park
Cockle Pond
Newtown
Forton Fields
St Vincent Leisure Centre
St Vincent School
Swimming Pool
Felicia Pk Urban Fm
Forton
Camdentown
Anns Hill
Cemetery
War Memorial Hospital
Theatre
Fire & Amb Sta
MUMBY ROAD
FORTON ROAD
HIGH STREET
SOUTH STREET
WEEVIL LANE
SPRING GARDEN LANE
ANNS HILL ROAD
BURY ROAD
HASLAR ROAD
ESPLANADE

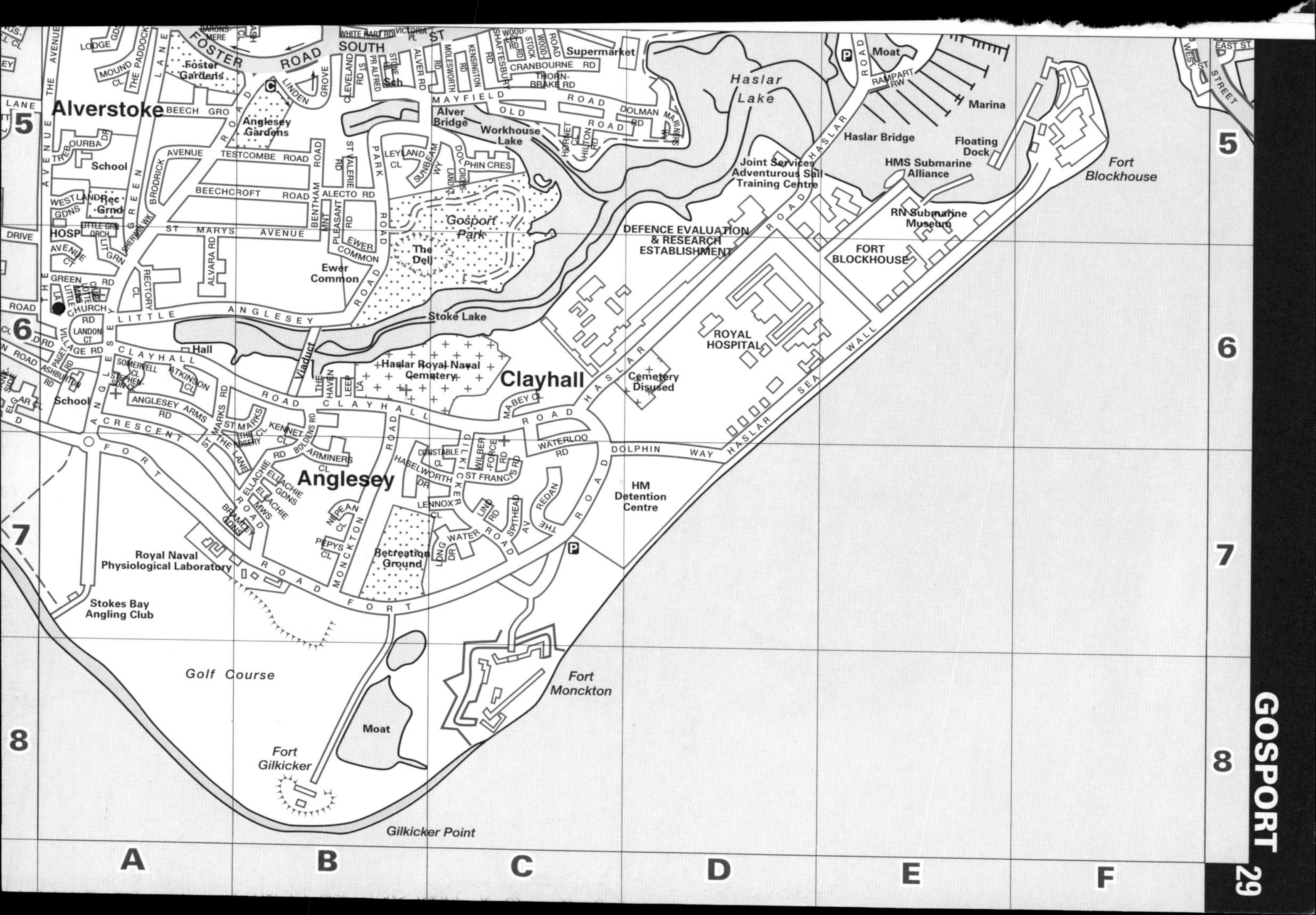
Alverstoke
Foster Gardens
Anglesey Gardens
Supermarket
Haslar Lake
Moat
Marina
Haslar Bridge
Floating Dock
HMS Submarine Alliance
Fort Blockhouse
Joint Services Adventurous Sail Training Centre
RN Submarine Museum
FORT BLOCKHOUSE
DEFENCE EVALUATION & RESEARCH ESTABLISHMENT
ROYAL HOSPITAL
Alver Bridge
Workhouse Lake
Gosport Park
The Dell
Ewer Common
Stoke Lake
Viaduct
Hall
Haslar Royal Naval Cemetery
Clayhall
Cemetery Disused
HM Detention Centre
School
Rec Grnd
HOSP
Anglesey
Recreation Ground
Royal Naval Physiological Laboratory
Stokes Bay Angling Club
Golf Course
Fort Monckton
Moat
Fort Gilkicker
Gilkicker Point
FOSTER ROAD
SOUTH ST
MAYFIELD ROAD
OLD ROAD
DOLMAN RD
CRANBOURNE RD
THORNBRAKE RD
TESTCOMBE ROAD
BEECHCROFT ROAD
ST MARYS AVENUE
PARK ROAD
LITTLE ANGLESEY
CLAYHALL ROAD
HASLAR ROAD
HASLAR SEA WALL
DOLPHIN WAY
WATERLOO RD
GILKICKER ROAD
THE REDAN
FORT ROAD
MONCKTON ROAD
CRESCENT ROAD
ANGLESEY ARMS RD
ST MARKS RD
THE AVENUE
A
B
C
D
E
F
5
6
7
8

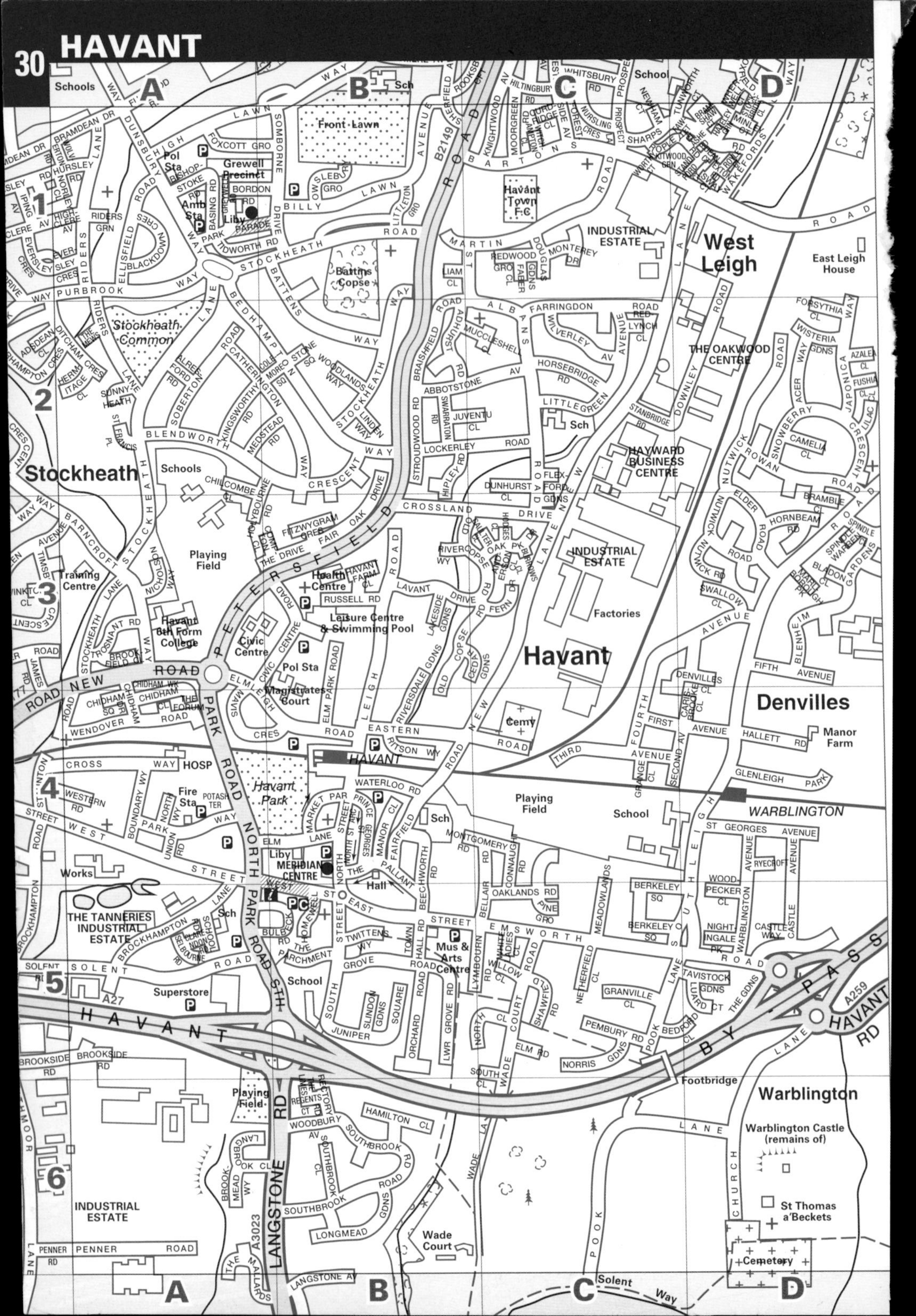
Stockheath
West Leigh
Havant
Denvilles
Warblington
Stockheath Common
Front Lawn
Grewell Precinct
Havant Town F.C.
INDUSTRIAL ESTATE
East Leigh House
THE OAKWOOD CENTRE
HAYWARD BUSINESS CENTRE
Factories
Leisure Centre & Swimming Pool
Civic Centre
Magistrates Court
Havant 6th Form College
Training Centre
Playing Field
Havant Park
MERIDIAN CENTRE
THE TANNERIES INDUSTRIAL ESTATE
Superstore
Mus & Arts Centre
Manor Farm
WARBLINGTON
Footbridge
Warblington Castle (remains of)
St Thomas a'Beckets
Cemetery
Wade Court
Solent Way
HAVANT BY-PASS
PETERSFIELD ROAD
NEW ROAD
LANGSTONE RD
A3023
A27
A259
B2149

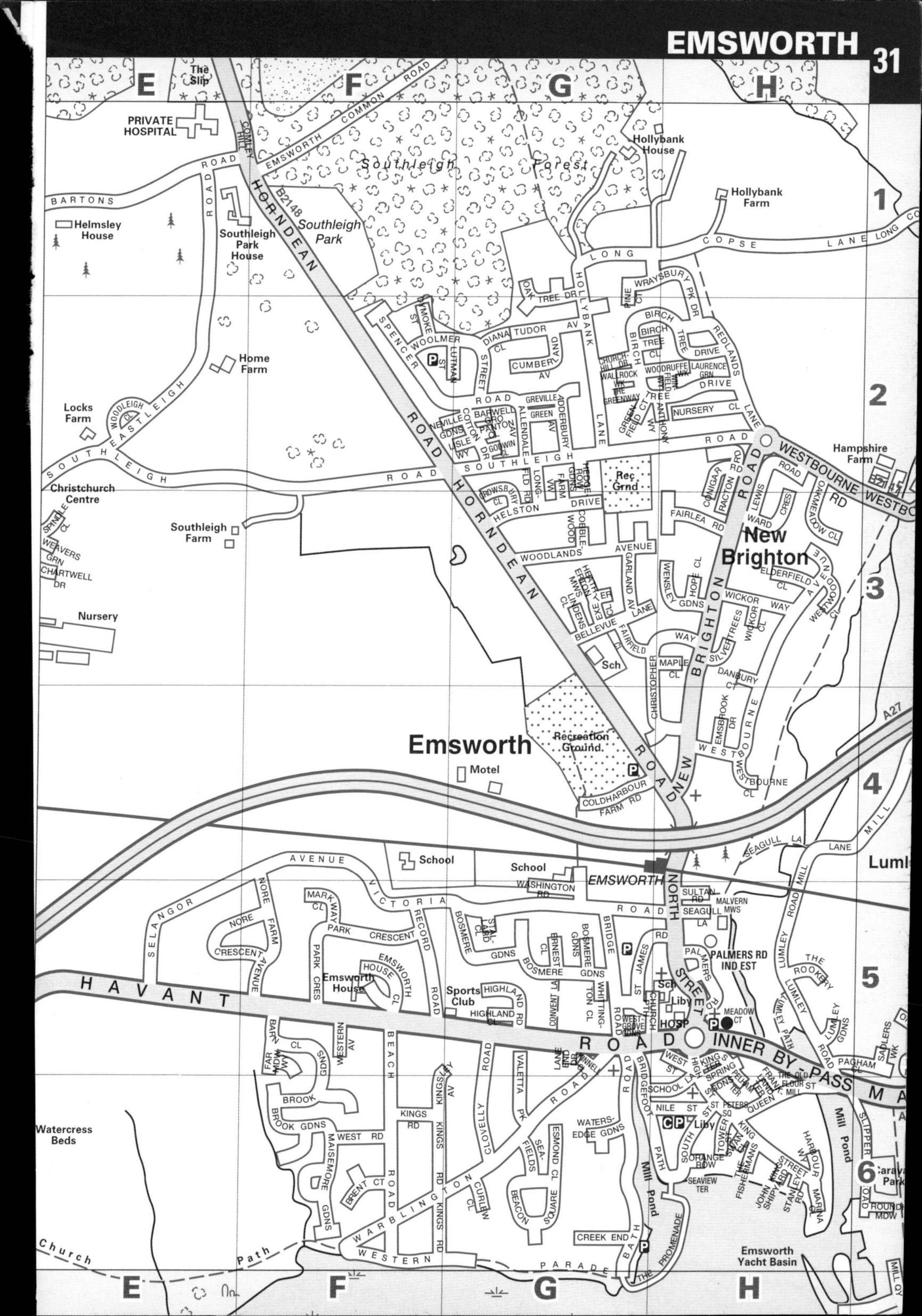

Southleigh Forest
Southleigh Park
Southleigh Park House
PRIVATE HOSPITAL
Helmsley House
Home Farm
Locks Farm
Hollybank House
Hollybank Farm
Hampshire Farm
Christchurch Centre
Southleigh Farm
Nursery
New Brighton
Emsworth
Motel
Recreation Ground
Rec Grnd
School
EMSWORTH
PALMERS RD IND EST
Emsworth House
Sports Club
Watercress Beds
Mill Pond
Emsworth Yacht Basin
HAVANT ROAD
HORNDEAN ROAD
SOUTHLEIGH ROAD
NEW BRIGHTON ROAD
WESTBOURNE ROAD
INNER BY-PASS
NORTH STREET
VICTORIA ROAD
WESTERN PARADE
WARBLINGTON ROAD
LONG COPSE LANE
EMSWORTH COMMON ROAD
BARTONS ROAD
Church Path

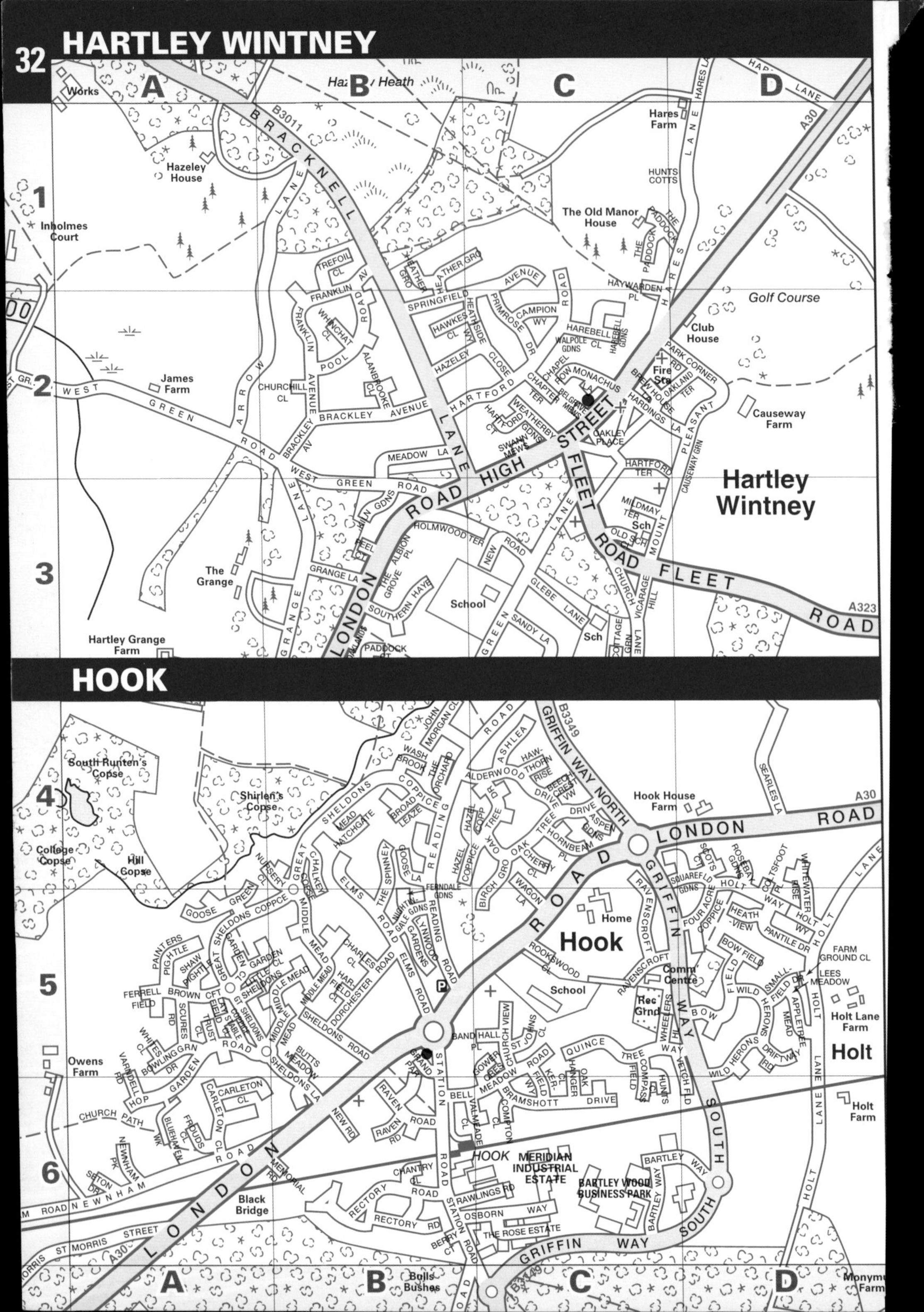
HARTLEY WINTNEY
Hartley Wintney
Works
Hazeley House
Inholmes Court
James Farm
The Grange
Hartley Grange Farm
The Old Manor House
Hares Farm
Club House
Causeway Farm
Golf Course
School
Sch
BRACKNELL LANE
HIGH STREET
LONDON ROAD
FLEET ROAD
WEST GREEN ROAD
HOOK
Hook
Holt
South Runten's Copse
Shirlen's Copse
College Copse
Hill Copse
Owens Farm
Black Bridge
Hook House Farm
Holt Lane Farm
Holt Farm
Home
School
Comm Centre
Rec Grnd
MERIDIAN INDUSTRIAL ESTATE
BARTLEY WOOD BUSINESS PARK
THE ROSE ESTATE
GRIFFIN WAY NORTH
GRIFFIN WAY SOUTH
LONDON ROAD
READING ROAD
STATION ROAD
Bulls Bushes

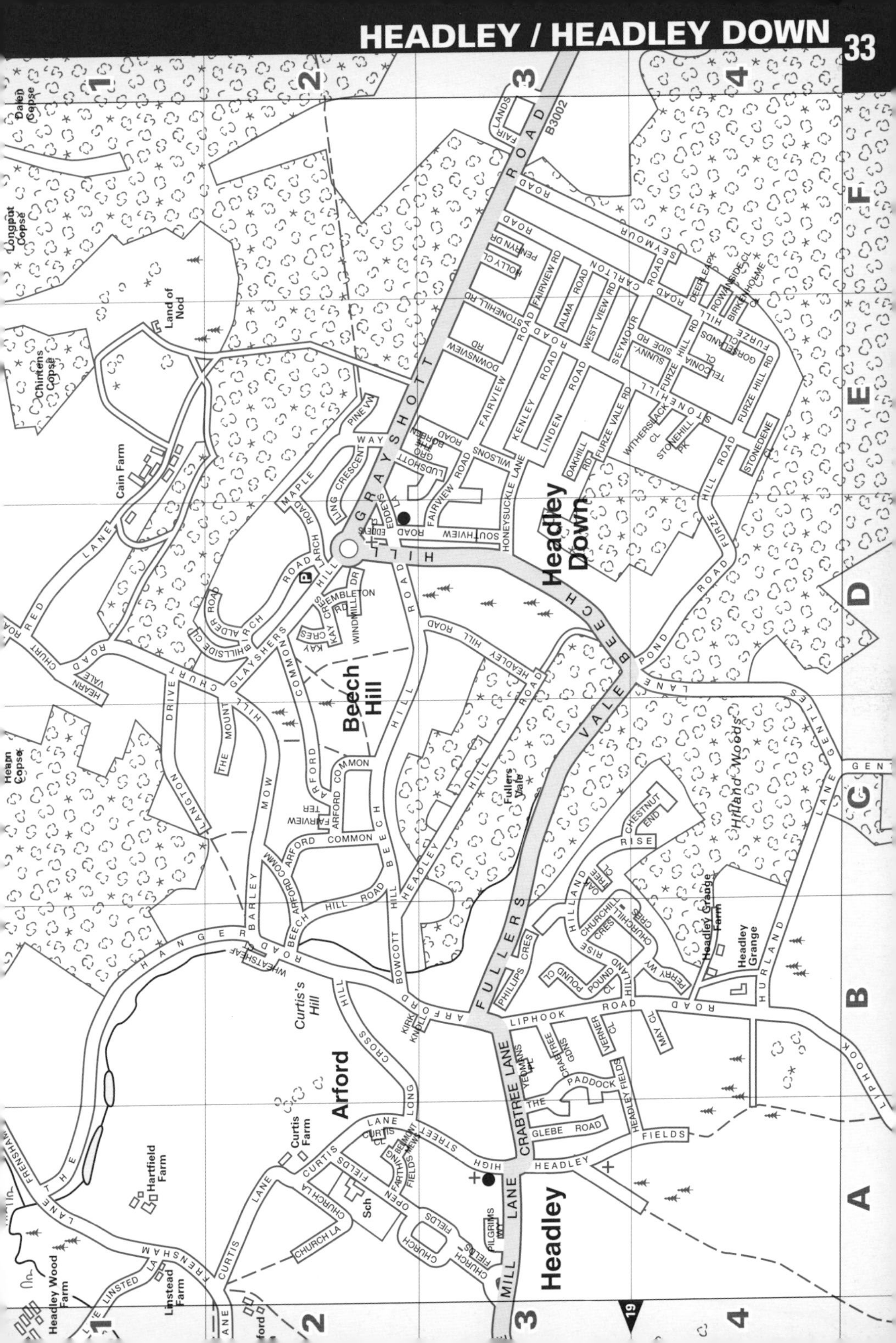
Headley Down
Headley
Beech Hill
Arford
Curtis's Hill
Fullers Vale
Hilland Woods
Land of Nod
Cain Farm
Chintens Copse
Longput Copse
Dalen Copse
Hearn Copse
Hartfield Farm
Curtis Farm
Headley Wood Farm
Linstead Farm
Headley Grange Farm
Headley Grange
Sch
GRAYSHOTT ROAD
B3002
BEECH HILL
VALE
FULLERS
CRABTREE LANE
MILL LANE
HIGH STREET
HEADLEY FIELDS
LIPHOOK ROAD
HURLAND LANE
GENTLES LANE
POND LANE
FURZE HILL ROAD
STONEHILL ROAD
SEYMOUR ROAD
CARLTON ROAD
FAIRVIEW RD
ALMA ROAD
WEST VIEW RD
KENLEY ROAD
LINDEN ROAD
FURZE VALE RD
OAKHILL RD
HONEYSUCKLE LANE
WILSONS ROAD
SOUTHVIEW ROAD
FAIRVIEW ROAD
DOWNSVIEW RD
LUDSHOTT GRO
EDDEYS LA
HOLLY CL
PENRYN DR
FAIR LANDS
PINE VW
LING CRESCENT
MAPLE WAY
LARCH ROAD
BIRCH ROAD
ALDER RD
HILLSIDE CL
CREMBLETON
WINDMILL DR
KAY CRES
HEADLEY HILL ROAD
GLAYSHERS HILL
COMMON
CHURT ROAD
RED LANE
HEARN VALE
THE MOUNT
DRIVE
LANGTON
BARLEY MOW HILL
ARFORD COMMON
FAIRVIEW TER
ARFORD ROAD
BEECH HILL ROAD
HANGER
WHEATSHEAF
BOWCOTT HILL
CROSS
LONG
KIRK KNOLL
CURTIS LANE
CURTIS CL
BELMONT MEWS
FARTHING FIELDS
OPEN FIELDS
CHURCH LA
CHURCH FIELDS
PILGRIMS WY
FRENSHAM LANE
THE
LINSTED LA
YEOMANS PL
CRABTREE GDNS
VERNER CL
MAY CL
THE PADDOCK
GLEBE ROAD
PHILLIPS CRES
HILLAND RISE
CHESTNUT END
OAK TREE CL
CHURCHILL CRES
POUND CL
POUND CL
PERRY WY
WITHERSLACK CL
STONEHILL PK
STONEDENE CL
TELCONIA CL
GORSELANDS CL
SUNNY-SIDE RD
DEERLEAP
ROWANSIDE CL
BIRKENHOLME CL
D
E
F
C
B
A
19

Tadley
Mount Pleasant
Heath End
Baughurst
Tadley Common
Golf Course
MULFORDS HILL
TADLEY HILL
MAIN RD
A340
B3051
Library
Police Station
Schools
Club House
Bishops Wood Stream
Gully Copse
Priors Copse
Smarts Copse
Burnhams Plantation
Oak Plantation
Great Copse
Hawley Farm
Manor Farm
Curtis Farm
Copse Close
Sports Centre
Playing Field
Comm' Centre
Caravan Park
CALLEVA PARK
Tadley Court
1. CHERITON CL
2. BRAMDEAN CL

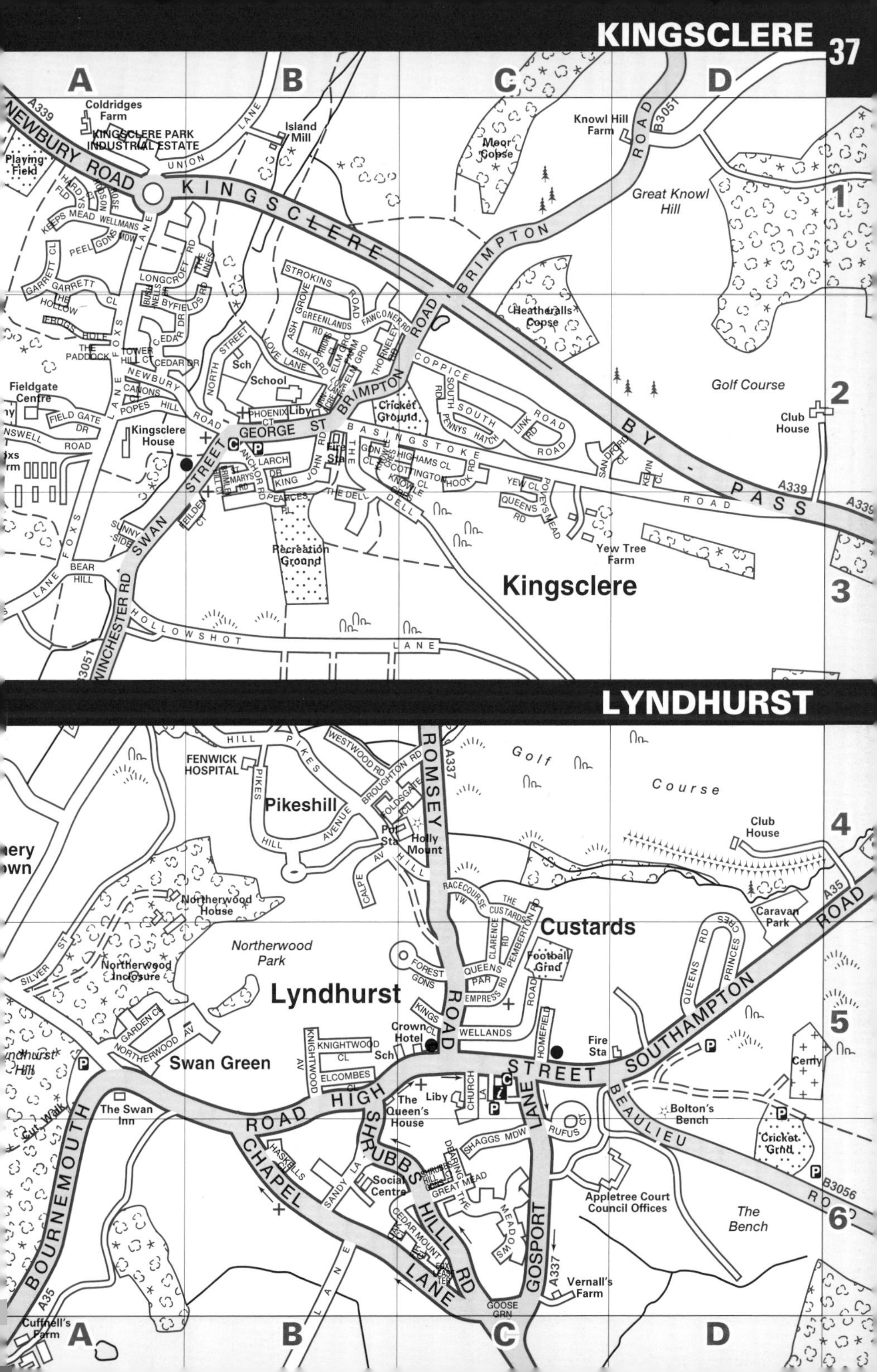
A
B
C
D
1
2
3
Coldridges Farm
KINGSCLERE PARK INDUSTRIAL ESTATE
Playing Field
NEWBURY ROAD
A339
UNION LANE
Island Mill
Moor Copse
Knowl Hill Farm
B3051
BRIMPTON ROAD
Great Knowl Hill
KINGSCLERE BY-PASS
Heatheralls Copse
Golf Course
Club House
Fieldgate Centre
Kingsclere House
School
Sch
Liby
Cricket Ground
GEORGE ST
SWAN STREET
Fire Sta
BASINGSTOKE ROAD
Recreation Ground
Yew Tree Farm
Kingsclere
WINCHESTER RD
HOLLOWSHOT LANE
BEAR HILL
FOXS LANE
STROKINS ROAD
GREENLANDS RD
ASH GROVE
LOVE LANE
COPPICE ROAD
SOUTH ROAD
LINK RD
SANDFORD CL
KEVIN CL
YEW CL
QUEENS RD
POVEYS MEAD
HIGHAMS CL
COTTINGTON CL
HOOK RD
THE DELL
PEARCES PL
KING JOHN RD
LARCH DR
ANCHOR RD
ST MARYS RD
FIELD GATE DR
POPES HILL
CANONS
TOWER HILL CT
CEDAR DR
LONGCROFT RD
BYFIELDS RD
GARRETT CL
THE HOLLOW
FROGS HOLE
THE PADDOCK
PEEL GDNS
KEEPS MEAD
WELLMANS MDW
SUNNY SIDE
FAWCONER RD
THORNELEY RD
PHOENIX CT
NORTH STREET
LYNDHURST
4
5
6
FENWICK HOSPITAL
Pikeshill
PIKES HILL
WESTWOOD RD
BROUGHTON RD
ROMSEY ROAD
A337
Golf Course
Club House
Pol Sta
Holly Mount
Northerwood House
Northerwood Park
Northerwood Inclosure
Custards
Football Grnd
Caravan Park
SOUTHAMPTON ROAD
A35
Lyndhurst
Swan Green
Crown Hotel
Sch
Fire Sta
HIGH STREET
The Swan Inn
BOURNEMOUTH ROAD
Cut Walk
The Queen's House
Liby
Social Centre
CHAPEL LANE
SHRUBBS HILL RD
GOSPORT LANE
BEAULIEU ROAD
B3056
Bolton's Bench
Cemy
Cricket Grnd
Appletree Court Council Offices
The Bench
Vernall's Farm
GOOSE GRN
Cuffnell's Farm
QUEENS RD
PRINCES CRES
CLARENCE RD
PEMBERTON RD
RACECOURSE VW
THE CUSTARDS
FOREST GDNS
QUEENS PAR
EMPRESS RD
WELLANDS
KINGS CL
HOMEFIELD
KNIGHTWOOD CL
KNIGHTWOOD AV
ELCOMBES CL
GARDEN CL
NORTHERWOOD AV
SILVER ST
RUFUS CT
SHAGGS MDW
GREAT MEAD
THE MEADOWS
CEDAR MOUNT
HASKELLS CL
SANDY LA
CHURCH LA
CALPE AV

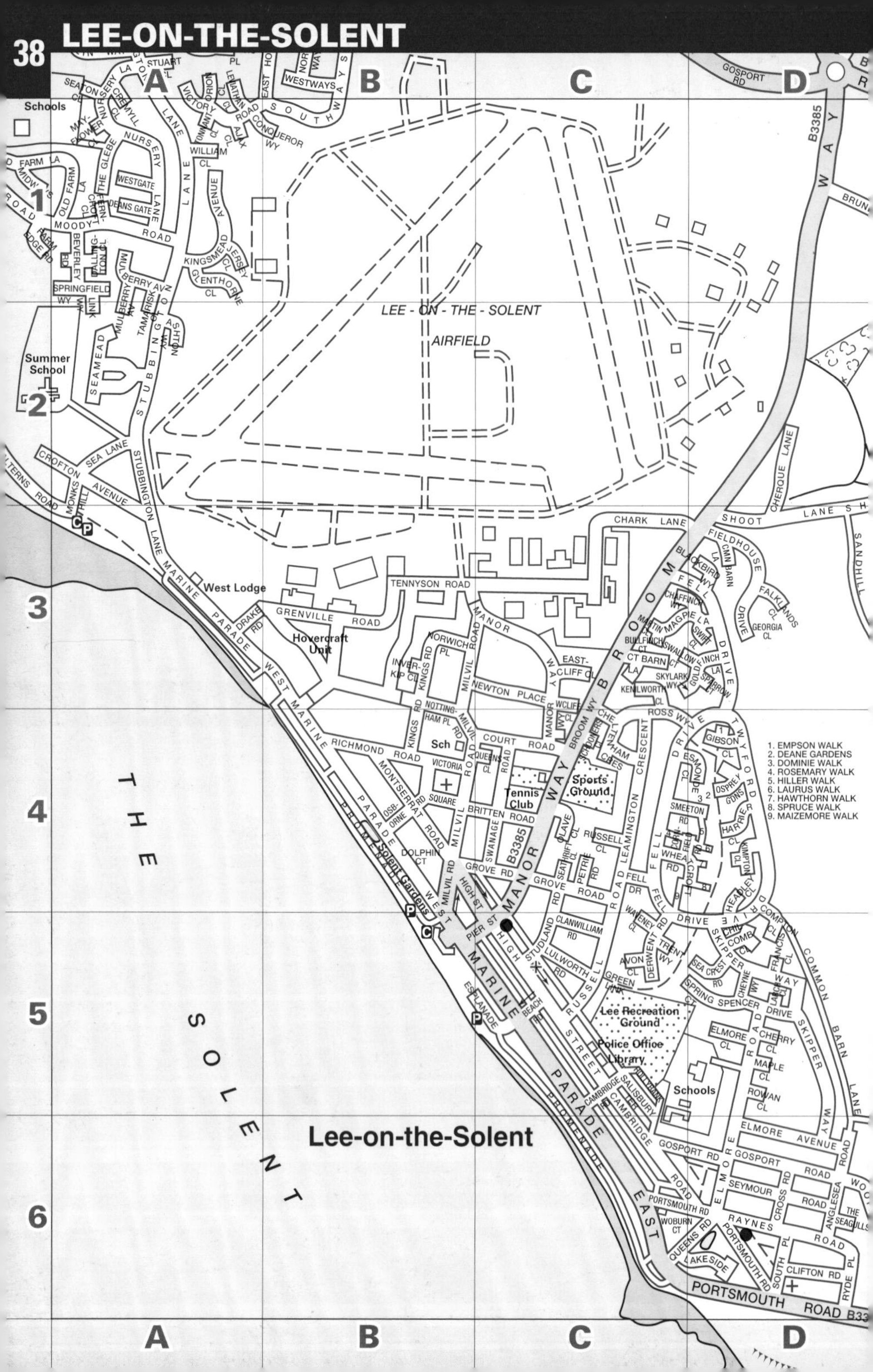
LEE - ON - THE - SOLENT
AIRFIELD
Lee-on-the-Solent
THE SOLENT
Schools
Summer School
West Lodge
Hovercraft Unit
Sch
Tennis Club
Sports Ground
Solent Gardens
Lee Recreation Ground
Police Office
Library
Schools
STUBBINGTON LANE
MARINE PARADE
WEST MARINE PARADE
MARINE PARADE EAST
MANOR WAY
BROOM WAY
GOSPORT RD
PORTSMOUTH ROAD
CHARK LANE
SHOOT LANE
TENNYSON ROAD
GRENVILLE ROAD
RICHMOND ROAD
COURT ROAD
BRITTEN ROAD
GROVE RD
HIGH ST
PIER ST
MILVIL RD
MONTSERRAT RD
VICTORIA SQUARE
LEAMINGTON CRESCENT
FELL DRIVE
TWYFORD DRIVE
ELMORE AVENUE
SEYMOUR ROAD
RAYNES ROAD
CLIFTON RD
SKIPPER WAY
COMMON BARN LANE
CHEROUE LANE
SANDHILL
B3385
B3333
1. EMPSON WALK
2. DEANE GARDENS
3. DOMINIE WALK
4. ROSEMARY WALK
5. HILLER WALK
6. LAURUS WALK
7. HAWTHORN WALK
8. SPRUCE WALK
9. MAIZEMORE WALK
A B C D
1 2 3 4 5 6

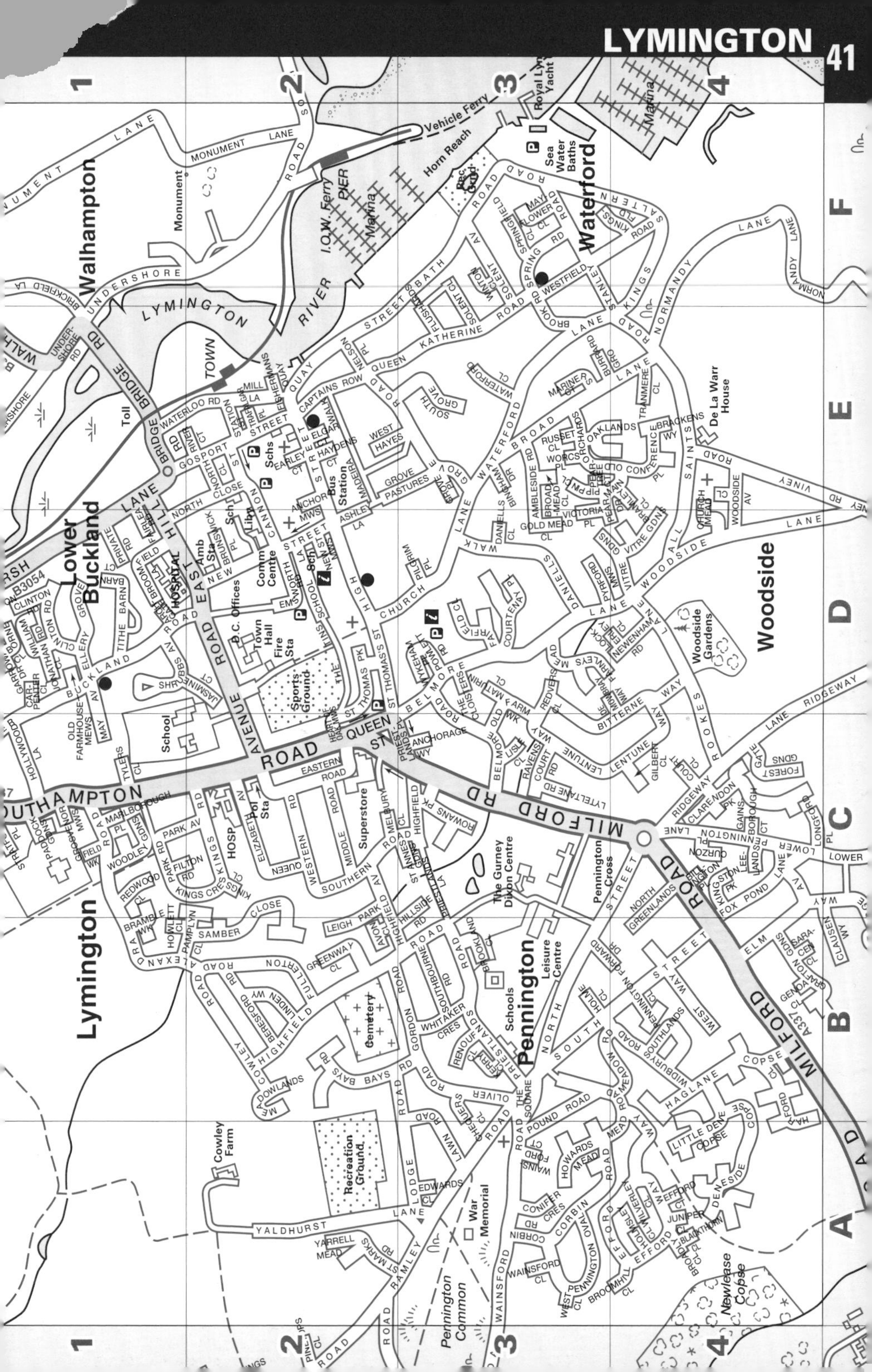
Walhampton
Lower Buckland
Lymington
Waterford
Woodside
Pennington
Monument
Marina
Vehicle Ferry
Horn Reach
I.O.W. Ferry
PIER
Sea Water Baths
Royal Lymington Yacht Club
LYMINGTON RIVER
TOWN
Toll
De La Warr House
Woodside Gardens
Sports Ground
Town Hall
Fire Sta
D.C. Offices
Comm Centre
Bus Station
Superstore
HOSP
Pol Sta
School
The Gurney Dixon Centre
Pennington Cross
Leisure Centre
Schools
Cemetery
Recreation Ground
Cowley Farm
War Memorial
Pennington Common
Newlease Copse
MILFORD RD
SOUTHAMPTON ROAD
AVENUE ROAD
QUEEN ST
HIGH STREET
B3054
A337

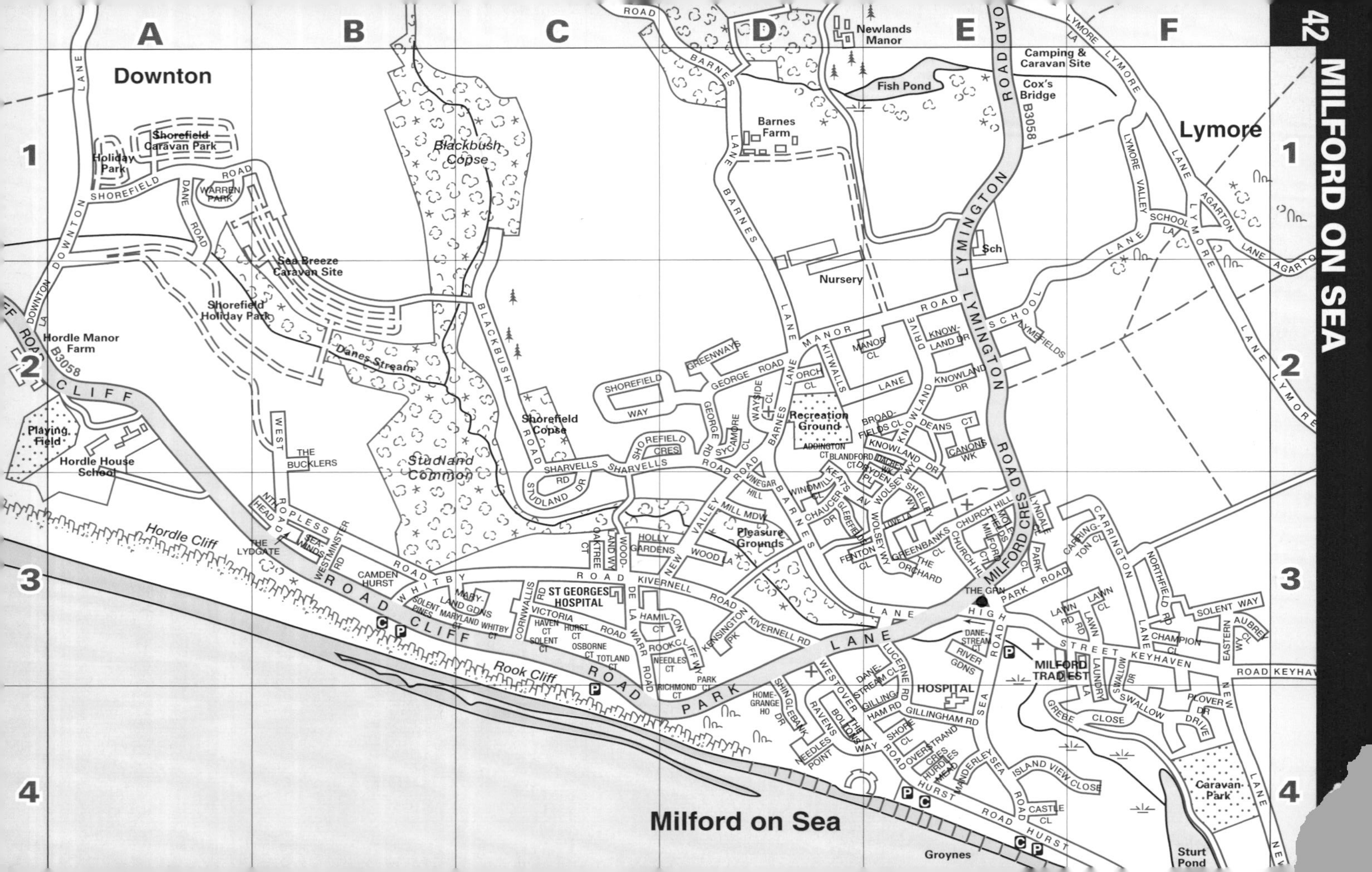
Downton
Shorefield Caravan Park
Holiday Park
Shorefield Road
Warren Park
Dane Road
Downton Lane
Sea Breeze Caravan Site
Shorefield Holiday Park
Hordle Manor Farm
B3058
Cliff Road
Playing Field
Hordle House School
Danes Stream
Blackbush Copse
Blackbush Road
West Road
The Bucklers
Hordle Cliff
The Lydgate
Westminster Rd
Camden Hurst
Whitby Road
Studland Common
Shorefield Copse
Sharvells Road
Studland Dr
Shorefield Way
George Road
Greenways
St Georges Hospital
Cornwallis
Victoria Rd
Kivernell Road
De La Warr Road
Rook Cliff
Park Lane
Pleasure Grounds
Vinegar Hill
Barnes Lane
Barnes Farm
Nursery
Manor Road
Kitwalls
Recreation Ground
Knowland Dr
Newlands Manor
Fish Pond
Camping & Caravan Site
Cox's Bridge
Lymington Road
Sch
Lymore
Lymore Lane
Lymore Valley
School La
Agarton Lane
Milford Cres
Church Hill
The Grn
High Street
Keyhaven Road
Milford Trad Est
Northfield Rd
Carrington Lane
Solent Way
Eastern Way
Swallow Dr
Plover Dr
Caravan Park
Sturt Pond
Hospital
Sea Road
Hurst Road
Island View Close
Needles Point
Milford on Sea
Groynes
A
B
C
D
E
F
1
2
3
4

Old Alresford
New Alresford
The Soke
Woodlands
Fobdown Farm
Tumulus
Manor Farm
School
Upton Park Farm
Watercress Beds
Old Alresford Place
Old Alresford House
Old Alresford Park
Roman Building (site of)
Little Weir
The Fulling Mill
Great Weir
Old Alresford Pond
River Arle
Fish Farm
Fish Pond
Fob Down
Recreation Ground
Works
Valdean Caravan Home Park
Liby
Arlebury Park
Fire Sta
Pol Sta
Bowling Green
Mid-Hants Railway
Playing Field
Sewards Bridge
Makins Court
Alresford Golf Course
OXDROVE WAY
DROVE LANE
THE AVENUE
POUND HILL
WEST ST
EAST STREET
BROAD ST
GREAT WEIR
JACKLYNS LANE
NEW ALRESFORD BY-PASS
TICHBORNE DOWN
SUN LANE
B3046
B3047
A31

New Milton
Old Milton
Barton on Sea
Barton Common
Golf Course
Club House
Hotel
Recreation Ground
Swimming Pool
Durlston Court
Superstore
School
Schools
Sports Centre
Cemy
Police Sta
Liby
Sch
Fire Sta
Rec Ground
College
Pond Copse
INDUSTRIAL ESTATE
WICK 1 IND EST
WICK 2 IND EST
GORE RD IND EST
WILLIAMS IND PK
KING GEORGE MOBILE HOME PK
LYMINGTON ROAD
CHRISTCHURCH RD
STATION ROAD
FERNHILL LANE
MILFORD ROAD
MARINE DRIVE
MANOR ROAD
GORE ROAD
A337
B3058

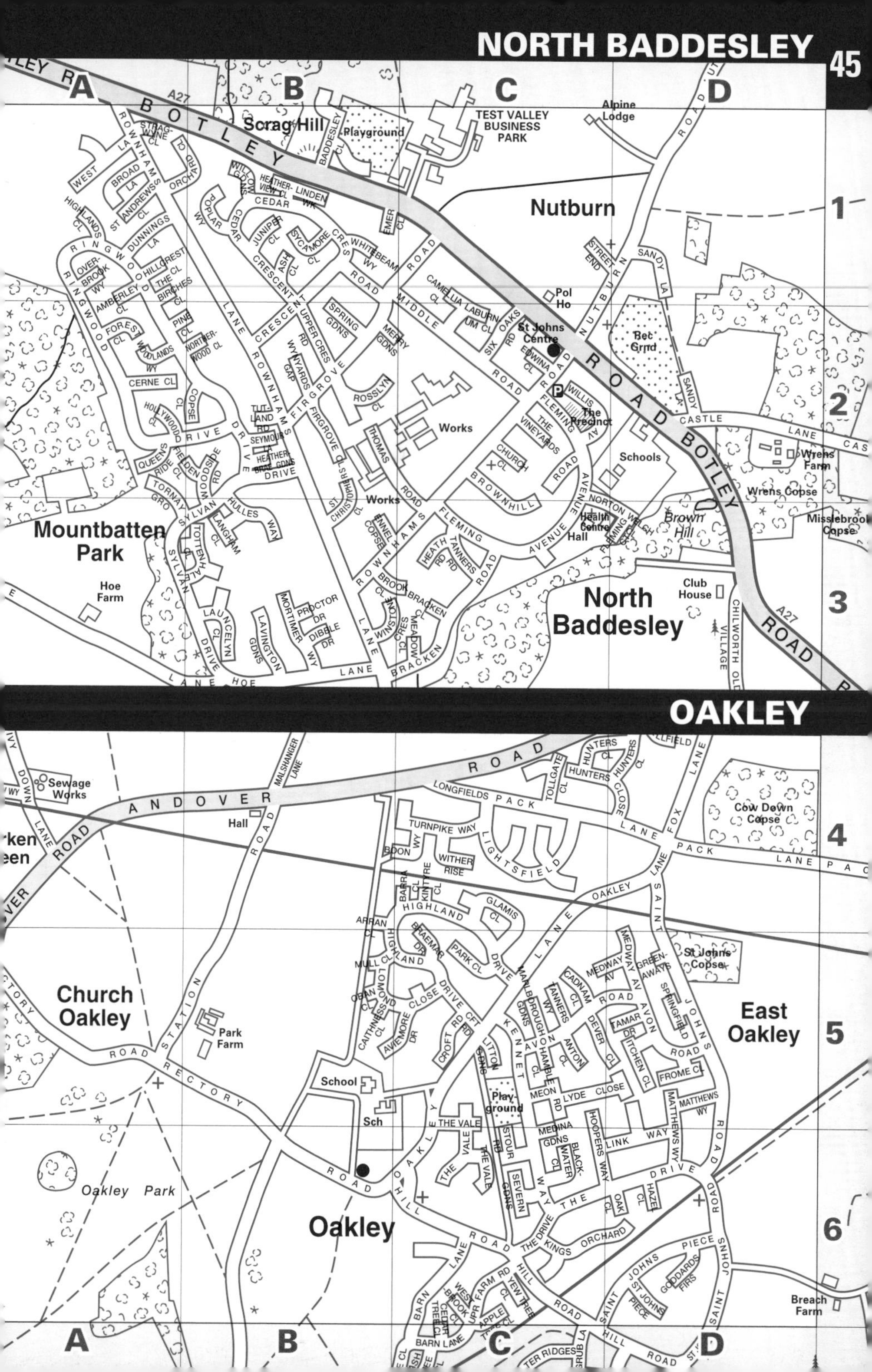
NORTH BADDESLEY
45
A
B
C
D
1
2
3
BOTLEY ROAD
A27
Scrag Hill
Playground
TEST VALLEY
BUSINESS
PARK
Alpine
Lodge
Nutburn
ROWNHAMS LANE
WEST LA
BROAD LA
ST ANDREWS CL
HIGHLANDS CL
DUNNINGS LA
RINGWOOD DRIVE
OVERBROOK WY
AMBERLEY CL
FOREST CL
WOODLANDS WY
HILLCREST
THE BIRCHES CL
PINE CL
NORTHERWOOD CL
CERNE CL
HOLLYWOOD CL
COPSE CL
QUEENS RIDE
ORCHARD CL
POPLAR WY
CEDAR WY
CEDAR CL
HEATHERVIEW CL
LINDEN WK
JUNIPER CL
ASH CL
SYCAMORE CL
WHITEBEAM WY
CRESCENT
UPPER CRES
SPRING GDNS
MERRY GDNS
FIRGROVE
WYNYARDS GAP
ROSSLYN CL
TUTLAND RD
SEYMOUR CL
HEATHERBRAE GDNS
THOMAS ROAD
ST CHRISTOPHERS CL
FENNEL COPSE
Works
MIDDLE ROAD
CAMELLIA CL
LABURNUM CL
SIX OAKS RD
St Johns Centre
EDWINA CL
STREET END
Pol Ho
Rec Grnd
SANDY LA
NUTBURN ROAD
WILLIS AV
The Precinct
FLEMING AV
THE VINEYARDS
CHURCH CL
BROWNHILL ROAD
Schools
NORTON WELCH CL
Health Centre
Hall
Brown Hill
CASTLE LANE
Wrens Farm
Wrens Copse
Misslebrook Copse
FLEMING AVENUE
HEATH RD
TANNERS RD
FLEMING ROAD
BROOK CL
BRACKEN CL
WINSTONE CRES
MEADOW CL
BRACKEN LANE
MORTIMER WY
PROCTOR DR
DIBBLE DR
LAVINGTON GDNS
LAUNCELYN CL
SYLVAN DRIVE
TORNAY GRO
HULLES WAY
LANGHAM CL
TOTTENHALE CL
WOODSIDE RD
FIELDEN CL
Mountbatten Park
Hoe Farm
HOE LANE
North Baddesley
Club House
CHILWORTH OLD VILLAGE
A27
VALLEY ROAD
OAKLEY
ANDOVER ROAD
MALSHANGER LANE
Sewage Works
DOWN LANE
Hall
Church Oakley
STATION ROAD
RECTORY ROAD
Park Farm
Oakley Park
LONGFIELDS
TURNPIKE WAY
BOON WY
WITHER RISE
LIGHTSFIELD
TOLLGATE CL
HUNTERS CL
HUNTERS CLOSE
FOX LANE
PACK LANE
Cow Down Copse
BARRA CL
KINTYRE CL
HIGHLAND DRIVE
GLAMIS CL
ARRAN CL
BRAEMAR DR
PARK CL
MULL CL
LOMOND CL
OBAN CL
CAITHNESS CL
AWEMORE DR
CLOSE
CROFT RD
OAKLEY LANE
SAINT JOHNS ROAD
MARLBOROUGH GDNS
TANNERS WY
CADNAM CL
MEDWAY AV
GREENAWAYS
St Johns Copse
East Oakley
AVON ROAD
SPRINGFIELD
KENNET CL
AVON CL
ANTON CL
DEVER CL
TAMAR DR
ITCHEN CL
FROME CL
HAMBLE RD
LITTON GDNS
Playground
MEON CL
LYDE CLOSE
MATTHEWS WY
School
Sch
THE VALE
MEDINA GDNS
BLACKWATER CL
HOOPERS WAY
LINK WAY
STOUR RD
SEVERN GDNS
THE DRIVE
OAK CL
HAZEL CL
HILL ROAD
Oakley
KINGS ORCHARD
ST JOHNS PIECE
GODDARDS FIRS
BARN LANE
WESTBROOK CL
CEDAR TREE CL
UPR FARM RD
YEW TREE CL
APPLE TREE CL
GRUB LA
Breach Farm
6
4
5

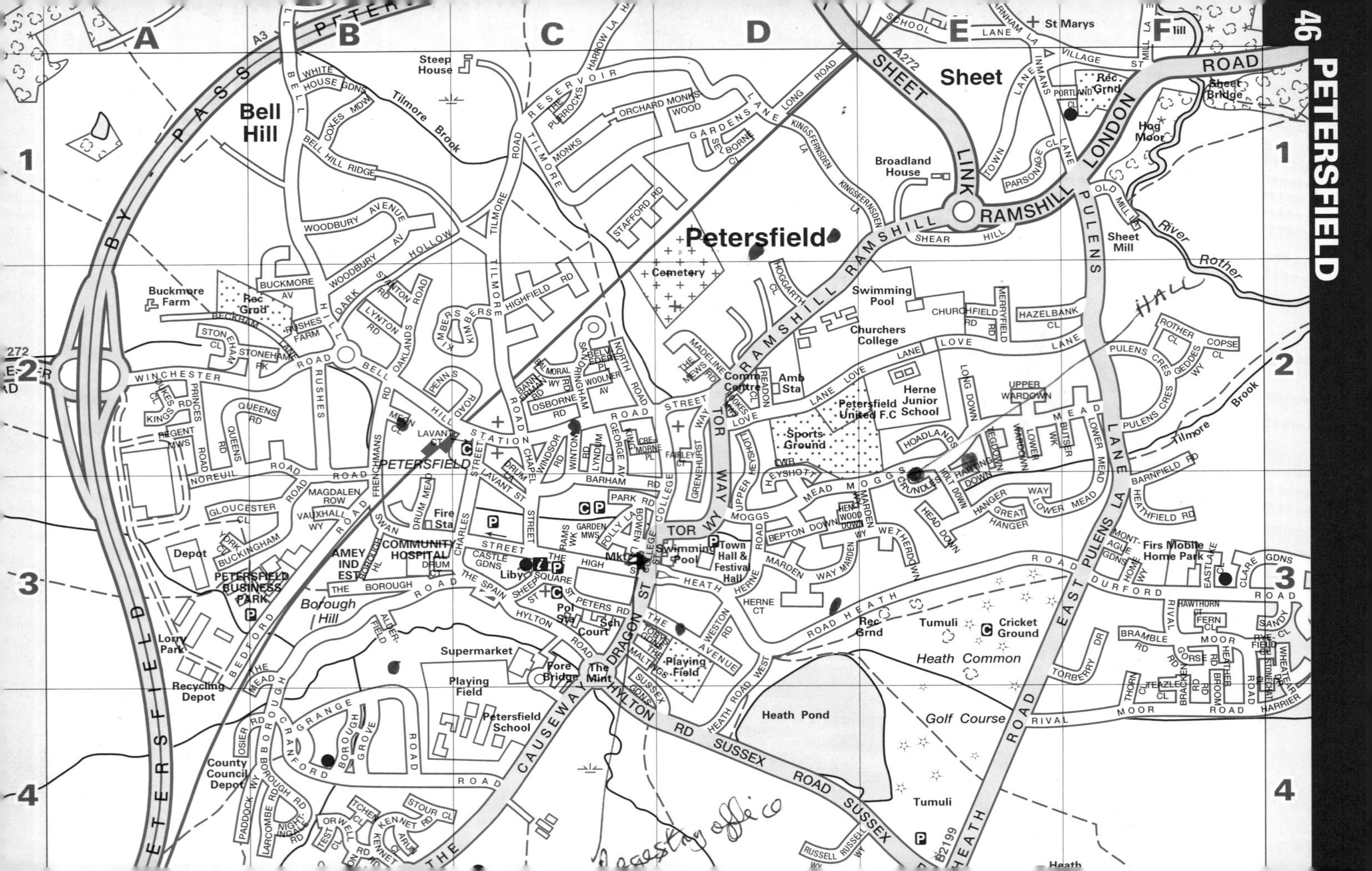

Petersfield
Sheet
Bell Hill
St Marys
Steep House
Broadland House
Sheet Mill
Hog Moor
Sheet Bridge
River Rother
Tilmore Brook
Cemetery
Swimming Pool
Churchers College
Amb Sta
Comm Centre
Herne Junior School
Petersfield United F.C
Sports Ground
Buckmore Farm
Rec Grnd
Fire Sta
COMMUNITY HOSPITAL
AMEY IND EST
Depot
PETERSFIELD BUSINESS PARK
Borough Hill
Lorry Park
Recycling Depot
County Council Depot
Supermarket
Playing Field
Petersfield School
Fore Bridge
The Mint
Liby
Pol Sta
Sch
Court
Mkt
Town Hall & Festival Hall
Firs Mobile Home Park
Tumuli
Cricket Ground
Heath Common
Golf Course
Heath Pond
Heath
LONDON ROAD
RAMSHILL
SHEET LINK
A272
A3
B2199
BY-PASS
PETERSFIELD
PULENS LANE
EAST PULENS LA
HEATH ROAD
HEATH ROAD WEST
SUSSEX ROAD
HYLTON RD
DRAGON ST
THE CAUSEWAY
TOR WAY
TILMORE ROAD
LONG ROAD
BELL HILL
WINCHESTER ROAD
RUSHES ROAD
FRENCHMANS ROAD
STATION ROAD
CHAPEL STREET
CHARLES STREET
HIGH ST
COLLEGE ST
THE SQUARE
THE SPAIN
BOROUGH ROAD
BEDFORD ROAD
NOREUIL ROAD
QUEENS RD
LOVE LANE
MOGGS MEAD
DURFORD ROAD

A
B
C
D
1
2
3
4
5
6
PORTSMOUTH
Old Portsmouth
HM NAVAL BASE AND DOCKYARD
HMS NELSON
Union Gate
MARY ROSE SHIP HALL
HMS VICTORY
Mary Rose Exhibition
Victory Gate
HMS WARRIOR
Common Hard
Landing Stage
HARBOUR STATION
Passenger Ferry
GUNWHARF QUAYS RETAIL & LEISURE PARK
HMS NELSON (Gunwharf)
Isle of White Car Ferry Terminal
The Point
Round Tower (site of)
King James's Gate (site of)
Victoria Pier
Fort Blockhouse
HMS DOLPHIN
Clarence Pier
Amusement Park
Hovercraft Terminal
Southsea Common
War Memorial
Tennis Courts & Bowling Green
Sea Life Centre
D'DAY MUSEUM
Southsea Castle
The Pyramids Indoor Leisure Centre
Spit Sand
Passenger ferry to Ryde (I of W)
Hovercraft Ferry to Ryde (I. of W.)
Car Ferry to Fishbourne (I of W)
THE CASCADES SHOPPING CENTRE
TRICORN CENTRE
Victoria Park
Swimming Pool
PORTSMOUTH & SOUTHSEA STATION
Civic Offices
Guildhall
University
United Services Rec Grnd
Royal Naval Athletics Ground
Running Track
ST GEORGES BUSINESS CENTRE
Old Infirmary House
Cathedral
Grammer School
Museum & Art Gallery
Governors Green
Kings Bastion
Pembroke Gdns
Recreation Ground
Aspex Art Gallery
Coll of Art
Law Cts
Pol Sta
WINSTON CHURCHILL AV
A2030
CAMBRIDGE RD
HIGH STREET
BROAD ST
ST GEORGES ROAD
ANGLESEA RD
MUSEUM RD
KINGS RD
ELM GROVE
PIER RD
SOUTHSEA TER
WESTERN PAR
CLARENCE PARADE
CLARENCE ESPLANADE
A288
QUEEN STREET
THE HARD
VICTORIA ROAD
CIRCULAR ROAD
MARKETWAY
COMMERCIAL ROAD

North Poulner
Hangersley
Poulner
Whites Copse
Rec Ground
Hightown
Lynes Farm
Lane End Farm
Ringwood
Kingfisher Lake
Headlands Business Park
Headlands Adventure Centre
Lifeland Copse
Up Mead
River Avon
Lin Brook
Bickerley Common
Mill Stream
Sports Ground
Swimming Pool
Playing Fields
Cemy
Sch
School
Liby
Fire Sta
Council Offices
Carvers Trad Est
Hightown Ind Est
The Furlong
Poulner Mobile Home Park
Poulner Hill
A31
A338
By-pass
Salisbury Road
Southampton Road
Christchurch Rd
Noualé Lane
Narrow Lane
Back Lane
Eastfield Lane
Northfield Road
North Poulner Rd
Crow Arch Lane
Barn Lane
Parsonage Barn Lane
Kingsfield
Hightown Road
Castleman Way
Mansfield Road
High Street
Market Pl
West Street
Bickerley Rd
Riverside
Gorley Road
Linford Road
Meadow Road
Seymour Road
Broadshard Lane
Highfield Drive
Wessex Estate
Merryweather Estate

Woodley
Halterworth
Harefield
Whitenap
Romsey
Cupernham
Halterworth Farm
Halterworth Lodge
School
Montfort College
The Mountbatten School
Beggarspath Wood
Whitenap Farm
Recreation Ground
Cemetery
Romsey & District Hospital
Primary School
Fishlake Meadows
Fish Lake
Romsey Industrial Estate
Budds Lane Industrial Estate
Works
Romsey School
Playing Field
Romsey Primary School
Rec Grnd
Rapids Leisure Pool
Sports Centre
Broadlands Park
Broadlands House
Romsey Abbey Sch
La Sagesse Convent
War Memorial Park
Middle Bridge
Mead Mill Farm
Test Mills
Burnt Mill
Mill Race
Mill Stream
Mainstone Farm
Council Offices
Fire Sta
Pol Sta
Bus Sta
Dukes Mill Shopping Centre
Sun Inn
Hunters Inn
WINCHESTER ROAD
SOUTHAMPTON RD
A27
BY-PASS
ROMSEY BY-PASS
GREATBRIDGE ROAD
MALMESBURY RD
ALMA RD
CHURCH ST
BELL ST
THE HUNDRED
BOTLEY ROAD
CUPERNHAM LANE
WOODLEY LANE
HALTERWORTH LANE
WHITENAP LANE
TADBURN RD
NORTHLANDS RD
MAINSTONE
A3090
B3398
CAUSEWAY
HOLLMAN DR
PRIESTLANDS
CHURCH LA
PRINCES RD
DUTTONS RD
MOUNTBATTEN AV
STATION RD
LATIMER ST
BROADWATER RD
PALMERSTON ST
MIDDLEBRIDGE ST
NEWTON LA
KNATCHBULL CL
BRIDGE RD
GREAT WELL DR
AVENUE
SELSDON AV
VINEY AV
A
B
C
D
E
F
1
2
3
4

Polygon
Blechynden
Fourposts
SOUTHAMPTON
SOUTHAMPTON CENTRAL
MOUNTBATTEN WAY
WEST QUAY ROAD
WESTERN ESPLANADE
CUMBERLAND PL
HAVELOCK RD
SHIRLEY ROAD
COMMERCIAL ROAD
WESTERN DOCKS
Main Dock Gate
CITY INDUSTRIAL PARK
WEST QUAY RETAIL PARK
RETAIL VILLAGE
WEST QUAY SHOPPING AREA
THE MARLANDS SHOPPING CENTRE
Mayflower Theatre
MOUNTBATTEN BUSINESS CENTRE
Leisure World & Cinema
THE QUAYS Sports & Lesiure Centre
Tudor House Museum
Merchants House Museum
Mayflower Park
Maritime Museum
FERRY PORT
Red Funnel Ferry Terminal
ROYAL PIER (Disused)
Town Quay
RIVER TEST
DOCKS
TOWN QUAY
Dock Gate 8
Bargate Museum
Lansdowne Hill
WATTS PARK
Polygon Hotel
Civic Centre
Library Art Gallery
Guildhall
BBC Broadcasting Centre
Pol Sta & Law Courts
Coach Station
Superstore
Footbridge
Hotels
Depot
Mills
Piers
Elmfield
Goods Sheds
Passenger &
HERBERT WALKER AVENUE
A3024
A305

E
F
G
H
1
2
3
4
5
6
Royal South Hampshire Hospital
Newtown
Northam
Millbank
Nichols Town
Belvidere
Kingsland Place
Chapel
Crosshouse
Ocean Village
St Marys Sports Hall
Fire Station
The Argyle Education Centre
Health Centre
Amb Sta
College of Art
Millais Gallery
Mountbatten Liby
The Southampton Institute
Playing Field
School
St. Mary's Stadium Southampton F.C.
Jonas Nichols Sq
Cricket Ground
Hoglands Park
City College
St Marys
Central Trading Estate
Gymnastics Club
Central Hall
East St Shopping Centre
Lorry Park
College
Footbridge
City Commerce Centre
Southampton Hall of Aviation
Club
Yacht Club
Canutes Pavilion
Multiplex Cinema
SS Shieldhall Museum
Ocean Village Marina
Marina
Police Station
Dock Gate 4
Trafalgar Dry Dock
Queens Park
Sch
Works
Willments Industrial Estate
Longbridge Ind Est
Shipbuilding & Engineering Works
Northern Anchorage
Bakers Wharf
Millbank Wharf
James Wharf
Dibles Wharf
Dibles Gut
Belvidere Wharf
Leamouth Wharf
Britannia Wharf
Phoenix Wharf
Burnley Wharf
Victoria Wharf
Sunderland Wharf
Baltic Wharf
American Wharf
Vancouver Wharf
Corporation Wharf
Crosshouse Hard
Spitfire Quay
Smiths Quay
River Itchen
Itchen Bridge
Toll
A3025
A355
A33
Northam Road
St Andrews Rd
Kingsway
St Marys Pl
Britannia Road
Belvidere Road
Marine Parade
Albert Road North
Central Bri
Terminus Terrace
Marsh La
Evans St
Threefield La
Queens Ter
Platform Road
Canute Road
Orchard Pl
Charlotte Pl
Dorset St
Oxford Avenue
Graham Road
Clovelly Road
Argyle Road
Northbrook Road
Durnford Rd
Derby Road
Northumberland Road
Harrington Road
Radcliffe Rd
Parsonage Rd
Augustine Rd
Kent St
Princes Ct
Graham St
York Cl
Bond Street
William Street
Millbank Street
Cable St
Belvidere Ter
Rochester St
Victoria St
Peel St
Wilson St
Chapel St
James Street
Coleman Street
Cumberland St
Ascupart St
Golden Grove
Melbourne Street
Longcroft St
Standford St
Paget St
Anglesea Ter
Elm Ter
Endle St
Ryde Ter
Crosshouse Road
Bridge Ter
Alcantara Cres
Andes Cl
Asturias Wy
Channel Wy
Cadland Ct
Neptune Wy
Ocean Way
Enterprise Wy
Maritime Wk
Maritime Way
Central Road
Cunard Road
West Road
Old Road
Royal Crescent Rd
Saltmarsh Road
Lawrence Rd
Chantry Rd
Andersons Rd
Western Ter
Maryfield
Cook Street
Houndwell Pl
Palmerston Road
Cossack Grn
Johnson St
Winton St
South Front
East St
St Georges St
Lime Street
Bell St
Challis Ct
Russell St
King St
Chandos St
College St
Richmond St
Duke St
Charles St
Bernard Street
Oxford St
Brunswick Sq
Latimer St
John St
Queens Way
Canal Walk
Strand
Houndwell

A
B
C
D
1
2
3
4
5
6
Manor House
HAVANT ROAD
A3023
School
Pound Marsh
ROAD
KINGS ROAD
Hayling Billy Coastal Path
Caravan & Camping Site
WOODLANDS LA
BRIGHTS LA
HIGHWORTH LA
SALTMARSH LANE
DENHILL CL
WEST LANE
WARDENS
DOVER CT
HAYLING ISLAND
Higworth Caravan Park
LULWORTH CL
KATRINA GDNS
School
Golf Course
Club House
Newtown
GLEBE CL
ATHERLEY RD
CHARLESTON CL
GILBERT MEAD
SYCAMORE DR
Gable Head
CHURCH ROAD
DUNDONALD CL
ITCHIA CL
GROVE
BURWOOD
EASTWOOD CL
TOURNERBURY LANE
Tournerbury Farm
POPLAR GRO
BEECH GROVE
LABURNAM GROVE
HAWTHORNE GRO
LEGION RD
School
PALMERSTON RD
Fire Sta
Sch
Liby
FURNISS WY
DANCES WAY
NEWTOWN LA
STATION ROAD
HAMFIELD DR
AUBREY CL
FATHOMS REACH
SPINNAKER CL
SOUTHLEIGH GRO
MANOR ROAD
RICHMOND DR
RICHMOND CL
JAMES CL
GRAYLAND
ST MARYS
CHERRYWOOD GDNS
South Hayling
Tourner Bury Plantations
THOMAS AVENUE
STAUNTON AVENUE
Community Centre
Hayling Park Playing Field
West Town
Pol Sta
GARDEN CL
SOUTH ROAD
WALNUT TREE CL
BRIARWOOD GDNS
FIR TREE RD
LINDEN GRO
ELWELL GRN
OAKWOOD
WILLOW RD
ASHWOOD CL
ELM CLOSE ESTATE
ELM GROVE
SPENCER CL
Health Centre
ST LEONARDS AVENUE
ST MARGARETS RD
MENGHAM CT
GOLDRING CL
MY LORDS LANE
Mengham House Barn Theatre
FERNHURST CL
HOLLOW LANE
THE PRECINCT
MENGHAM RD
MENGHAM LANE
STEAD CL
TEAL
Mengham
SWANS WK
BACON LANE
WESTMEAD CL
STAMFORD AV
WINSTON CL
NICHOLAS CT
MARK ANTHONY CT
Sch
TIMBERS
OAKS
WEST FIELD CT
Westfield
SELSMORE ROAD
RAMSEY RD
RITCHIE CL
OSPREY DR
SALTERNS
RAILS
MAGDALA RD
GREEN LA
LENNOX LODGE
BEACH ROAD
WESTFIELD AV
VICTORIA AV
AVENUE
LYNDHURST CL
SEA GROVE AVENUE
MENGHAM AV
NORTH CRES
NORMAN RD
SEA FRONT
WARD CT
NORFOLK CRES
ANNES
ST JOHNS CL
SOLENT RD
ORCHARD CL
HOLM CT
ALEXANDRA AV
TUDOR CL
CHICHESTER AVENUE
GRAND PAR
ORCHARD RD
SEA FRONT ESTATE
Mengham Park
Amusement Park
MANOR WAY
WEBB LANE
THE SANDERLINGS
WEBB CL
BOUND LANE
WYBORN CL
HAROLDE
ST ANDREWS
OLD SCHOOL
The Beach
SUNTRAP GDNS
Coastguard Lookout
Hayling Bay

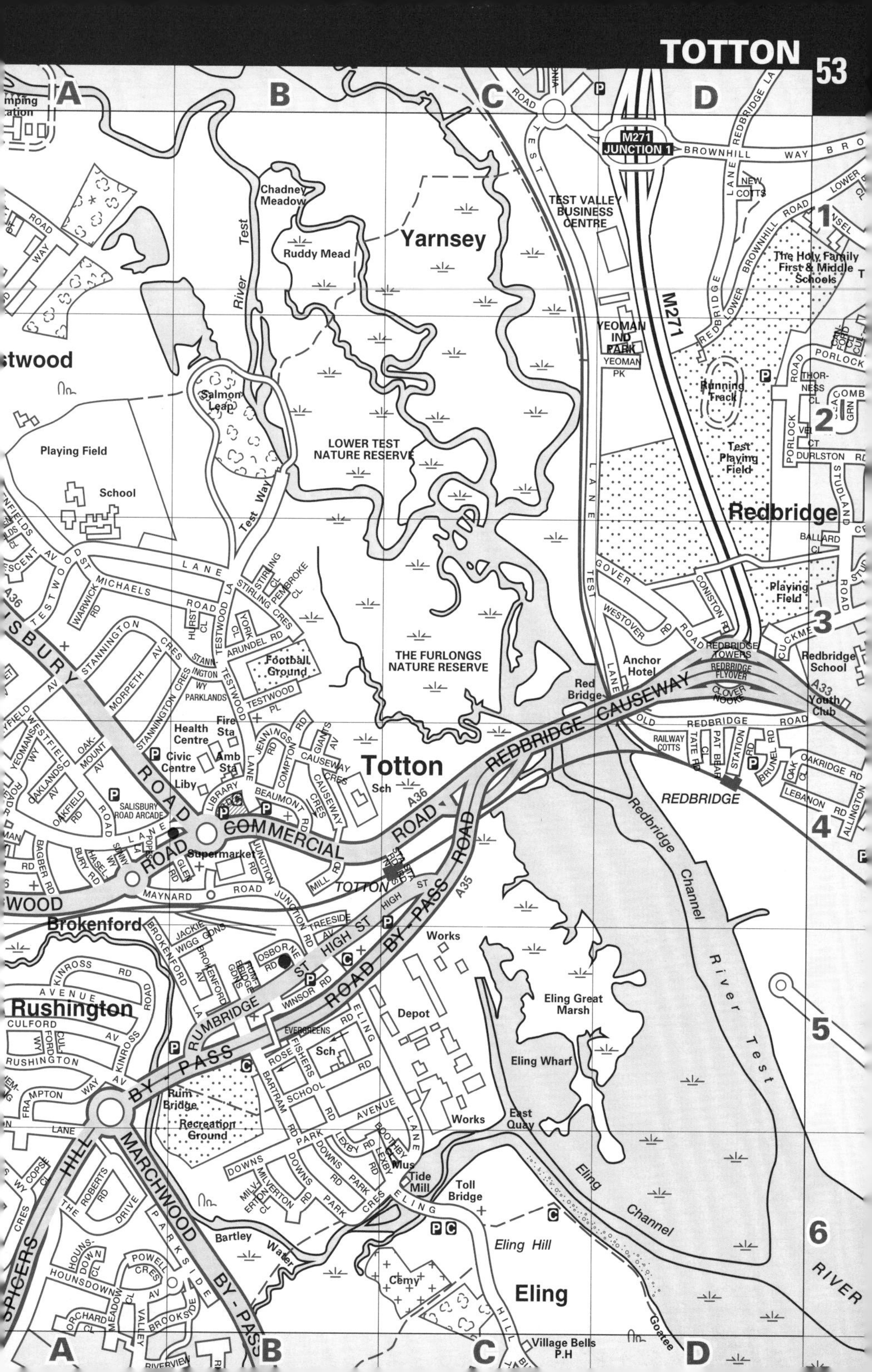
A
B
C
D
1
2
3
4
5
6
M271 JUNCTION 1
BROWNHILL WAY
Chadney Meadow
Ruddy Mead
Yarnsey
River Test
TEST VALLEY BUSINESS CENTRE
The Holy Family First & Middle Schools
M271
YEOMAN IND PARK
Running Track
Test Playing Field
Redbridge
Salmon Leap
LOWER TEST NATURE RESERVE
Playing Field
School
Testwood
Test Way
THE FURLONGS NATURE RESERVE
Football Ground
Health Centre
Fire Sta
Civic Centre
Amb Sta
Liby
Totton
Sch
SALISBURY ROAD ARCADE
COMMERCIAL ROAD
REDBRIDGE CAUSEWAY
Red Bridge
Anchor Hotel
REDBRIDGE TOWERS
REDBRIDGE FLYOVER
Redbridge School
Youth Club
A33
A36
A35
Supermarket
TOTTON
REDBRIDGE
Redbridge Channel
River Test
Brokenford
Works
Rushington
Depot
Eling Great Marsh
Eling Wharf
Sch
Rum Bridge Recreation Ground
Works
East Quay
Tide Mill
Mus
Toll Bridge
Eling Channel
Eling Hill
Bartley Water
Cemy
Eling
Village Bells P.H
Goatee
RIVER
BY-PASS
MARCHWOOD BY-PASS
SPICERS HILL
RUMBRIDGE ST
HIGH ST
SALISBURY ROAD

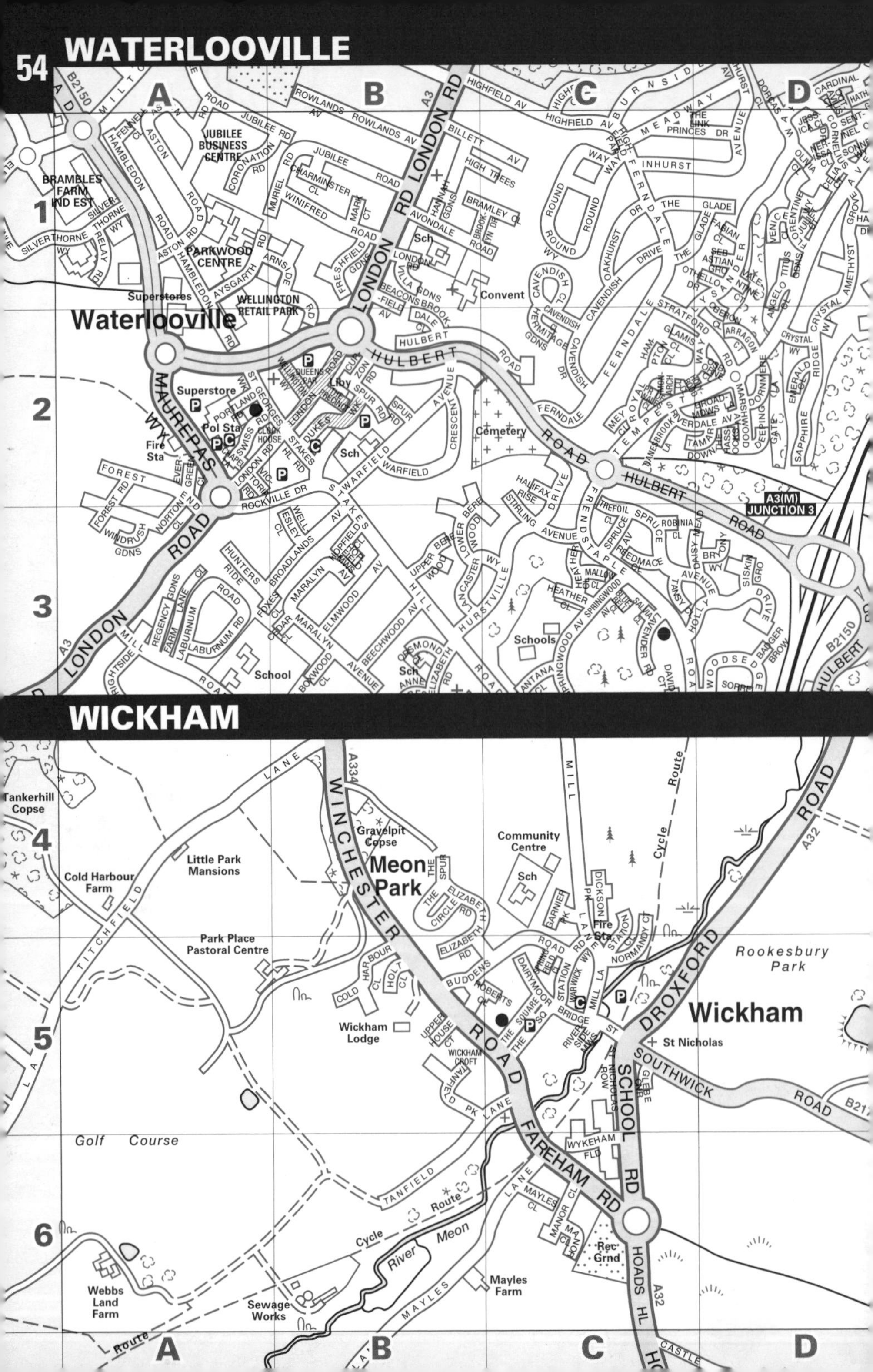

54
WATERLOOVILLE
Waterlooville
Brambles Farm Ind Est
Jubilee Business Centre
Parkwood Centre
Wellington Retail Park
Superstores
Superstore
Pol Sta
Fire Sta
Convent
Cemetery
Schools
School
Sch
Liby
A3(M) Junction 3
London Road
Hulbert Road
Maurepas Wy
Stakes Hill Road
Highfield Av
Rowlands Av
Jubilee Rd
Hambledon Road
Aston Road
Rockville Dr
Forest Rd
Warfield Av
Stratford
Ferndale
Cavendish Drive
Hurstville
Springwood Av
Woodsedge
B2150
A3
WICKHAM
Wickham
Meon Park
Rookesbury Park
Tankerhill Copse
Gravelpit Copse
Cold Harbour Farm
Little Park Mansions
Park Place Pastoral Centre
Community Centre
Fire Sta
Wickham Lodge
St Nicholas
Golf Course
Webbs Land Farm
Sewage Works
Mayles Farm
Rec Grnd
River Meon
Cycle Route
Winchester Road
Fareham Rd
Droxford Road
Southwick Road
School Rd
Hoads Hl
Titchfield Lane
Mill Lane
Mayles Lane
Tanfield
A334
A32

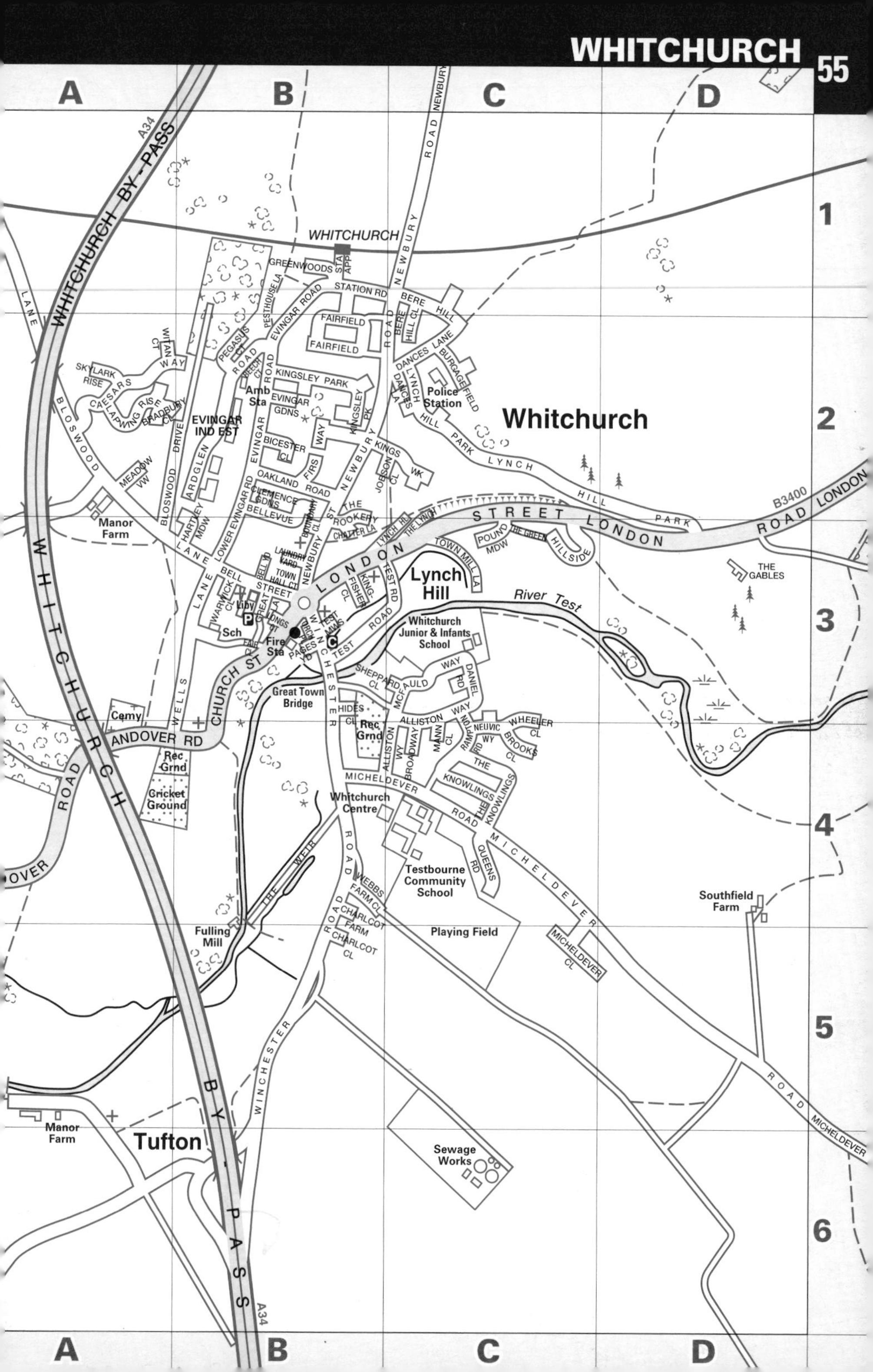
A
B
C
D
1
2
3
4
5
6
Whitchurch
Lynch Hill
Tufton
WHITCHURCH BY-PASS
A34
WHITCHURCH
NEWBURY ROAD
STATION RD
GREENWOODS
STA APP
BERE HILL
BERE HILL CL
FAIRFIELD
EVINGAR ROAD
PESTHOUSE LA
PEGASUS CT
WITAN WAY
WITAN CT
SKYLARK RISE
CAESARS
LAPWING RISE
BRADBURY CL
BLOSWOOD LANE
BLOSWOOD DRIVE
LANE
KINGSLEY PARK
KINGSLEY PK
Amb Sta
EVINGAR GDNS
EVINGAR IND EST
ARDGLEN
WAY
BICESTER CL
FIRS
OAKLAND ROAD
CLEMENCE GDNS
BELLEVUE
LOWER EVINGAR RD
HARTLEY MDW
MEADOW VW
Manor Farm
DANCES LANE
DANCES LA
LYNCH HILL PARK
BURGAGE FIELD
Police Station
KINGS WK
JOBSON CL
THE ROOKERY
CHATTER LA
LYNCH RD
THE LYNCH
LONDON STREET
LONDON ROAD
B3400
POUND MDW
THE GREEN
HILLSIDE
TOWN MILL LA
THE GABLES
River Test
LAUNDRY YARD
TOWN HALL CT
NEWBURY ST
BELL ST
BELL STREET
WARWICK CL
Liby
P
GREAT
LONGS
Sch
Fire Sta
CHURCH ST
PAGES
WINCHESTER
TEST MWS
TEST RD
TEST ROAD
KINGFISHER CL
C
Whitchurch Junior & Infants School
SHEPPARD CL
MCFAULD WAY
DANIEL RD
Great Town Bridge
HIDES CL
Rec Grnd
ALLISTON WY
ALLISTON WAY
BROADWAY
MANN CL
RAMPTON RD
NEUVIC WY
WHEELER CL
BROOKS CL
THE KNOWLINGS
MICHELDEVER ROAD
Whitchurch Centre
WELLS LANE
Cemy
ANDOVER RD
ANDOVER ROAD
Cricket Ground
THE WEIR
WEBBS FARM CL
CHARLCOT FARM
CHARLCOT CL
Testbourne Community School
Playing Field
QUEENS RD
MICHELDEVER CL
Southfield Farm
Fulling Mill
WINCHESTER ROAD
Sewage Works
MICHELDEVER ROAD
BY-PASS

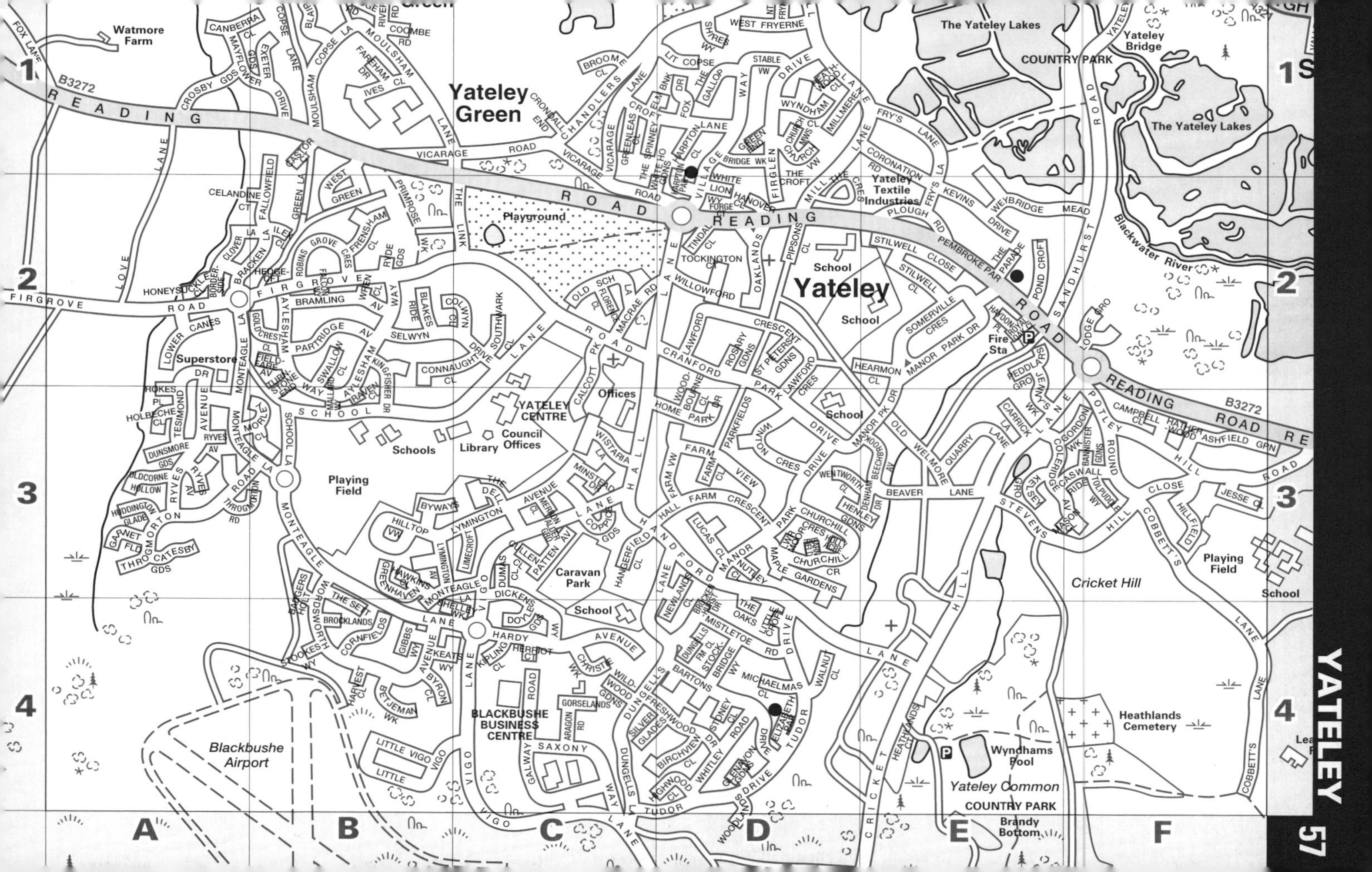
Watmore Farm
FOX LANE
B3272
READING ROAD
Yateley Green
The Yateley Lakes
COUNTRY PARK
Yateley Bridge
Blackwater River
SANDHURST ROAD
POND CROFT
THE PARADE
PEMBROKE PAR
Yateley Textile Industries
Yateley
School
Playground
Fire Sta
Superstore
Offices
YATELEY CENTRE
Council Offices
Library
Schools
Playing Field
Caravan Park
Cricket Hill
Heathlands Cemetery
Wyndhams Pool
Yateley Common
COUNTRY PARK
Brandy Bottom
BLACKBUSHE BUSINESS CENTRE
Blackbushe Airport
FIRGROVE ROAD
LOVE LANE
MONTEAGLE LA
SCHOOL LA
VIGO LANE
CRICKET HILL
COBBETT'S LANE
STEVENS HILL
POTLEY HILL
HALL LANE
HANDFORD LANE
CALCOTT PK
CRONDALL END
VICARAGE ROAD
MOULSHAM LANE
DUNGELLS LA
TUDOR DRIVE
WOODLANDS DRIVE
OLD WELMORE
MANOR PARK DR

The Index includes some names for which there is insufficient space on the maps. These names are indicated by an * and are followed by the nearest adjoining thoroughfare.

A Avenue SO45 24 A1
Abbey Cl SO45 35 B3
Abbey Pass SO23 56 E3
Abbey Pk Ind Est SO51 49 F4
Abbey Water SO51 49 A3
Abbey Way GU14 25 B1
Abbots Cl GU51 26 B2
Abbotstone Av PO9 30 B2
Abbotswood Cl, Romsey SO51 49 E1
Abbotswood Cl, Tadley RG26 34 E4
Abbotts Rd SO50 22 B6
A'Becket Ct PO1 47 B3
Abingdon Cl PO12 28 B4
Above Bar St SO15 50 D1
Acacia Gdns PO8 21 C3
Acacia Rd SO41 36 B1
Acer Way PO9 30 D2
Ackender Rd GU34 12 B3
Ackworth Rd PO6 20 C6
Ackworth Rd Ind Est PO6 20 D6
Acorn Bsns Centre PO6 20 A3
Acorn Cl BH25 44 D1
Acorn Gdns PO8 21 B2
Acre Ct SP10 14 C3
Acre Path SP10 14 C3
Adam Cl RG26 34 B2
Adams Dr GU51 26 D2
Adams Rd SO45 35 B4
Adams Way GU34 12 D1
Adderbury Av PO10 31 G2
Addington Ct SO41 42 D2
Addison Cl SO51 49 E1
Addison Rd, Brockenhurst SO42 17 C5
Addison Rd, Eastleigh SO50 22 D1
Addison Sq BH24 48 C3
Adelaide Pl PO16 23 E3
Adelaide Rd SP10 14 C3
Adhurst Rd PO9 30 B2
Adlington Pl GU14 25 C3
Admers Cres GU30 39 B6
Admirality Rd PO1 47 B2
Admirals Cl SO45 24 D2
Admirals Walk PO1 47 B1
Admirals Way, Andover SP10 14 D2
Admirals Way, Southampton SO45 35 C2
Admiralty Cl PO12 28 B2
Agarton La SO41 42 F1
Ainsley Gdns SO50 22 C1
Aircraft Esp GU14 25 B4
Airport Service Rd PO6 20 D6
Ajax Cl PO13 38 A1
Alamein Rd GU11 13 C1
Alanbrooke Cl RG27 32 B2
Albany Cl, Fleet GU51 26 C2
Albany Cl, New Milton BH25 44 B4
Albany Ct, Fleet GU51 26 C2
Albany Ct, Southampton SO32 15 A4
Albany Dr SO32 15 A4
Albany Rd, Fleet GU51 26 B3
Albany Rd, Romsey SO51 49 B3
Albany Rd, Southampton SO32 15 A5
Albemarle Rd PO12 28 B1
Albert Ct SO23 56 C1
Albert Rd, Aldershot GU11 13 D2
Albert Rd, Alton GU34 12 B4
Albert Rd, Eastleigh SO50 22 D1
Albert Rd, Farnborough GU14 25 B4
Albert Rd, New Milton BH25 44 B2
Albert Rd, Portsmouth PO6 20 C3
Albert Rd, Southampton SO32 15 B5
Albert Rd North SO14 51 G5
Albert Rd South SO14 51 F5
Albert St, Fleet GU51 26 A3
Albert St, Gosport PO12 28 C3
Albert Walk RG21 16 D4
Albert Yd RG21 16 C4
Albion Pl, Hook RG27 32 B3
Albion Pl, Southampton SO14 50 D4
Albion Rd SP6 27 F2
Alcantara Cres SO14 51 G5
Aldbury Ct BH25 44 B6
Alder Cl, Alton GU34 12 B1
Alder Cl, Romsey SO51 49 F4
Alder Gro GU46 57 C3
Alder Rd GU35 33 D2
Alderfield GU31 46 B3
Alders Ct SO24 43 D4
Aldershot Rd, Church Crookham GU52 26 C6
Aldershot Rd, Fleet GU51 26 B3
Alderwood Dr RG27 32 B4
Aldrich Rd PO1 47 C1
Aldroke St PO6 20 C3
Alec Rose La PO1 47 D2
Alecto Rd PO12 29 B5
Alencon Link RG21 16 B2
Alexander Gro PO16 23 B4
Alexandra Av PO11 52 B5
Alexandra Cl SO45 35 B3
Alexandra Ct, Bordon GU35 18 D4
Alexandra Ct, Farnborough GU14 25 B5
Alexandra Rd, Aldershot GU11 13 A2
Alexandra Rd, Alton GU34 12 C1
Alexandra Rd, Andover SP10 14 A3
Alexandra Rd, Basingstoke RG21 16 A3
Alexandra Rd, Farnborough GU14 25 B4
Alexandra Rd, Fordingbridge SP6 27 E3
Alexandra Rd, Hythe SO45 35 B2
Alexandra Rd, Lymington SO41 41 B2
Alexandra Rd, Southampton SO15 50 A1
Alexandra St PO12 28 A3
Alexandra Ter SO22 56 B4
Alfred Rd PO1 47 C1
Alice Rd GU11 13 C2
Alison Rd GU11 13 A2
All Saints Rd SO41 41 D4
Allan Gro SO51 49 E3
Allaway Av PO6 20 A2
Allee Dr GU30 39 B2
Allen Cl GU34 12 D1
Allendale Av PO10 31 G2
Allenwater Dr SP6 27 D2
Alliston Way RG28 55 C4
Allnutt Av RG21 16 F3
Alma Rd, Bordon GU35 18 D4
Alma Rd, Headley Down GU35 33 E3
Alma Rd, Romsey SO51 49 B3
Alma Sq GU14 25 B5
Alma St PO12 28 A3
Almond Cl PO8 21 C4
Almond Ct GU52 26 D5
Almswood Rd RG26 34 C1
Alpine Rd GU35 18 C6
Alresford Rd, Havant PO9 30 A2
Alresford Rd, Winchester SO23 56 F3
Alswitha Ter SO23 56 D1
Alton Bsns Centre GU34 12 E3
Alton By-Pass GU34 12 E4
Alton Rd GU51 26 D2
Alvara Rd PO12 29 A6
Alver Rd PO12 29 B5
Alverstoke Gdns GU11 13 A2
Amber Cl GU35 18 D5
Amberley Cl SO52 45 A2
Amberley Grange GU11 13 A3
Amberley Rd PO12 28 A1
Amberslade Walk SO45 35 A5
Ambleside SO32 15 A5
Ambleside Rd SO41 41 D3
Ambrose Rd RG26 34 E2
Amery Hill GU34 12 C2
Amery St GU34 12 C3
Amethyst Gro PO7 54 D1
Amey Ind Est GU31 46 B3
Amherst Rd GU35 18 C1
Anchor Gate Rd PO1 47 C1
Anchor La PO1 47 B1
Anchor Mws SO41 41 D2
Anchor Rd RG20 37 B2
Anchor Yd RG21 16 D3
Anchorage Way SO41 41 C3
Anderson Cl PO9 30 C3
Andersons Rd SO14 51 G5
Andes Cl SO14 51 G5
Andlers Ash Rd GU33 40 A6
Andover By-Pass SP11 14 A6
Andover Rd, Basingstoke RG23 45 A5
Andover Rd, Southampton SO15 50 A1
Andover Rd, Whitchurch RG28 55 A4
Andover Rd, Winchester SO23 56 C1
Andover Way GU11 13 D5
Andrew Bell St PO32 47 D1
Andrew Cl SO45 35 B6
Andrewartha Rd GU14 25 C4
Andrewes Cl SO32 15 C4
Andrews Cl GU52 26 B5
Androse Gdns BH24 48 B4
Angelo Cl PO7 54 D2
Anglesea Rd, Lee-on-the-Solent PO13 38 D6
Anglesea Rd, Portsmouth PO1 47 C2
Anglesea Ter SO14 51 G4
Anglesey Arms Rd PO12 29 A6
Anglesey Cl SP10 14 B6
Anglesey Rd PO12 29 A6
Anmore Rd PO7 36 C4
Anne Cres PO7 54 B3
Annes Ct PO11 52 A5
Annes Way GU52 26 C5
Anns Hill Rd PO12 28 A2
Anson Cl, Aldershot GU11 13 A1
Anson Cl, Ringwood BH24 48 E2
Anstey La GU34 12 D1
Anstey Mill Cl GU34 12 E1
Anstey Mill La GU34 12 E1
Anstey Rd, Alton GU34 12 D2
Anstey Rd, Romsey SO51 49 E1
Anthony Way PO10 31 G2
Anton Cl, Basingstoke RG23 45 C5
Anton Cl, Romsey SO51 49 E3
Anton Mill Rd SP10 14 A4
Anton Rd SP10 14 B4
Anton Trading Est SP10 14 A4
Anzio Cl GU11 13 C1
Apollo Dr GU35 18 D4
Appledown Cl SO24 43 D6
Applegate Pl PO8 21 A2
Appleshaw Cl RG26 34 D3
Appleton Mws SP10 14 B4
Appletree Cl BH25 44 C4
Appletree Mead RG27 32 D5
Apsley Cl SP10 14 A6
Aragon Rd GU46 57 C4
Arbour Ct SO22 56 B2
Archers Rd SO50 22 C3
Archery La, Fareham PO16 23 D2
Archery La, Winchester SO23 56 B3
Archery Rise GU34 12 B4
Archgate SO41 41 D1
Arden Walk BH25 44 D2
Ardglen Rd RG28 55 B2
Arford Common GU35 33 C2
Arford Rd GU35 33 B3
Argyle Cl GU35 18 C5
Argyle Rd SO14 51 E1
Arle Cl SO24 43 C3
Arle Gdns SO24 43 C3
Arlington Ct BH25 44 C5
Arlington Pl SO23 56 D1
Arlington Ter GU11 13 B2
Armada Dr SO45 35 A4
Arminers Cl PO12 29 B7
Armitage Av SO45 35 A6
Armory La PO1 47 B3
Armstrong Cl SO42 17 B3
Armstrong La SO42 17 B3
Armstrong Rd SO42 17 B3
Arnhem Cl GU11 13 D1
Arnold Rd SO50 22 C6
Arnolds Cl BH25 44 B5
Arnside Rd PO7 54 A1
Arnwood Av SO45 35 A6
Arragon Ct PO7 54 D2
Arran Cl, Basingstoke RG23 45 B4
Arran Cl, Portsmouth PO6 20 B2
Arreton Ct PO12 28 A4
Arrow Cl SO50 22 C2
Arrow La RG27 32 A2
Arthur Rd SO50 22 D2
Arthur St GU11 13 C2
Artillery Rd, Badshot Lea GU11 13 C1
Artillery Rd, North Camp GU11 25 C6
Artists Way SP10 14 A1
Arun Cl GU31 46 B4
Arun Ct RG21 16 F3
Arundel Cl, Alresford SO24 43 C6
Arundel Cl, Fleet GU51 26 C2
Arundel Cl, New Milton BH25 44 A2
Arundel Dr PO16 23 A1
Arundel Rd SO40 53 B3
Arundel St PO1 47 D2
Arundel Way PO1 47 D2
Ascot Cl GU34 12 C4
Ascot Ct GU11 13 C2
Ascupart St SO14 51 F3
Ash Cl, Gosport PO12 29 B5
Ash Cl, Romsey SO51 49 F4
Ash Cl, Southampton SO52 45 B1
Ash Copse PO8 21 A3
Ash Gro, Liphook GU30 39 C4
Ash Gro, Newbury RG20 37 B2
Ash Gro, Ringwood BH24 48 D3
Ash Gro, Southampton SO40 15 B2
Ash La RG26 34 A2
Ash Rd SO40 15 A3
Ash Walk SO24 43 D4
Ashburn Garth BH24 48 E4
Ashburton Cl SO24 43 B5
Ashburton Ct SO23 56 C2
Ashburton Rd, Alresford SO24 43 B5
Ashburton Rd, Gosport PO12 29 A6
Ashburton Rd, Southsea PO5 47 D5
Ashbury Rd GU35 18 D5
Ashby Pl PO5 47 D5
Ashdell Rd GU34 12 D3
Ashdene Rd SO40 15 B2
Ashdown SO45 24 B2
Ashdown Av GU14 25 C3
Ashdown Rd SO45 24 B2
Ashdown Walk BH25 44 D3
Ashdown Way SO51 49 E3
Ashe Rd PO9 30 D1
Ashfield Grn GU46 57 F3
Ashford Cl, Fordingbridge SP6 27 C3
Ashford Cl, Portsmouth PO6 20 B2
Ashford Cres SO45 35 C3
Ashford Rd SP6 27 B4
Ashford Works Ind Est SP6 27 C3
Ashington Cl PO8 21 A5
Ashington Pk BH25 44 D3
Ashlawn Gdns SP10 14 B5
Ashlea RG27 32 C4
Ashleigh Cl SO45 35 B6
Ashlett Cl SO45 24 D2
Ashlett Mws SO45 24 D2
Ashlett Rd SO45 24 D2
Ashley Cl BH24 48 E4
Ashley Ct PO12 28 A3
Ashley Gdns SO53 22 A1
Ashley La, Hordle SO41 36 A1
Ashley La, Lymington SO41 41 D2
Ashley Mdws SO51 49 D2
Ashley Rd, Farnborough GU14 25 C2
Ashley Rd, New Milton BH25 44 C2
Ashley Walk PO6 20 C4
Ashling Cl PO7 36 B4
Ashling Gdns PO7
Ashling Park Rd PO7
Ashmead GU35
Ashmore Av BH25
Ashton Way PO13
Ashurst Cl, Southampton SO40
Ashurst Cl, Tadley RG26
Ashurst Rd PO6
Ashwood Cl PO11
Aspen Cl GU35
Aspen Gdns RG27
Aspen Pl BH25
Aspen Way PO8
Astley St PO5
Aston Rd PO7
Astra Ct SO45
Astra Walk PO12
Asturias Way SO14
Asylum Rd SO15
Atheling Rd SO45
Atherley Rd PO11
Atherstone Walk PO5
Atholl Rd GU35
Atkinson Cl PO12
Aubrey Cl, Hayling Island PO11
Aubrey Cl, Lymington SO41
Auchinleck Way GU11
Auckland Av SO42
Auckland Pl SO42
Auckland Rd East PO5
Auckland Rd West PO5
Audemer Ct BH24
Augustine Rd SO14
Avenue Cl GU30
Avenue Ct PO12
Avenue De Caen PO5
Avenue Rd, Brockenhurst SO42
Avenue Rd, Fareham PO14
Avenue Rd, Farnborough GU14
Avenue Rd, Fleet GU51
Avenue Rd, Gosport PO12
Avenue Rd, Lymington SO41
Avenue Rd, New Milton BH25
Avenue Rd, Winchester SO22
Avery La PO12
Aviemore Dr RG23
Avocet Way PO8
Avon Cl, Lee-on-the-Solent PO13
Avon Cl, Lymington SO41
Avon Cl, Petersfield GU31
Avon Cres SO51
Avon Ct SP10
Avon Meade SP6
Avon Rd RG23
Avondale Rd, Aldershot GU11
Avondale Rd, Fleet GU51
Avondale Rd, Waterlooville PO7
Award Rd GU52
Ayesgarth GU52
Ayjay Cl GU11
Aylesham Way GU46
Ayling Ct GU9
Ayling Hill GU11
Ayling La GU11
Aylward St PO1
Aysgarth Rd PO7
Aysha Cl BH25
Azalea Av GU35
Azalea Cl PO9

B Avenue SO45
Back La, Brockenhurst SO42
Back La, Ringwood BH24
Back of The Walls SO14
Bacon La PO11
Badajos Rd GU11
Baddesley Cl SO52
Baden Cl BH25
Baden Powell Way SO51
Badger Brow PO7

ers Cl GU52 26 A3
ers Holt GU46 57 B4
ers Walk SO45 35 A5
ninston La SO45 24 D4
hot Lea Rd GU9 13 B6
hot Pk GU9 13 C6
er Rd SO40 53 A4
ur Dr GU33 40 B4
d Cl,
Milton BH25 44 C1
d Cl,
thampton SO16 53 D3
d Ct PO12 28 B4
er Lawn Rd SO42 17 D1
oral Cl GU34 12 A3
oral Rd SP10 14 A3
oral Walk BH25 44 A2
oral Way GU31 46 C2
Hall Pl RG27 32 B5
St SO32 15 C5
side GU9 13 A4
erman Rd GU31 46 C2
ing St SO51 49 B4
ister Gdns GU46 57 F3
ume Rd PO6 20 B6
ara Cl GU52 26 C5
rry Cl GU52 26 B4
lona Cl SP10 14 C2
ay Mws SO45 35 B6
ate Centre SO14 50 D4
ate St SO14 50 D4
am Cl PO12 28 B2
am Rd GU31 46 C3
Mow Hill GU35 33 B2
ws La SP10 14 A6
ws Rd RG26 34 D3
Cl PO10 31 F5
Ct SO41 41 D1
Fld GU46 57 D3
Green Cl PO7 36 C4
La RG23 45 C6
croft Way PO9 30 A3
es Cl GU14 25 C1
es La SO41 42 D1
ield Rd GU31 46 F3
ide Way GU33 40 B5
smere PO12 29 A5
Cl RG23 45 C4
ck Rd GU11 13 B1
gton Cl SO50 22 B1
Av BH25 44 C1
Wood Dr BH25 44 C1
y Way RG27 32 C6
ey Wood Bsns Pk
7 32 C6
n Cft BH25 44 C5
n Cl,
rshot GU11 13 A2
n Cl,
sey SO51 49 D2
n Common La
5 44 C5
n Common Rd
5 44 C6
n Court Av BH25 44 B6
n Court Rd BH25 44 B4
n Cross PO8 21 B1
n Dr BH25 44 B5
n Grn BH25 44 C6
n Ho BH25 44 A6
n Way BH25 44 A5
n Wood Rd BH25 44 A6
ns Dr GU46 57 D4
ns Rd,
ingbridge SP6 27 E3
ns Rd,
ant PO9 30 C1
m Rd SO40 53 B5
ell Gro PO10 31 G2
g Dr GU11 13 D5
g Rd PO9 30 A1
g Vw RG21 16 E2
gbourne Cl GU52 26 B5
gbourne Rd GU52 26 B6
gstoke Rd,
GU34 12 A3
gstoke Rd,
bury RG20 37 B2
gwell St SO32 15 C5
nthwaite Gdns
5 18 C2
elors Barn Rd
14 C2
a PO16 23 E3
Rd,
worth PO10 31 G6
Rd,
ngton SO41 41 F3
Sq PO1 47 B3
g La PO1 47 A4
burg Rd PO12 28 C4
s Way PO9 30 B1
Hill SO32 15 A5
Row PO1 47 B4
urst Rd RG26 34 A2
Rd SO41 41 B2

Beach Av BH25 44 A6
Beach Rd,
Emsworth PO10 31 F5
Beach Rd,
Hayling Island PO11 52 B4
Beach Rd, Lee-on-the-Solent
PO13 38 C5
Beacon Ct SP6 27 E2
Beacon Hill Rd GU52 26 D6
Beacon Sq PO10 31 G6
Beaconsfield Av,
Portsmouth PO6 20 C4
Beaconsfield Av,
Waterlooville PO7 54 B1
Beaconsfield Rd RG21 16 D4
Beales Cl SP10 14 C3
Bear Hill RG20 37 A3
Bearwood Gdns GU51 26 B2
Beatty Cl BH24 48 E2
Beaufort Av PO16 23 A1
Beaufort Dr SO32 15 B5
Beaufort Rd,
Bordon GU35 18 C2
Beaufort Rd, Fleet GU52 26 C4
Beaufort Rd,
Winchester SO22 56 B4
Beaulieu Cl BH25 44 A2
Beaulieu Ct,
Andover SP10 14 C1
Beaulieu Ct,
Basingstoke RG21 16 F3
Beaulieu Rd,
Eastleigh SO50 22 C2
Beaulieu Rd,
Lyndhurst SO43 37 D5
Beaulieu Rd,
Southampton SO45 35 A6
Beaumaris Gdns SO45 35 A2
Beaumond Grn SO23 56 B3
Beaumont Gro GU11 13 A1
Beaumont Rd SO40 53 B4
Beaver Ind Est GU30 39 B5
Beaver La GU46 57 E3
Beavers Cl, Alton GU34 12 B1
Beavers Cl, Tadley RG26 34 C2
Beavers Mws GU35 19 E3
Beck St PO1 47 C2
Beckham La GU31 46 A2
Becton La BH25 44 C4
Becton Mead BH25 44 C4
Bedford Cl,
Bordon GU35 18 C5
Bedford Cl,
Fordingbridge SP6 27 E2
Bedford Cl, Havant PO9 30 C5
Bedford Pl SO15 50 D1
Bedford Rd GU31 46 A3
Bedford St,
Gosport PO12 28 A2
Bedford St,
Southsea PO5 47 D3
Bedford Walk RG21 16 C3
Bedhampton Way PO9 30 A1
Beech Cl SO51 49 F4
Beech Ct RG28 55 B2
Beech Gro,
Gosport PO12 29 A5
Beech Gro,
Hayling Island PO11 52 D3
Beech Hill GU35 33 D3
Beech Hill Rd GU35 33 B2
Beech Rd,
Alresford SO24 43 D4
Beech Rd,
Southampton SO40 15 B2
Beech Ride GU52 26 A4
Beech Tree Dr GU9 13 C6
Beech Way PO8 21 B3
Beechbrook Av GU46 57 E3
Beechcrest Vw RG27 32 C4
Beechcroft Cl SO53 22 A1
Beechcroft La BH24 48 C2
Beechcroft Rd PO12 29 A5
Beechcroft Way SO53 22 A1
Beeches Hill SO32 15 C4
Beechnut Ind Est
GU11 13 C2
Beechnut Rd GU12 13 D2
Beechwood SP6 27 D4
Beechwood Av,
New Milton BH25 44 A1
Beechwood Av,
Waterlooville PO7 54 B3
Beechwood Ct GU33 40 C2
Beechwood Rd GU34 12 A4
Beechworth Rd PO9 30 B5
Beehive Walk PO1 47 B3
Beggars La SO23 56 F2
Behrendt Cl PO12 28 A2
Belgrave Mws RG27 32 C2
Bell Cl SO45 24 A3
Bell Hill GU31 46 B1
Bell Hill Ridge GU31 46 B1
Bell Ho SO24 43 D6
Bell Meadow Rd RG27 32 B6
Bell Rd, Andover SP10 14 C3

Bell Rd,
Portsmouth PO6 20 A3
Bell St, Romsey SO51 49 B3
Bell St,
Southampton SO14 51 E4
Bell St,
Whitchurch RG28 55 B3
Bell Yd RG28 55 B3
Bellair Rd PO9 30 C5
Belland Dr GU11 13 A2
Belle Vue Rd SP10 14 C4
Bellevue RG28 55 B2
Bellevue La PO10 31 G3
Bellevue Rd SO50 22 C3
Bellvue Ter PO5 47 C4
Belmont Cl,
Andover SP10 14 C4
Belmont Cl,
Southampton SO45 35 B5
Belmont Mws GU35 33 A2
Belmont Pl PO5 47 D4
Belmont Rd SP10 14 C4
Belmont St PO5 47 D4
Belmore La SO41 41 D3
Belmore Rd SO41 41 C3
Belsize Rd GU14 25 A4
Belstone Rd SO40 53 A4
Belvedere Pl GU31 46 C2
Belvedere Rd,
Farnborough GU14 25 B4
Belvedere Rd,
Southampton SO45 35 B5
Belvidere Rd SO14 51 G2
Belvidere Ter SO14 51 G1
Belvoir Cl PO16 23 B3
Bemisters La PO12 28 E4
Benbow Cl PO8 21 C1
Benbow St PO1 47 B2
Beneden Grn SO24 43 C6
Benedict Cl SO51 49 F3
Benificial St PO1 47 B2
Bennet Cl GU34 12 B2
Bentham Rd PO12 29 B5
Bepton Down GU31 46 D3
Bere Hill RG28 55 C1
Bere Hill Cl RG28 55 C2
Bere Hill Cres SP10 14 D4
Bere Rd PO7 36 C5
Berehurst GU34 12 B4
Beresford Cl,
Andover SP10 14 A6
Beresford Cl,
Eastleigh SO53 22 A1
Beresford Gdns SO53 22 A1
Beresford Rd,
Eastleigh SO53 22 A1
Beresford Rd,
Lymington SO41 41 B2
Berkeley Cl GU51 26 C2
Berkeley Sq PO9 30 C5
Bernard Av PO6 20 D3
Bernard St SO14 50 D5
Bernwood Gro SO45 24 A6
Berry Ct RG27 32 B6
Berryfield Rd SO41 36 C3
Berrylands GU33 40 D1
Bertram Rd BH25 44 D1
Beryton Cl PO12 28 A2
Beryton Rd PO12 28 A2
Betjeman Walk GU46 57 B4
Bevan Rd PO8 21 A3
Beverley Gdns SO51 49 E1
Beverley Rd,
Lee-on-the-Solent
PO13 38 A1
Beverley Rd,
Southampton SO45 35 A6
Bevis Cl SO45 24 B3
Bevis Rd PO12 28 B4
Bevois St SO14 51 F3
Bicester Cl RG28 55 B2
Bickerley Gdns BH24 48 B4
Bickerley Rd BH24 48 A3
Bickerley Ter BH24 48 A3
Bilbao Ct SP10 14 D2
Bilberry Ct SO23 56 C2
Billett Av PO7 54 B1
Billington Pl SO41 41 C4
Billy Lawn Av PO9 30 B1
Bingham Dr SO41 41 E3
Bingley Cl GU34 12 B2
Binley Ct RG26 34 F3
Birch Av GU51 26 B1
Birch Cl, Bordon GU35 18 D4
Birch Cl, Liss GU33 40 C4
Birch Cl, Romsey SO51 49 F4
Birch Gro, Bordon GU35 18 C6
Birch Gro, Hook RG27 32 C5
Birch Gro,
New Milton BH25 44 C4
Birch Par GU51 26 B2
Birch Rd, Bordon GU35 33 D2
Birch Rd, Tadley RG26 34 B1
Birch Tree Cl PO10 31 G2
Birch Tree Dr PO10 31 G2
Birchdale SO45 35 C5

Birchett Rd GU11 13 C2
Birchview Cl GU46 57 D4
Birdlip Cl PO8 21 B2
Birkenholme Cl GU35 33 E4
Bishearne Gdns GU33 40 B4
Bishop Ct BH24 48 C3
Bishop St PO1 47 C2
Bishops Cl, Fleet GU52 26 B4
Bishops Cl, Tadley RG26 34 D2
Bishops La SO32 15 B6
Bishops Way SP10 14 A2
Bishopstoke Rd,
Eastleigh SO50 22 D3
Bishopstoke Rd,
Havant PO9 30 A1
Bishopswood Ct RG26 34 C2
Bishopswood La RG26 34 A2
Bishopswood Rd RG26 34 C2
Bittern Cl PO12 28 B1
Bitterne Way SO41 41 C3
Black Swan Yd SP10 14 B3
Blackbird Way PO13 38 C3
Blackbush Rd SO41 42 C2
Blackbushe Bsns Centre
GU46 57 C4
Blackdown Cres PO9 30 A1
Blackfield Rd SO45 24 A4
Blackthorn Cl,
Bordon GU35 18 D4
Blackthorn Cl,
Lymington SO41 41 A4
Blackwater Cl,
Basingstoke RG21 16 F2
Blackwater Cl,
Oakley RG23 45 C6
Blackwater Cl,
Portsmouth PO6 20 A3
Blackwater Valley Rd
GU14 25 C1
Bladon Cl PO9 30 D3
Blair Cl BH25 44 A1
Blaire Pk GU46 57 B1
Blaise Cl GU14 25 C2
Blake Rd PO12 28 C3
Blakes La RG26 34 E2
Blakes Ride GU46 57 B2
Blanchard Rd SO32 15 B5
Blandford Ct SO41 42 D2
Bleachs Yd Ind Est
GU30 39 B6
Blechynden Ter SO15 50 B2
Blendworth Cres PO9 30 A2
Blendworth La PO8 21 D1
Blenheim Cl GU34 12 C2
Blenheim Cres SO41 36 A1
Blenheim Ct GU14 25 C3
Blenheim Gdns PO9 30 D3
Blenheim Mws SO45 35 B6
Blenheim Pk GU11 25 B6
Blenheim Rd,
Aldershot GU11 25 B6
Blenheim Rd,
Eastleigh SO50 22 C4
Blenheim Rd,
Waterlooville PO8 21 A3
Blossom Sq PO1 47 B1
Bloswood Dr RG28 55 A3
Bloswood La RG28 55 A1
Blount Rd PO1 47 C4
Blue Anchor La SO14 50 D5
Blue Ball Cnr SO23 56 F2
Blue Ball Hill SO23 56 F2
Blue Hayes Cl SP10 14 A4
Blue Timbers Cl GU35 18 D5
Bluebell Cl PO7 54 C3
Bluebell Rd GU35 19 F2
Bluehaven Walk RG27 32 A6
Blythswood Ct BH25 44 B5
Boakes Pl SO40 15 B2
Boldens Rd PO12 29 B7
Bolle Rd GU34 12 A4
Bolley Av GU35 18 A1
Bond Cl RG26 34 D1
Bond St SO14 51 H1
Bonfire Cnr PO1 47 B1
Boon Way RG23 45 B4
Boothby Cl SO40 53 B5
Borden Gate SP10 14 B4
Borderside GU46 57 A2
Bordon Cl RG26 34 D3
Bordon Rd PO9 30 A1
Bordon Trading Est
GU35 18 A2
Borough Gro GU31 46 B4
Borough Hill GU31 46 B3
Borough Rd GU31 46 B4
Borovere Cl GU34 12 B4
Borovere Gdns GU34 12 B3
Borovere La GU34 12 B4
Borsberry Cl SP10 14 C2
Bosmere Gdns PO10 31 G5
Boston Rd PO6 20 B2
Bosville SO50 22 C1
Botley Rd,
Bishops Waltham
SO32 15 B6

Botley Rd,
North Baddesley SO52 45 A1
Botley Rd,
Romsey SO51 49 C3
Boulter's Rd GU12 13 D2
Bound La PO11 52 C5
Boundary Cl RG28 55 B3
Boundary Rd GU14 25 B3
Boundary Way,
Havant PO9 30 A4
Boundary Way,
Portsmouth PO6 20 D1
Boundstone SO45 35 A4
Bounty Rd RG21 16 B4
Bourne Cl PO8 21 B2
Bourne Ct,
Aldershot GU11 13 B3
Bourne Ct,
Andover SP10 14 C1
Bourne Ct,
Basingstoke RG21 16 F2
Bourne Rd SO15 50 A1
Bournemouth Av PO12 28 A1
Bournemouth Rd SO43 37 A6
Bouverie Cl BH25 44 B4
Bow Fld RG27 32 D5
Bow La SO51 49 D2
Bow St GU34 12 B4
Bowcott Hill GU35 33 B2
Bowen La GU31 46 C3
Bowenhurst Gdns
GU52 26 B6
Bowenhurst Rd GU52 26 B6
Bowers Cl PO8 21 B4
Bowerwood Rd SP6 27 C4
Bowes Lyon Ct PO8 21 B1
Bowland Rise BH25 44 D2
Bowling Grn Dr RG27 32 A5
Bowmonts Rd RG26 34 F3
Bowyer Cl RG21 16 A4
Boxall's Gro GU11 13 C4
Boxall's La GU11 13 B4
Boxwood Cl PO7 54 B3
Bracher Cl SP10 14 B2
Bracken Cl SO52 45 C3
Bracken La GU46 57 A2
Bracken Rd,
Petersfield GU31 46 F4
Bracken Rd,
Southampton SO52 45 B3
Brackens Way SO41 41 E4
Brackenwood Dr RG26 34 D2
Brackley Av RG27 32 B2
Bracknell La RG27 32 A1
Bradbury Cl RG28 55 A2
Braehead SO45 35 A4
Braemar Av PO6 20 D4
Braemar Dr RG23 45 C4
Braine Lalleud Rd RG21 16 D2
Braintree Rd PO6 20 A2
Braishfield Rd,
Havant PO9 30 B2
Braishfield Rd,
Romsey SO51 49 E1
Bramber Rd PO12 28 A1
Bramble Cl,
Eastleigh SO50 22 D1
Bramble Cl,
Havant PO9 30 D3
Bramble Dr SO51 49 F2
Bramble Hill SO24 43 C5
Bramble Rd GU31 46 F3
Bramble Walk SO41 41 B1
Bramblys Cl RG21 16 B4
Bramblys Dr RG21 16 B4
Bramdean Cl RG26 34 D3
Bramdean Dr PO9 30 A1
Bramley Cl, Alton GU34 12 D2
Bramley Cl,
Lymington SO41 41 D4
Bramley Cl,
Waterlooville PO7 54 B1
Bramley Gdns PO12 29 A7
Bramley Walk GU35 18 A5
Bramling Av GU46 57 B2
Bramshaw Ct PO9 30 D1
Bramshot Dr GU51 26 C1
Bramshott Dr RG27 32 C6
Brandon Cl GU34 12 A2
Brandy Mt SO24 43 D4
Branksome Cl BH25 44 D2
Branksomewood Rd
GU51 26 A1
Bransley Cl SO51 49 D1
Branson Rd GU35 18 D3
Breamore Cl BH25 44 A2
Brecon Av PO6 20 D2
Brent Ct PO10 31 F6
Brew House La RG27 32 C2
Brewers St PO1 47 D1
Brewhouse Yd SO24 43 D4
Brewster Cl PO8 21 A5
Briar Cl PO8 21 B3
Briar Ct SO45 35 B4
Briar Way,
Romsey SO51 49 E2

Briar Way, Tadley RG26 34 E3
Briar Wood GU33 40 C2
Briarfield Gdns PO8 21 B2
Briarleas Ct GU14 25 C5
Briarwood Cl PO16 23 C4
Briarwood Gdns PO11 52 C4
Brick Kiln La GU34 12 A3
Brickfield La SO41 41 F1
Brickwoods Cl SO51 49 E2
Bridge Ct RG26 34 F3
Bridge Mdws GU33 40 B5
Bridge Rd,
Aldershot GU11 13 C3
Bridge Rd,
Alresford SO24 43 B4
Bridge Rd,
Emsworth PO10 31 G5
Bridge Rd,
Lymington SO41 41 E1
Bridge Rd,
Romsey SO51 49 C3
Bridge St,
Andover SP10 14 B3
Bridge St,
Fareham PO17 54 C5
Bridge St,
Fordingbridge SP6 27 F3
Bridge St,
Winchester SO23 56 E3
Bridge Ter SO14 51 G5
Bridge Walk GU46 57 D1
Bridgefoot Dr PO16 23 E3
Bridgefoot Path PO10 31 G5
Bridges Cl SO50 22 B3
Bridget Cl PO8 21 C1
Bridle Ct GU11 13 A2
Bridport St PO1 47 D2
Brights La PO11 52 B2
Brightside PO7 54 A3
Brightstone Rd PO6 20 B4
Brimley Hill Ct RG20 37 B2
Brimpton Rd,
Newbury RG20 37 B2
Brimpton Rd,
Tadley RG26 34 A2
Brindle Cl GU11 13 C4
Brinksway GU51 26 B2
Brinton La SO45 35 B2
Brintons Rd SO14 51 E1
Britain St PO1 47 B2
Britannia Cl GU35 19 E4
Britannia Rd SO14 51 G2
Britannia Way PO12 28 B1
Briton St SO14 50 D5
Britten Rd PO13 38 B4
Broad Grn SO14 51 E2
Broad Halfpenny La
RG26 34 F1
Broad La,
Lymington SO41 41 E3
Broad La,
North Baddesley SO52 45 A1
Broad La,
Southampton SO14 50 D5
Broad Leaze RG27 32 B4
Broad St,
Alresford SO24 43 D3
Broad St,
Portsmouth PO1 47 B3
Broadcut PO16 23 E1
Broadfields Cl SO41 42 E2
Broadlands GU14 25 D3
Broadlands Av,
Eastleigh SO50 22 C1
Broadlands Av,
Waterlooville PO7 54 B3
Broadlands Rd SO42 17 B2
Broadly Cl SO41 41 A4
Broadmead Cl SO41 41 D3
Broadmeadows La PO7 54 C2
Broadshard Ct BH24 48 C2
Broadshard La BH24 48 C1
Broadwater Rd SO51 49 B4
Broadway RG28 55 C4
Brockenhurst Dr GU46 57 D4
Brockenhurst Rd GU11 13 C3
Brockhampton La PO9 30 A5
Brockhurst Rd PO12 28 A2
Brocklands GU46 57 B4
Brodrick Av PO12 29 A5
Brokenford Av SO40 53 B5
Brokenford La SO40 53 A5
Brook Av, Farnham GU9 13 B4
Brook Av,
New Milton BH25 44 C1
Brook Av North BH25 44 D1
Brook Cl SO52 45 B3
Brook Gdns PO10 31 F6
Brook Rd SO41 41 E3
Brook St SO32 15 C5
Brook Ter SP6 27 E4
Brook Way SO51 49 D1
Brookdale PO7 54 B1
Brookfield Cl PO9 30 A3
Brookland Cl SO41 41 B3
Brooklands GU11 13 A2
Brooklands Rd SO32 15 C5
Brookley Rd SO42 17 C3
Brookly Gdns GU51 26 C1
Brooklyn Ct BH25 44 B1
Brooklyn Dr PO7 54 B1
Brookmead Way PO9 30 A6
Brooks Cl,
Ringwood BH24 48 D4
Brooks Cl,
Whitchurch RG28 55 C4
Brookside SO40 53 A6
Brookside Cl PO7 36 C5
Brookside Rd,
Brockenhurst SO42 17 C3
Brookside Rd,
Havant PO9 30 A5
Brookside Walk RG26 34 F3
Brookvale Cl RG21 16 A3
Brookwood Av SO50 22 C3
Brookwood Ind Est
SO50 22 C3
Brookwood Rd GU14 25 C2
Broom Acres GU52 26 B5
Broom Rd GU31 46 F3
Broom Way PO13 38 C3
Broome Cl GU46 57 C1
Broomfield La SO41 41 D1
Broomfield Rd GU35 18 A5
Broomhill Cl SO41 41 A3
Brougham La PO12 28 A2
Brougham St PO12 28 A2
Broughham Rd PO5 47 D3
Broughton Rd SO43 37 B4
Brown Cft RG27 32 A5
Brownhill Rd SO52 45 C2
Brownhill Way SO16 53 D1
Browning Cl SO50 22 B3
Brownsea Cl BH25 44 A2
Broxhead Ind Est
GU35 19 E1
Bruce Cl PO16 23 B1
Brune La PO13 38 D1
Brunel Rd,
Southampton SO15 53 D4
Brunel Rd, Totton SO40 53 A1
Brunswick Pl,
Lymington SO41 41 D2
Brunswick Pl,
Southampton SO15 50 D1
Brunswick Sq SO14 51 E5
Brunswick St PO5 47 D3
Bruntile Cl GU14 25 C5
Bruyn Ct SP6 27 F3
Bruyn Rd SP6 27 F3
Bryanstone Cl GU52 26 C5
Brympton Cl SP6 27 C3
Bryony Way PO7 54 D3
Bryson Rd PO6 20 A3
Buckingham Cl GU34 12 A3
Buckingham Rd GU31 46 A3
Buckingham St PO1 47 D1
Buckingham Walk BH25 44 A2
Buckland Cl SO50 22 C1
Buckland Dene SO41 41 C1
Bucklers Rd PO12 28 C1
Buckmore Av GU31 46 B2
Buddens Rd PO17 54 B5
Budds Cl RG21 16 B4
Budds La,
Bordon GU35 18 B2
Budds La,
Romsey SO51 49 A1
Budds La Ind Est
SO51 49 A1
Bugle St SO14 50 D5
Bulbeck Rd PO9 30 A5
Buller Ct GU14 25 B5
Bullers Rd GU9 13 A6
Bullfinch Ct PO13 38 C3
Bullrush Cl SO45 35 A5
Bulls Copse La PO8 21 A2
Bunnian Pl RG21 16 D1
Burford La SO42 17 D2
Burgage Fld RG28 55 C2
Burgate Flds SP6 27 F2
Burgess Rd RG21 16 B1
Burgh Hill Rd GU30 39 A1
Burley Rd SO42 17 A4
Burlington Ct GU11 13 B2
Burma Rd SO51 49 B4
Burnaby Rd PO1 47 C2
Burnett Cl SO45 35 C4
Burnham Rd,
Fordingbridge SP6 27 E2
Burnham Rd,
Tadley RG26 34 C1
Burnhams Walk PO12 28 D4
Burnley Cl RG26 34 D3
Burns Av GU52 26 D5
Burns Cl SO50 22 B5
Burns Rd SO50 22 B5
Burnside, Fleet GU51 26 B2
Burnside,
Waterlooville PO7 54 C1
Burrard Gro SO41 41 E3
Burrill Av PO6 20 D3
Burrows Cl PO9 30 C3
Burwood Gro PO11 52 C3
Bury Cl PO12 28 B4
Bury Cres PO12 28 B4
Bury Rd PO12 28 A4
Bush St East PO5 47 D4
Bush St West PO5 47 D4
Bushells Farm SP6 27 E4
Bushnells Dr RG20 37 A2
Busket La SO23 56 E3
Busketts Way SO40 15 A3
Butcher St PO1 47 B2
Butlers La BH24 48 E1
Butser Walk GU31 46 E2
Buttercup Cl SO45 35 B5
Buttermere Cl GU35 18 C1
Buttermere Gdns SO24 43 D5
Butterys Ct*,
Normandy St GU34 12 C2
Butts Ash Av SO45 35 B6
Butts Ash Gdns SO45 35 B6
Butts Ash La SO45 35 A6
Butts Bridge Hill SO45 35 B4
Butts Bridge Rd SO45 35 B5
Butts Farm La SO32 15 D4
Butts Lawn SO42 17 C2
Butts Mdw RG27 32 B5
Butts Mws GU34 12 B4
Butts Rd GU34 12 B4
Byeways SO45 35 A4
Byfields Rd RG20 37 A2
By-Pass Rd SO40 53 A5
Byron Cl,
Fareham PO16 23 A1
Byron Cl, Fleet GU51 26 C3
Byron Cl,
Southampton SO32 15 D5
Byron Cl, Yateley GU46 57 B4
Byron Rd SO50 22 D2
Byways GU46 57 B3

C Avenue SO45 24 A1
Cable St SO14 51 G1
Cabot Way BH25 44 A1
Cadhay Cl BH25 44 A1
Cadland Ct SO14 51 G6
Cadnam Cl,
Aldershot GU11 13 D5
Cadnam Cl,
Basingstoke RG23 45 C5
Cadogan Rd BH24 48 C3
Caesar Ct GU11 13 A2
Caesars Way RG28 55 A2
Caird Av BH25 44 D2
Caithness Cl RG23 45 B5
Caker Stream Rd GU34 12 E2
Cakers La GU34 12 E4
Calcott Pk GU46 57 C3
Caldecote Walk PO5 47 D3
Calender Cl GU34 12 B4
Calleva Pk RG7 34 B1
Calpe Av SO43 37 B4
Calshot Ct SO14 51 G6
Calshot Rd SO45 24 D2
Calthorpe Sq GU51 26 B2
Calton Gdns GU11 13 D4
Calvecroft GU30 39 C3
Cam Walk RG21 16 F3
Camber Pl PO1 47 B4
Camber Quay PO1 47 B3
Cambridge Rd,
Aldershot GU11 13 B1
Cambridge Rd,
Lee-on-the-Solent
PO13 38 C5
Cambridge Rd,
Portsmouth PO1 47 C3
Cambridge Rd West
GU14 25 B4
Camden Hurst SO41 42 B3
Camden St PO12 28 A3
Camden Walk GU51 26 D2
Camelia Cl PO9 30 D2
Camellia Cl SO52 45 C1
Camellia Gdns BH25 44 C2
Camp Rd, Bordon GU35 18 C3
Camp Rd,
Farnborough GU14 25 B5
Campbell Cl,
Aldershot GU11 13 D5
Campbell Cl,
Fleet GU51 26 A2
Campbell Cl,
Yateley GU46 57 F3
Campbell Rd SO50 22 D5
Campion Cl GU35 19 F2
Campion Dr SO51 49 F1
Campion Way RG27 32 C2
Canada Ct PO12 28 C1
Canada Way,
Bordon GU35 18 C3
Canada Way,
Liphook GU30 39 C4
Canal Cl SO51 49 C2
Canal Walk,
Romsey SO51 49 C2
Canal Walk,
Southampton SO14 51 E4
Canberra Cl GU46 57 A1
Candover Cl RG26 34 E3
Canes La GU35 19 E2
Canister Ho SO23 56 D2
Cannon St SO41 41 D2
Canon St SO23 56 C4
Canons Ct RG20 37 A2
Canons Walk SO41 42 E2
Canterbury Rd GU14 25 C3
Canute Rd,
Southampton SO14 51 F6
Canute Rd,
Winchester SO23 56 F4
Captains Pl SO14 51 F5
Captains Row,
Lymington SO41 41 E2
Captains Row,
Portsmouth PO1 47 B4
Cardew Rd GU33 40 D5
Careys Cotts SO42 17 C2
Cargate Av GU11 13 B2
Cargate Gro GU11 13 B3
Cargate Hill GU11 13 B2
Cargate Ter GU11 13 B2
Carisbrooke Cl,
Alresford SO24 43 C6
Carisbrooke Cl,
Havant PO9 30 D4
Carisbrooke Cres SO53 22 A1
Carisbrooke Ct,
New Milton BH25 44 A2
Carisbrooke Ct,
Romsey SO51 49 D1
Carleton Cl RG27 32 A6
Carlton Cres GU52 26 C5
Carlton Rd,
Bordon GU35 33 F4
Carlton Rd,
Gosport PO12 28 C4
Carlton Way PO12 28 C4
Carlyle Rd PO12 28 B3
Carlyon Cl GU14 25 B2
Carmarthen Av PO6 20 D2
Carnarvon Rd PO12 28 A4
Carnival Sq GU51 26 B2
Caroline Pl PO12 28 B3
Carpenter Cl,
Lymington SO41 41 D1
Carpenter Cl,
Southampton SO45 35 B3
Carpenters SO24 43 C5
Carrick La GU46 57 E3
Carrington Cl SO41 42 F3
Carrington Cres RG26 34 D2
Carrington La SO41 42 F3
Carronade Walk PO6 20 C6
Carthona Dr GU52 26 B4
Carvers La BH24 48 B3
Carvers Trading Est
BH24 48 B3
Cascades App 47 D1
Caslake Cl BH25 44 B4
Cassino Cl GU11 13 C1
Castle Av, Havant PO9 30 D5
Castle Av,
Winchester SO23 56 C3
Castle Cl,
Lymington SO41 42 E4
Castle Cl,
Southsea PO5 47 D4
Castle Gdns GU31 46 C3
Castle Hill SO23 56 C3
Castle La, North Baddesley
SO52 45 D2
Castle La,
Southampton SO14 50 D4
Castle Rd PO5 47 D4
Castle Sq RG21 16 D2
Castle St GU52 26 B4
Castle Ter SO23 56 C2
Castle Way,
Havant PO9 30 D5
Castle Way,
Southampton SO14 50 D4
Castleman Way BH24 48 B4
Castons Walk RG21 16 D4
Castons Yd RG21 16 D4
Castor Ct, Fleet GU52 26 D5
Castor Ct, Yateley GU46 57 B1
Caswall Ride GU46 57 F3
Catesby Gdns GU46 57 A3
Catherington La PO8 21 B1
Catherington Way PO9 30 A2
Causeway SO51 49 A4
Causeway Cotts RG27 32 D3
Causeway Cres SO40 53 B4
Causeway Fm PO8 21 B3
Cavalier Way GU34 12 A4
Cavalry Ct GU11 13 A2
Cavell Dr PO6 20 B2
Cavendish Cl,
Romsey SO51 49 E1
Cavendish Cl,
Waterlooville PO7 54 C1
Cavendish Corner Carava
BH24
Cavendish Dr PO7
Cavendish Gdns GU52
Cavendish Mws GU11
Cavendish Rd GU11
Cawtes Pl PO16
Cecil Av SO40
Cecil Gro PO5
Cecil Pl PO5
Cedar Cl PO7
Cedar Cres,
Southampton SO52
Cedar Cres,
Waterlooville PO8
Cedar Ct SO32
Cedar Dr RG20
Cedar Gdns,
Havant PO9
Cedar Gdns,
New Milton BH25
Cedar Lawn SO51
Cedar Mt SO43
Cedar Rd,
Eastleigh SO50
Cedar Rd,
Farnborough GU14
Cedar Tree Cl RG23
Cedar Walk SO22
Cedric Cl SO45
Celandine Av PO8
Celandine Ct GU46
Celia Ct PO7
Cement Ter SO14
Cemetery La PO7
Central Bri SO14
Central Rd,
Bordon GU35
Central Rd,
Southampton SO14
Central Station Bri
SO15
Central Trading Est
SO14
Centre Pl BH24
Cerne Cl SO52
Chadderton Gdns PO1
Chadwick Rd SO50
Chaffey Cl BH24
Chaffinch Cl BH25
Chaffinch Way PO13
Chalcraft Cl GU30
Chalcrafts GU34
Chalet Hill GU35
Chalewood Rd SO45
Chalfont Dr GU14
Chalkey Copse RG27
Chalkridge Rd PO6
Chalky La SO32
Challenger Dr PO12
Challis Ct SO14
Chaloner Cres SO45
Chamberlain Gro PO14
Chamberlayne Rd SO50
Chambers Av SO51
Champion Cl SO41
Champion Way GU52
Champney Cl GU35
Chandlers La GU46
Chandos St SO14
Channel Ct BH25
Channel Way SO14
Chantry Cl RG27
Chantry Rd,
Southampton SO14
Chantry Rd,
Waterlooville PO8
Chantry St SP10
Chapel Gdns GU35
Chapel Hill RG21
Chapel La,
Blackfield SO45
Chapel La,
Fawley SO45
Chapel La,
Lyndhurst SO43
Chapel La,
Waterlooville PO7
Chapel Rd SO14
Chapel Row RG27
Chapel St,
Petersfield GU31
Chapel St,
Southampton SO14
Chapel St,
Southsea PO5
Chappell Cl GU30
Chapter Ter RG27
Charing Cl BH24
Chark La PO13
Charlcot Cl RG28
Charlcot Fm RG28
Charlcote Cl GU14
Charlecote Mws SO23
Charles Cl RG27
Charles Dalton Ct SP10

es Dickens St PO1 47 D2
es Ley Ct SO45 24 C2
es St,
rsfield GU31 46 C3
es St,
:hampton SO14 51 F4
eston Cl PO11 52 A3
eston Rd SO45 35 D6
ejoy Gdns SO14 51 G1
otte Mws PO12 29 A6
otte Pl SO14 51 E1
otte St PO1 47 D1
ton Cl SO41 36 A2
ton Rd SP10 14 A2
ninster Cl PO7 54 B1
ock Cl SO41 36 A2
wood Cl SP10 14 C5
wood Dr SP6 27 E2
well Dr PO9 31 E3
e Cl GU33 40 D5
e Ct GU35 19 E2
e Rd,
don GU35 19 E2
e Rd, Liss GU33 40 D5
ewater Ct GU11 13 B2
ield Cl GU14 25 B4
am Cl PO12 28 C2
am Dr PO1 47 C4
worth Av PO6 20 C4
worth Rd,
eigh SO50 22 D1
worth Rd,
borough GU14 25 C3
worth Way BH25 44 A1
er La RG28 55 B3
cer Cl PO16 23 A1
cer Dr SO41 42 D3
ntsingers Rd
4 12 C2
eney Cl SO45 35 A6
ton Park Rd GU34 12 A4
ner Ct RG21 16 F3
ea Ho RG21 16 D3
enham Cres PO13 38 C4
ers Cl SO41 41 A3
ers Rd RG21 16 D3
bourg Rd SO50 22 B5
ton Cl,
ey RG26 34 D3
ton Cl,
erlooville PO8 21 B1
ton Rd,
eigh SO50 22 C6
ton Rd,
port PO12 28 A4
ton Rd,
chester SO22 56 A1
ue La PO13 38 D3
y Cl, Hook RG27 32 C4
y Cl, Lee-on-the-Solent
3 38 D5
y Gdns SO32 15 D5
y Tree Av PO8 21 B5
y Way GU34 12 B1
yhill Gro GU11 13 A3
ywood Gdns PO11 52 C3
ille Ct SO51 49 A3
ille St SO51 49 B3
well Gdns SO53 22 A2
St SO23 56 F3
Ter SO23 56 F4
ton Cres GU52 26 B6
er Pl RG21 16 B4
er Rd SO23 56 F3
nut Av,
over SP10 14 A6
nut Av,
eigh SO50 22 A5
nut Av,
Milton BH25 44 C4
nut Av,
erlooville PO8 21 C4
nut Cl,
n GU34 12 B1
nut Cl,
ook GU30 39 D5
nut Cl,
sey SO51 49 F4
nut Cl,
erlooville PO7 36 C5
nut Ct GU35 18 D5
nut Dr SO40 15 C1
nut End GU35 33 C4
nut Gro GU51 26 C1
nut Rd SO42 17 D3
nut Rise SO50 22 A5
nut Walk SO24 43 D5
e Way PO13 38 D5
ey Ct SO23 56 D4
ster Av PO11 52 C5
ester Rd BH24 48 E2
am Cl PO9 30 A4
am Dr PO9 30 A3
am Rd PO6 20 D2
am Sq PO9 30 A4
am Walk PO9 30 A3

Chilcomb Cl PO13 38 D5
Chilcombe Cl PO9 30 A2
Childerstone Cl GU30 39 B4
Chilmark Ct GU33 40 B4
Chiltern Cl, Fleet GU52 26 C5
Chiltern Cl, New Milton BH25 44 B4
Chiltern Ct SO24 43 D5
Chiltern Dr BH25 44 A4
Chiltlee Cl GU30 39 C4
Chiltlee Manor GU30 39 B4
Chiltley La GU30 39 C6
Chiltley Way GU30 39 C5
Chilworth Gro PO12 28 A3
Chilworth Old Village SO52 45 D3
Chinnock Cl GU52 26 A4
Chippendale Cl RG26 34 B2
Chipstead Rd PO6 20 B3
Chiswick Ho RG21 16 D2
Chivers Cl PO5 47 D4
Christchurch Bay Rd BH25 44 A6
Christchurch Rd, New Milton BH25 44 A4
Christchurch Rd, Ringwood BH24 48 B3
Christchurch Rd, Winchester SO22 56 B4
Christie Walk GU46 57 C4
Christopher Way PO10 31 H4
Christy Ct RG26 34 E3
Church Av GU14 25 B1
Church Brook RG26 34 C4
Church Circle GU14 25 B4
Church Cl, Andover SP10 14 B3
Church Cl, Southampton SO52 45 C2
Church Ct GU51 26 B2
Church Flds, Bordon GU35 19 G2
Church Flds, Bordon GU35 33 A3
Church Fm SP6 27 E4
Church Gro GU51 26 A1
Church Hill, Aldershot GU12 13 D3
Church Hill, Lymington SO41 42 E3
Church La, Aldershot GU11 13 D3
Church La, Basingstoke RG21 16 C3
Church La, Bordon GU35 19 H1
Church La, Bordon GU35 33 A2
Church La, Brockenhurst SO42 17 D4
Church La, Fawley SO45 24 B2
Church La, Havant PO9 30 D6
Church La, Hook RG27 32 C3
Church La, Liphook GU30 39 B1
Church La, Lymington SO41 41 D2
Church La, Lyndhurst SO43 37 C5
Church La, New Milton BH25 44 B3
Church La, Romsey SO51 49 A3
Church La, Southampton SO14 50 D5
Church La East GU11 13 C3
Church La West GU11 13 B3
Church Mead SO41 41 D4
Church Mws GU46 57 D1
Church Path, Emsworth PO10 31 G5
Church Path, Fareham PO16 23 D2
Church Path, Farnborough St GU14 25 B1
Church Path, Gosport PO12 28 D4
Church Path, Hook RG27 32 A6
Church Path, Reading Rd, Farnborough GU14 25 B5
Church Path, Waterlooville PO8 21 D2
Church Pl, Fareham PO16 23 E2
Church Pl, Romsey SO51 49 A3
Church Rd, Aldershot GU11 13 D4
Church Rd, Fleet GU51 26 A1
Church Rd, Gosport PO12 29 A6
Church Rd, Hayling Island PO11 52 C3

Church Rd, Liphook GU30 39 C1
Church Rd, Romsey SO51 49 A3
Church Rd, Tadley RG26 34 D4
Church Rd East GU14 25 C4
Church Rd West GU14 25 B4
Church Row*, Hylton Rd GU31 46 C3
Church Sq RG21 16 C3
Church St, Aldershot GU11 13 B2
Church St, Alton GU34 12 C2
Church St, Basingstoke RG21 16 C2
Church St, Fordingbridge SP6 27 E4
Church St, Liss GU33 40 A3
Church St, Romsey SO51 49 B3
Church St, Whitchurch RG28 55 B4
Church Vw, Hook RG27 32 C5
Church Vw, Yateley GU46 57 D1
Churchfield Ct GU30 39 B5
Churchfield Rd GU31 46 E2
Churchfields SO45 24 D1
Churchill Av, Aldershot GU12 13 D3
Churchill Av, Southampton SO32 15 A4
Churchill Cl, Alton GU34 12 C4
Churchill Cl, Hook RG27 32 B2
Churchill Cr GU46 57 D3
Churchill Cres, Bordon GU35 33 B3
Churchill Cres, Yateley GU46 57 D3
Churchill Ct, New Milton BH25 44 B3
Churchill Ct, Waterlooville PO8 21 A2
Churchill Dr PO10 31 G2
Churchill Way, Andover SP10 14 C1
Churchill Way, Basingstoke RG21 16 C2
Churchill Way East RG21 16 E2
Churchill Way West RG21 16 A2
Churt Rd GU35 33 D2
Circular Rd PO1 47 C1
City Bsns Centre SO23 56 D1
City Commerce Centre SO14 51 F5
City Ind Pk SO15 50 B3
City Rd SO23 56 C1
Civic Centre Rd, Havant PO9 30 A3
Civic Centre Rd, Southampton SO14 50 C2
Civic Way PO16 23 D2
Clacton Rd PO6 20 A2
Clandon Ct GU14 25 C3
Clandon Dr SO50 22 B1
Clanwilliam Rd PO13 38 C5
Clare Gdns, Petersfield GU31 46 F3
Clare Gdns, Southampton SO45 24 A6
Clarence Esp PO5 47 C5
Clarence Par PO5 47 D5
Clarence Rd, Fleet GU51 26 B3
Clarence Rd, Gosport PO12 28 D3
Clarence Rd, Lyndhurst SO43 37 C5
Clarence St PO1 47 D1
Clarendon Cl SO51 49 E1
Clarendon Pk SO41 41 C4
Clarendon Pl PO1 47 D2
Clarendon Rd, Havant PO9 30 A5
Clarendon Rd, Southsea PO5 47 D5
Clark Mws*, Church St RG28 55 B3
Clarks Cl BH24 48 B3
Clayhall Rd PO12 29 A6
Claylands Ct SO32 15 B5
Claylands Rd SO32 15 B5
Clemence Gdns RG28 55 B2
Clevedon Cl GU14 25 C3
Cleveland Rd PO12 29 B5
Cliddesden Rd RG21 16 D4
Cliff Cres BH25 44 B6
Cliff Rd SO41 42 A2
Cliff Ter BH25 44 B6
Cliffdale Gdns PO6 20 D2
Clifford St SO14 51 F2
Clifton Hill SO22 56 B2
Clifton Rd, Lee-on-the-Solent PO13 38 D6

Clifton Rd, Southsea PO5 47 D5
Clifton Rd, Winchester SO22 56 B2
Clifton Ter, Basingstoke RG21 16 D1
Clifton Ter, Southsea PO5 47 D5
Clifton Ter, Winchester SO22 56 B2
Clifton Walk RG21 16 C3
Clinton Rd SO41 41 D1
Clock Ho PO7 54 A2
Clock St PO1 47 B2
Clockhouse Rd GU14 25 A1
Closeworth Rd GU14 25 C5
Cloughs Rd BH24 48 C3
Clovelly Rd, Emsworth PO10 31 G6
Clovelly Rd, Southampton SO14 51 E1
Clover Cl GU35 19 F2
Clover La GU46 57 A2
Clover Nooke SO15 53 D3
Clover Way SO51 49 F2
Clyde Ct SP10 14 C1
Coachways SP10 14 A4
Coat Gdns SO45 35 B3
Cobbett's La GU17, 46 57 F3
Cobblewood PO10 31 G3
Cobden St PO12 28 B3
Coe Cl GU11 13 B2
Coghlan Cl PO16 23 C1
Coker Cl SO22 56 B1
Colborne Cl SO41 41 D1
Colchester Rd PO6 20 A2
Cold Harbour Cl PO17 54 B5
Colden La SO24 43 D2
Coldharbour Ct SP10 14 C3
Coldharbour Farm Rd PO10 31 G4
Coldhill La PO8 21 A1
Colebrook Pl SO23 56 E4
Colebrook St SO23 56 E3
Coleford Bridge Rd GU16 25 D1
Coleman St SO14 51 F3
Colemore Sq PO9 30 B2
Colenso Rd PO16 23 B2
Colenzo Dr SP10 14 C2
Coleridge Av GU46 57 E3
Coleville Av SO45 24 C2
Collard Way GU33 40 C5
College La PO1 47 B2
College Rd, Portsmouth PO1 47 B2
College Rd, Ringwood BH24 48 B3
College St, Petersfield GU31 46 C3
College St, Portsmouth PO1 47 B2
College St, Southampton SO14 51 E5
College St, Winchester SO23 56 D4
College Walk SO23 56 E4
Collingwood GU14 25 D4
Collins La BH24 48 B3
Collyers Cres GU30 39 D4
Collyers Rd SO42 17 C5
Colpoy St PO5 47 D3
Colson Cl SO23 56 F1
Colson Rd SO23 56 F2
Coltsfoot Pl RG27 32 D5
Coltsfoot Rd GU35 19 F2
Coltsfoot Walk SO51 49 F1
Colville Dr SO32 15 D5
Colville Rd PO6 20 C2
Colwell Rd PO6 20 B4
Colwyn Cl GU46 57 B2
Comfrey Cl SO51 49 F2
Comley Hill PO9 31 E1
Commercial Pl PO1 47 D1
Commercial Rd, Portsmouth PO1 47 D2
Commercial Rd, Southampton SO15 50 B2
Commercial Rd, Totton SO40 53 B4
Commodore Ct GU14 25 A5
Common Barn La, Lee-on-the-Solent PO13 38 D3
Common Barn La, Lee-on-the-Solent PO13 38 D5
Compass Fld RG27 32 C5
Compass Pt PO16 23 C4
Compton Cl, Eastleigh SO50 22 B1
Compton Cl, Fleet GU52 26 C6
Compton Cl, Havant PO9 30 B3

Compton Cl, Hook RG27 32 C6
Compton Cl, Lee-on-the-Solent PO13 38 D4
Compton Rd, Fleet GU52 26 C6
Compton Rd, New Milton BH25 44 B3
Compton Rd, Southampton SO40 53 B4
Compton Rd, Winchester SO22 56 B4
Compton Walk SO14 51 E1
Conde Way GU35 18 C5
Conference Pl SO41 41 E4
Conholt Rd SP10 14 B5
Conifer Cl, Bordon GU35 18 C6
Conifer Cl, Fleet GU52 26 B6
Conifer Cl, Southampton SO45 35 A3
Conifer Cl, Tadley RG26 34 A1
Conifer Cl, Waterlooville PO8 21 B6
Conifer Cl, Winchester SO22 56 A1
Conifer Cres SO41 41 A3
Conigar Rd PO10 31 H3
Coniston Gro SO24 43 D6
Coniston Rd, Bordon GU35 18 C2
Coniston Rd, Eastleigh SO50 22 B4
Coniston Rd, Ringwood BH24 48 C4
Coniston Rd, Southampton SO16 53 D3
Coniston Way GU52 26 A6
Connaught Cl, Bordon GU35 18 D5
Connaught Cl, New Milton BH25 44 A4
Connaught Cl, Yateley GU46 57 B2
Connaught Rd, Fleet GU51 26 B3
Connaught Rd, Havant PO9 30 C5
Conqueror Way PO13 38 A1
Consort Cl SO50 22 D1
Consort Rd SO50 22 D1
Constable Cl PO12 29 B7
Constable Ct SP10 14 A2
Constables Gate SO23 56 B3
Convent La PO10 31 G5
Conway Cl BH25 44 D2
Cook Cl BH24 48 E2
Cook St SO14 51 E4
Coombe Dr GU51 26 D2
Coombe Farm Av PO16 23 B4
Coombe Rd, Gosport PO12 28 B1
Coombe Rd, Yateley GU46 57 B1
Cooper Ho GU35 18 C5
Cooper Rd SO40 15 B1
Copper St PO5 47 C4
Coppice Cl, Farnham GU9 13 A5
Coppice Cl, Tadley RG26 34 A2
Coppice Gdns GU46 57 C3
Coppice Hill SO32 15 C6
Coppice Rd RG20 37 C2
Copse Av, Farnham GU9 13 A4
Copse Av, New Milton BH25 44 C2
Copse Cl, Hythe SO45 35 A5
Copse Cl, Liss GU33 40 C4
Copse Cl, North Baddesley SO52 45 B2
Copse Cl, Petersfield GU31 46 F2
Copse Cl, Totton SO40 53 A6
Copse La, Fleet GU52 26 A6
Copse La, Yateley GU46 57 B1
Copse Rd BH25 44 C2
Copsewood Rd, Ashurst SO40 15 B1
Copsewood Rd, Hythe SO45 35 A3
Copthorne La SO45 24 D2
Corbin Rd SO41 41 A3
Corbould Rd SO45 35 A6
Corfe Cl SO24 43 C6
Corfe Way GU14 25 D4
Cormorant Dr SO45 35 D4
Corn Hill SO32 15 C4
Corn Market SO51 49 B3
Cornelius Dr PO7 54 D1
Corner Mead PO7 36 B5
Cornfield Rd PO13 38 C4
Cornfields, Andover SP10 14 C5

Cornfields, Yateley GU46 57 B4
Cornwall Rd GU35 18 C5
Cornwallis Rd SO41 42 C3
Coronado Rd PO12 28 B2
Coronation Rd, Aldershot GU11 13 D4
Coronation Rd, Waterlooville PO7 54 A1
Coronation Rd, Yateley GU46 57 E1
Coronation Ter SO14 51 F3
Corringway GU52 26 C4
Corunna Main SP10 14 C2
Cosham Park Av PO6 20 C4
Cossack Grn SO14 51 E3
Cossack La SO23 56 E2
Cossack Lane Ho SO23 56 E2
Cotswold Ct GU51 26 B2
Cottage Cl PO7 36 B5
Cottage Grn RG27 32 C3
Cottage Gro, Gosport PO12 28 B3
Cottage Gro, Southsea PO5 47 D3
Cottage Mws SP6 27 E3
Cottagers La SO41 36 B2
Cottington Cl RG20 37 B2
Cotton Cl GU11 13 B1
Cotton Dr PO10 31 G2
Cottrell Flats GU14 25 C5
Cotwell Av PO8 21 B5
Coulmere Rd PO12 28 A2
Council Rd RG21 16 C4
Court Barn La PO13 38 C3
Court Cl, Liphook GU30 39 B5
Court Cl, Lymington SO41 41 C4
Court Cl, Portsmouth PO6 20 D3
Court Dr GU52 26 C4
Court La PO6 20 D4
Court Mead PO6 20 D3
Court Rd, Aldershot GU11 13 C1
Court Rd, Lee-on-the-Solent PO13 38 C4
Courtenay Pl SO41 41 D3
Courtenay Rd GU9 13 A5
Courtlands Ter PO8 21 A4
Courtmoor Av GU52 26 B4
Courtmount Gro PO6 20 C2
Courtmount Path PO6 20 D3
Covey Way SO24 43 B5
Cow La PO6 20 A4
Cowdray Pk GU34 12 C4
Cowley Rd SO41 41 B2
Cowper Av BH25 44 C4
Cowslip Cl GU35 19 F2
Cowslip Way SO51 49 F1
Coxes Mdw GU31 46 B1
Coxheath Rd GU52 26 A5
Coxmoor Cl GU52 26 D5
Coxstone La BH24 48 B4
Crabbe Ct PO5 47 D3
Crabtree Gdns GU35 33 B3
Crabtree La GU35 33 A3
Cranborne Pl BH25 44 A1
Cranborne Rd PO6 20 C2
Cranbourne Rd PO12 29 C5
Cranbury Rd SO50 22 C5
Cranford Av GU52 26 A6
Cranford Park Dr GU46 57 D2
Cranford Rd GU31 46 B4
Cranmore Gdns GU11 13 A3
Cranmore La GU11 13 A3
Cranworth Rd SO22 56 B1
Crasswell St PO1 47 D1
Craven St SO14 51 E2
Craven Walk SO14 51 E2
Crawters La*, Bowen La GU31 46 C3
Creech Vw PO7 36 B5
Creek End PO10 31 G6
Creek Rd PO12 28 D4
Cremorne Pl GU31 46 C2
Crescent Ct BH25 44 B6
Crescent Dr BH25 44 B6
Crescent Rd, Fareham PO16 23 B3
Crescent Rd, Gosport PO12 29 A6
Crescent Rd, North Baddesley SO52 45 B2
Crescent Rd, Southampton SO14 51 F5
Cress Gdns SP10 14 A4
Cressey Rd SO51 49 B3
Crestland Cl PO8 21 B5
Crete Cotts SO45 35 A6
Crete La SO45 35 A6
Crete Rd SO45 35 A6
Cricket Dr PO8 21 A3
Cricket Lea GU35 19 F2
Cricklemede SO32 15 C6
Cricklewood Cl SO32 15 D5
Crimea Rd GU11 13 C1
Crisspyn Cl PO8 21 B2
Crockford Ho SO24 43 D4
Croft Av SP10 14 B5
Croft Gdns, Alton GU34 12 B2
Croft Gdns, Andover SP10 14 B5
Croft La GU46 57 C1
Croft Rd, Aldershot GU11 13 D3
Croft Rd, Basingstoke RG23 45 C5
Croft Rd, Ringwood BH24 48 E1
Crombie Cl PO8 21 A4
Cromer Rd PO6 20 A2
Cromwell Gdns GU34 12 B2
Cromwell Ho SO23 56 C1
Crondall End GU46 57 C1
Crooked La BH25 44 D5
Crookham Cl RG26 34 E4
Crookham Rd GU51 26 A4
Cropleigh Ct GU14 25 A1
Crosby Gdns GU46 57 A1
Cross & Pillory La GU34 12 C3
Cross Keys Pass SO23 56 E3
Cross La, Andover SP10 14 A2
Cross La, Waterlooville PO8 21 B3
Cross Rd PO13 38 D6
Cross St, Aldershot GU11 13 C1
Cross St, Basingstoke RG21 16 C3
Cross St, Farnborough GU14 25 B5
Cross St, Portsmouth PO1 47 B2
Cross St, Southampton SO32 15 C5
Cross St, Winchester SO23 56 C2
Cross Way PO9 30 A4
Crossbill Cl PO8 21 B1
Crossborough Gdns RG21 16 E3
Crossborough Hill RG21 16 F3
Crosshouse Rd SO14 51 G5
Crossland Cl PO12 29 C5
Crossland Dr PO9 30 B3
Crossmead Av BH25 44 C3
Crossways SP10 14 A2
Crouch La PO8 21 A1
Crow Arch La BH24 48 C4
Crow Arch La Ind Est BH24 48 C4
Crow La BH24 48 D4
Crowder Ter SO22 56 B3
Crowleys Dr GU34 12 D3
Crown Dr GU9 13 B6
Crown Gdns GU51 26 C3
Crown La GU9 13 B6
Crowsbury Cl PO10 31 G3
Croye Cl SP10 14 A3
Crundles GU31 46 E3
Crystal Way PO7 54 D2
Cuckoo La SO14 50 D5
Culford Av SO40 53 A5
Culford Way SO40 53 A5
Cullen Cl GU46 57 C3
Cullens Mws GU11 13 B2
Culley Vw SO24 43 C5
Culver Mws SO23 56 C4
Culver Rd, New Milton BH25 44 A3
Culver Rd, Winchester SO23 56 C4
Culverley Cl SO42 17 C4
Culverwell Gdns SO23 56 C4
Cumberland Av, Eastleigh SO53 22 A1
Cumberland Av, Emsworth PO10 31 G2
Cumberland Cl SO53 22 A1
Cumberland Pl SO15 50 C1
Cumberland St, Portsmouth PO1 47 B1
Cumberland St, Southampton SO14 51 F3
Cumbria Ct GU14 25 D4
Cunard Rd SO14 51 E6
Cunningham Av SO32 15 A4
Cunningham Cl BH24 48 E2
Cunningham Rd PO8 21 C1
Cunnington Rd GU14 25 C4
Cupernham Cl SO51 49 D2
Cupernham La SO51 49 D1
Curdridge Cl PO9 30 C1
Curie Rd PO6 20 B2
Curlew Cl, Emsworth PO10 31 G6
Curlew Cl, Southampton SO45 35 D5
Curlew Dr SO45 35 C4
Curlew Sq SO50 22 A4
Curlew Walk SO45 35 C4
Curtis Cl GU35 33 A2
Curtis Ct GU52 26 B5
Curtis La GU35 33 A2
Curtis Rd GU34 12 D3
Curzon Dr GU52 26 C6
Curzon Howe Rd PO1 47 B2
Curzon Pl SO41 41 C4
Curzon Rd PO7 54 B2
Cusden Dr SP10 14 B1
Cypress Cres PO8 21 A3
Cypress Rd GU35 18 A4
Cyprus Av SO40 15 C2

D Avenue SO45 24 C1
Dacres Walk SO41 42 E2
Dairymoor PO17 54 C5
Daisy La PO12 28 A4
Daisy Mead PO7 54 D3
Dale Rd SO45 35 A3
Dallington Cl PO13 38 A1
Danbury Ct PO10 31 H3
Dances Cl SP10 14 C2
Dances La RG28 55 C2
Dances Way PO11 52 A3
Dando Rd PO7 36 D5
Dane Cl SO45 24 B4
Dane Rd SO41 42 A1
Danecrest Rd SO41 36 A2
Danemark Ct SO23 56 D1
Danes Cl BH25 44 C6
Danesbrook La PO7 54 C2
Danestream Cl SO41 42 D3
Danestream Ct SO41 42 E3
Daneswood Rd BH25 44 D2
Daniel Rd RG28 55 C3
Daniells Cl SO41 41 D3
Daniells Walk SO41 41 D3
Dark Hollow GU31 46 B2
Dark La SO45 24 A4
Darwin Rd SO50 22 D2
Dashwood Cl GU34 12 A4
David Ct SO51 49 D4
Davidia Ct PO7 54 C3
Davis Fld BH25 44 B2
Dawkins Way BH25 44 B3
De La Warr Rd SO41 42 C3
De Mowbray Way SO41 41 D3
Deal Rd PO6 20 A2
Dean Ct PO9 30 D1
Dean Rd PO6 20 C3
Dean St PO1 47 C2
Deane Gdns PO13 38 D4
Deanes Park Rd PO16 23 F3
Deans Ct SO41 42 E2
Deans Gate PO13 38 A1
Deansfield Cl SO51 49 E2
Deanswood Rd RG26 34 C2
Dearing Cl SO43 37 C6
Deep Dell PO8 21 B3
Deeping Gate PO7 54 D2
Deerleap GU35 33 E4
Deerleap Cl SO45 35 B4
Deerleap La SO40 15 C1
Deerleap Way SO45 35 B4
Dell Cl PO7 20 D1
Dell Piece East PO8 21 D3
Dell Piece West PO8 21 C3
Dellcrest Path PO7 20 D1
Delme Dr PO16 23 F2
De-Lucy Av SO24 43 B5
Denbigh Cl SO50 22 B1
Denbigh Dr PO16 23 A1
Dene Cl, Bordon GU35 18 D5
Dene Cl, Ringwood BH24 48 E1
Dene Ct SP10 14 C4
Dene Path SP10 14 C4
Dene Rd, Andover SP10 14 C4
Dene Rd, Southampton SO40 15 B2
Dene Way SO40 15 B1
Deneside Copse SO41 41 A4
Denewulf Cl SO32 15 B5
Denham Dr GU46 57 E3
Denhill Cl PO11 52 A2
Denholm Cl BH24 48 E1
Denman Cl GU51 26 D2
Denmead RG26 34 D3
Denning Cl GU52 26 A4
Dennis Way GU33 40 C5
Denny Cl SO45 24 C2
Denvilles Cl PO9 30 D3
Derby Rd, Eastleigh SO50 22 B5
Derby Rd, Southampton SO14 51 F2
Derlyn Ct PO16 23 B3
Derlyn Rd PO16 23 B3
Derrybrian Gdns BH25 44 C3
Dersingham Cl PO6 20 B2
Derwent Cl GU35 18 C1
Derwent Ct SP10 14 C1
Derwent Gdns SO24 43 D6
Derwent Rd PO13 38 C5
Desborough Rd SO50 22 C6
Dever Cl RG23 45 C5
Devils La GU30 39 D5
Devon Rd GU35 18 C4
Devonshire Gdns SO45 35 B6
Devonshire Pl, Aldershot GU11 13 A2
Devonshire Pl, Basingstoke RG21 16 A4
Devonshire Rd SO15 50 C1
Dew La SO50 22 B3
Deweys La BH24 48 A3
Diamond Cl SP6 27 E4
Diamond Ct SP6 27 E4
Diamond St*, Flint St PO5 47 C4
Diana Cl PO10 31 G2
Dibben Walk SO51 49 F1
Dibble Dr SO52 45 B3
Dibden Lodge Cl SO45 35 A2
Dickens Way GU46 57 C3
Dickenson Walk SO24 43 C6
Dickers La GU34 12 D2
Dickson Pk PO17 54 C4
Dilly La BH25 44 B5
Dinorben Av GU52 26 A4
Dinorben Beeches GU52 26 A4
Dinorben Cl GU52 26 A4
Ditcham Cres PO9 30 A2
Dock Rd PO12 28 C4
Doe Copse Way BH25 44 A1
Dolman Rd PO12 29 C5
Dolphin Cres PO12 29 C5
Dolphin Ct PO13 38 B4
Dolphin Ho SO23 56 D2
Dolphin Pl BH25 44 B6
Dolphin Way PO12 29 C7
Dome Alley SO23 56 D4
Dominie Walk PO13 38 D4
Dominy Cl SO45 35 C2
Donaldson Rd PO6 20 B5
Doncaster Rd SO50 22 C6
Donnelly St PO12 28 A3
Dorchester Rd RG27 32 B5
Dorian Gro SO24 43 B5
Dorking Cres PO6 20 C4
Dornmere La PO7 54 D2
Dorothy Dymond St PO1 47 D2
Dorrien Rd PO12 28 B2
Dorrita Av PO8 21 A4
Dorset Cl PO8 21 B2
Dorset St SO14 51 E1
Doswell Way RG21 16 E1
Douai Cl GU14 25 B1
Douglas Gdns PO9 30 C1
Douglas Way SO45 35 A2
Douro Cl RG26 34 A2
Dover Cl SO24 43 C6
Dover Ct PO11 52 B2
Dovercourt Rd PO6 20 D5
Dowden Gro GU34 12 C1
Down Gate SO24 43 C6
Downley Rd PO9 30 D2
Downs Park Av SO40 53 B6
Downs Park Cres SO40 53 B6
Downs Park Rd SO40 53 B6
Downs Way GU34 12 A4
Downsland Par RG21 16 A3
Downsland Rd RG21 16 A3
Downsview Rd GU35 33 E3
Downton La SO41 42 A2
Downwood Cl SP6 27 C3
Doyle Gdns GU46 57 C4
Dragon St GU31 46 C3
Dragoon Ct GU11 13 A2
Drake Cl, New Milton BH25 44 B2
Drake Cl, Ringwood BH24 48 E1
Drake Rd PO13 38 A3
Drakes Cl SO45 35 A4
Draymans Way GU34 12 C3
Drift Rd, Bordon GU35 18 A6
Drift Rd, Fareham PO16 23 E1
Driftway Rd RG27 32 D5
Drinkwater Cl SO50 22 C3
Drove La SO24 43 A4
Droxford Cres RG26 34 D3
Droxford Rd PO17 54 C5
Drum Ct GU31 46 B3
Drum La GU31 46 C2
Drum Mead GU31 46 B3
Drummond Rd SO45 35 B2
Dryden Cl PO16 23 A2
Dryden Pl SO41 42 D2
Dryden Way GU30 39 A2
Duart Ct BH25 44 D2
Duchess Cl GU34 12 B3
Duck Island La BH24 48 B4
Ducklands GU35 18 D4
Duckmead La GU33 40 D3
Duddleston Heath Dr PO8 21 B6
Dudley Av, Fordingbridge SP6 27 E2
Dudley Av, Lymington SO41
Dudley Cl GU35
Dudley Ct GU52
Dudley Ter GU33
Dugald Drummond St PO1
Duisburg Way PO5
Duke St SO14
Dukes Cl, Alton GU34
Dukes Cl, Petersfield GU31
Dukes Rd PO12
Dukes Walk PO7
Dukeswood Dr SO45
Dumas Cl GU46
Dummer Mws SO23
Dundonald Cl PO11
Dundridge La SO32
Dunfield Copse SO45
Dunford Cl BH25
Dungells Fm Cl GU46
Dungells La GU46
Dunhurst Cl PO9
Dunmow Hill GU51
Dunmow Rd SP10
Dunnings La SO52
Dunsbury Way PO9
Dunsmore Cl PO5
Dunsmore Gdns GU46
Durban Cl SO51
Durford Rd GU31
Durham St, Gosport PO12
Durham St, Portsmouth PO1
Durland Cl BH25
Durley Av PO8
Durley Rd PO12
Durlston Rd SO16
Durnford Rd SO14
Durngate Pl SO23
Durngate Ter SO23
Durnsford Av GU52
Duttons Rd SO51
Dymoke St PO10
Dyram Cl SO50
Dysart Av PO6

Eagle Av PO8
Earley Ct SO41
Earlsdon St PO5
East Bank Rd SO42
East Bargate SO14
East Cosham Rd PO6
East Ct PO6
East Hill, Lymington SO41
East Hill, Winchester SO23
East Hill Cl PO16
East Hill Dr GU33
East Park Ter SO14
East St, Alresford SO24
East St, Andover SP10
East St, Fareham PO16
East St, Havant PO9
East St, Portsmouth PO1
East St, Southampton SO14
East St Shopping Cen SO14
East Station Rd GU12
East Strand SO14
East Surrey St PO1
East View Rd BH24
Eastbrooke Rd GU34
Eastcliff Cl PO13
Eastcroft Rd PO12
Eastern Av SP10
Eastern Rd, Bordon GU35
Eastern Rd, Havant PO9
Eastern Rd, Lymington SO41
Eastern Way, Fareham PO16
Eastern Way, Lymington SO41
Eastfield Av RG21
Eastfield Cl SP10
Eastfield Ct BH24
Eastfield La BH24
Eastfield Rd SP10
Eastgate St, Southampton SO14
Eastgate St, Winchester SO23
Eastlake Cl GU31
Eastlands BH25
Eastleigh Rd PO9
Eastmead GU14
Easton La SO23
Eastrop Bsns Area RG21
Eastrop La RG21

op Roundabout
1 16 E2
op Way RG21 16 E2
ays SO32 15 C5
ood Cl PO11 52 D3
ood Ct SO51 49 B3
Rd SO23 56 F2
ezer La BH24 48 B4
swell Rd RG20 37 A2
s Cl GU35 33 D2
s La GU35 33 D2
Rd GU12 13 D2
Rise PO16 23 C4
St PO1 47 D1
Rd SO22 56 B4
Villas SO22 56 B4
y Gdns PO6 20 C5
vood Ct GU33 40 D6
urgh Rd PO1 47 C2
ton Cl SO32 15 B4
Haisman Cl SO15 50 A1
nds Cl BH25 44 B4
Cl GU52 26 D5
s La PO7 36 D4
d Cl SO45 24 A4
d Ct GU14 25 A2
d Rd, Alton GU34 12 C1
d Rd,
hampton SO45 35 B2
d St GU11 13 B1
d Ter SO24 43 D4
ds Cl SO41 41 A3
a Cl,
wood BH24 48 D1
a Cl,
hampton SO52 45 C2
Ct SO41 41 A4
Way SO41 41 A4
s Cl GU34 12 D1
s Ct GU12 13 D2
s Hill GU9 13 B4
on Cl GU52 26 A6
ine Cl PO8 21 C4
ne Walk PO8 21 C4
Acres SO51 49 D3
Gdns PO8 21 A3
Cnr RG21 16 C3
es Cl SO43 37 B5
Gro GU14 25 D4
Rd PO9 30 D3
erry Rd GU35 19 F2
erry Way PO8 21 C4
eld Cl PO10 31 H3
Av BH25 44 A4
Cl BH25 44 A5
St PO5 47 D3
e Gdns SO51 49 B2
Ct SO41 41 E2
l SO45 35 C4
d PO6 20 C5
ill SO40 53 C6
a SO40 53 B5
PO12 28 C3
th Cres SO41 36 C3
th Dr GU52 26 B6
th Gdns SO45 35 B5
th Par GU46 57 D4
th Rd,
am PO17 54 B4
th Rd,
ooville PO7 54 B3
th Way,
igh SO50 22 D2
th Way,
ampton SO32 15 A5
Gdns PO12 29 B7
Mws PO12 29 B7
Rd PO12 29 B7
Gro SO41 41 D1
GU14 25 A3
uarters GU14 25 A3
am Cl SO24 43 C4
Rd PO9 30 A1
gton SO41 41 B4
Milton BH25 44 C2
k GU46 57 C1
k Rd SP10 14 B4
GU35 18 D4
se Est PO11 52 B4
SO22 56 A1
,
gh SO50 22 B5
, Gosport PO12 28 B3
,
g Island PO11 52 C3
,
ry RG20 37 B2
, Southsea PO5 47 D4
ve Fm RG20 37 B2
ve Rd GU14 25 A1
PO9 30 A4
k Rd PO9 30 B4
GU11 13 D4
Alresford SO24 43 C5

Elm Rd, Havant PO9 30 C5
Elm Rd, Southampton SO32 15 D5
Elm Rd, Winchester SO22 56 A1
Elm St, Southampton SO14 51 G4
Elm St, Southsea PO5 47 D4
Elm Ter, Liss GU33 40 A3
Elm Ter, Southampton SO14 51 G4
Elm Vw BH24 48 E4
Elmeswelle Rd PO8 21 A2
Elmhurst RG26 34 E3
Elmhurst Rd, Fareham PO16 23 C4
Elmhurst Rd, Gosport PO12 28 C4
Elmleigh Rd PO9 30 A3
Elmore Av PO13 38 D6
Elmore Cl PO13 38 D5
Elmore Rd PO13 38 D6
Elms Cl SP6 27 A2
Elms Rd, Aldershot GU11 13 C2
Elms Rd, Fleet GU51 26 D2
Elms Rd, Hook RG27 32 B4
Elmsfield Ct*, Liphook Rd GU35 19 F2
Elmtree Cl SO40 15 B2
Elmtree Gdns, Eastleigh SO50 22 C5
Elmtree Gdns, Romsey SO51 49 F4
Elmwood Av, Fordingbridge SP6 27 C3
Elmwood Av, Waterlooville PO7 54 B3
Elmwood Cl GU34 12 A4
Elphinstone Rd PO5 47 D5
Elston Pl GU12 13 D3
Elston Rd GU12 13 D3
Elvin Cl SO41 36 A1
Elwell Grn PO11 52 B4
Embankment Way BH24 48 C4
Embleton Rd GU35 33 D2
Emer Cl SO52 45 B1
Emerald Cl PO7 54 D2
Empress Rd SO43 37 C5
Empson Walk PO13 38 D4
Emsbrook Dr PO10 31 H4
Emsworth Common Rd PO10 31 F1
Emsworth House Cl PO10 31 F5
Emsworth Rd, Havant PO9 30 C5
Emsworth Rd, Lymington SO41 41 D2
Endeavour Cl PO12 28 D4
Endeavour Way SO45 35 B1
Endle St SO14 51 G4
Ennel Copse SO52 45 B3
Ennerdale Gdns SO24 43 D6
Ennerdale Rd GU35 18 C2
Enterprise Way SO14 51 F6
Eperston Rd PO8 21 A2
Epsom Down GU34 12 C4
Erica Cl PO8 21 C5
Erica Way PO8 21 B5
Erles Rd GU30 39 C4
Ernest Cl PO10 31 G5
Erskine Rd SO22 56 A4
Esmond Cl PO10 31 G6
Esmonde Cl PO13 38 C4
Esplanade, Gosport PO12 28 E4
Esplanade, Lee-on-the-Solent PO13 38 B5
Essex Cl GU35 18 C3
Essex Rd, Basingstoke RG21 16 B3
Essex Rd, Bordon GU35 18 C3
Ettrick Ct GU14 25 A5
Euskirchen Walk RG21 16 D1
Euston Gro BH24 48 C4
Evans St SO14 51 E4
Eveley Cl GU35 18 A6
Evelyn Av GU11 13 D4
Evelyn Mws SO24 43 C4
Evergreen Cl PO7 54 A2
Evergreens SO40 53 B5
Everon Gdns BH25 44 C3
Eversfield Cl SP10 14 A3
Eversley Cres PO9 30 A1
Everton Rd SO41 36 A1
Evingar Gdns RG28 55 B2
Evingar Ind Est RG28 55 B2
Evingar Rd RG28 55 B2
Ewart Ct SO45 35 B2
Ewer Common PO12 29 B6
Exchange Rd PO1 47 D2
Exeter Cl, Eastleigh SO50 22 B1

Exeter Cl, Emsworth PO10 31 G3
Exeter Gdns GU46 57 B1
Exmoor Rd SO14 51 F1
Exmouth Rd PO12 28 A1
Exmouth St SO14 51 E2
Exton Rd PO9 30 D1
Eynon Mws BH24 48 B4

Faber Cl PO9 30 C1
Fabers Yd SO23 56 C2
Fabian Cl, Basingstoke RG21 16 A4
Fabian Cl, Waterlooville PO7 54 D1
Factory Rd SO50 22 C4
Fair Cl RG28 55 B3
Fair Fld SO51 49 C2
Fair Oak Dr PO9 30 B3
Fair Vw SO24 43 C6
Fairfax Mws GU14 25 C4
Fairfield RG28 55 B2
Fairfield Cl, Emsworth PO10 31 G3
Fairfield Cl, Lymington SO41 41 D3
Fairfield Cl, Southampton SO45 35 B3
Fairfield Rd, Havant PO9 30 B4
Fairfield Rd, New Milton BH25 44 A5
Fairfield Rd, Winchester SO22 56 A1
Fairfield Sq PO6 20 A2
Fairhome Cl PO12 28 A1
Fairland Cl GU52 26 C3
Fairlands GU35 33 F3
Fairlawn Rd RG26 34 F4
Fairlea Rd, Emsworth PO10 31 H3
Fairlea Rd, Lymington SO41 41 D1
Fairley Ct GU31 46 D2
Fairlie BH24 48 D1
Fairlie Pk BH24 48 D1
Fairmead Walk PO8 21 B5
Fairmile GU52 26 B5
Fairoak Way RG26 34 A1
Fairthorne Gdns PO12 28 A4
Fairview Cl, Romsey SO51 49 E2
Fairview Cl, Southampton SO45 35 B4
Fairview Dr, Romsey SO51 49 D2
Fairview Dr, Southampton SO45 35 B3
Fairview Par SO45 35 B4
Fairview Rd GU35 33 D3
Fairview Ter GU35 33 C2
Fairway Rd SO45 35 A3
Fairy Cross Way PO8 21 B6
Falaise Cl GU11 13 C1
Falcon Flds, Southampton SO45 24 C2
Falcon Flds, Tadley RG26 34 D1
Falcon Rd PO8 21 A1
Falcon Sq SO50 22 A5
Falcon Way GU46 57 B2
Falkland Ct GU14 25 C5
Falklands Cl PO13 38 D3
Fallowfield GU46 57 B2
Far Meadow Way PO10 31 F5
Fareham Dr GU46 57 B1
Fareham Rd PO17 54 C5
Farley Ct GU14 25 C4
Farm Cl, Ringwood BH24 48 B2
Farm Cl, Yateley GU46 57 D3
Farm Ground Cl RG27 32 D5
Farm La North BH25 44 B5
Farm La South BH25 44 B6
Farm Lane Cl PO7 54 A3
Farm Vw, Emsworth PO10 31 G2
Farm Vw, Yateley GU46 57 D3
Farmhouse Way PO8 21 A3
Farmside Gdns PO6 20 C6
Farnborough Rd, Aldershot GU11 13 A1
Farnborough Rd, Farnborough GU14 25 A6
Farnham Rd, Bordon GU35 18 D1
Farnham Rd, Liss GU33 40 A6
Farnleys Mead SO41 41 D4
Farriers Walk PO12 28 D4
Farringdon Rd PO9 30 C2
Farringdon Way RG26 34 E4
Farrs Av SP10 14 C4
Farthing Flds GU35 33 A2
Farthing La PO1 47 B4
Fathersfield SO42 17 C3
Fathoms Reach PO11 52 B3

Fawcett Rd BH25 44 A2
Fawconer Rd RG20 37 B2
Fawlet Ct PO9 30 D1
Fawley By-Pass SO45 24 C2
Fawley Rd, Fawley SO45 24 A2
Fawley Rd, Hythe SO45 35 B6
Fawley Rd, Portsmouth PO6 20 B6
Feathers La RG21 16 D3
Feathers Yd RG21 16 D3
Feilden Ct RG20 37 A3
Felix Rd PO12 28 B2
Fell Dr PO13 38 C3
Fellows Rd GU14 25 C4
Feltham Cl SO51 49 F2
Feltons Pl PO6 20 C6
Fenleigh Cl BH25 44 C4
Fennel Gdns SO41 41 D1
Fennell Cl PO7 54 A1
Fenton Cl SO41 42 D3
Ferbies GU52 26 B5
Ferdown Ct*, Dickers La GU34 12 D2
Fermor Dr GU11 13 B1
Fern Cl GU31 46 F3
Fern Dr, Fleet GU51 26 A5
Fern Dr, Havant PO9 30 C3
Fern Rd SO45 35 A4
Ferncote Rd GU35 18 D4
Ferncroft Cl PO13 38 A1
Ferndale PO7 54 C1
Ferndale Gdns RG27 32 B5
Fernglade BH25 44 C1
Fernhill La BH25 44 C2
Fernhill Rd BH25 44 B1
Fernhills Rd SO45 35 C5
Fernhurst Cl PO11 52 A4
Fernlea GU35 18 A5
Ferrell Fld RG27 32 A5
Ferrol Rd PO12 28 C2
Ferry Port SO14 50 D6
Ferry Rd SO45 35 A3
Fey Rd PO12 28 C4
Fibbards Rd SO42 17 C3
Field Cl SO51 49 D3
Field Gate Dr RG20 37 A2
Field Pl GU30 39 B5
Field Walk SO41 41 C1
Field Way PO7 36 C5
Fielden Cl SO52 45 A2
Fielders Ct GU34 12 B3
Fieldfare Av GU46 57 B2
Fieldhouse Dr PO13 38 D3
Fieldmore Rd PO12 28 B1
Fieldway BH24 48 C2
Fifth Av, Havant PO9 30 D3
Fifth Av, Portsmouth PO6 20 B3
Fifth St SO45 24 A2
Filton Rd SO41 41 C1
Finch Cl RG26 34 E4
Findon Rd PO12 28 B1
Fir Av BH25 44 D2
Fir Cl, Fleet GU51 26 A3
Fir Cl, Lyndhurst SO43 37 C6
Fir Gro GU35 18 B6
Fir Rd SO40 15 A2
Fir Tree All GU11 13 C2
Fir Tree Gdns PO8 21 C3
Fir Tree Rd PO11 52 C4
Fir Tree Way GU52 26 D3
Fircroft GU51 26 A2
Fircroft Dr SO53 22 A1
Firethorn Cl GU52 26 B4
Firglen Dr GU46 57 D2
Firgrove Cl SO52 45 B2
Firgrove Cres PO6 20 B6
Firgrove Ct GU14 25 A2
Firgrove Par GU14 25 A2
Firgrove Rd, Bordon GU35 18 A6
Firgrove Rd, Farnborough GU14 25 A2
Firgrove Rd, Southampton SO52 45 B2
Firgrove Rd, Yateley GU46 57 B2
Firs Cl GU14 25 B4
Firs Way RG28 55 B2
First Av, Havant PO9 30 C4
First Av, Portsmouth PO6 20 B3
First Marine Av BH25 44 B6
First St SO45 24 C2
Firtree Cres SO41 36 A2
Firview GU30 39 B5
Fisgard Rd PO12 28 B1
Fishermans Quay SO41 41 E2
Fishers Rd SO40 53 B5
Fishlake Mdws SO51 49 B1
Fitzhugh St SO15 50 C2
Fitzwygram Cres PO9 30 B3
Five Acres Cl GU35 19 E2
Five Elms Dr SO51 49 E4
Five Heads Rd PO8 21 C1

Five Post La PO12 28 B2
Flag Walk PO8 21 A4
Flaxfield Ct RG21 16 B3
Flaxfield Rd RG21 16 B3
Flaxfields End SP6 27 D4
Fleet Rd, Fleet GU51 26 A3
Fleet Rd, Hook RG27 32 C2
Fleming Av SO52 45 C2
Fleming Ct SO52 45 C3
Fleming Pl SO51 49 C3
Fletcher Cl RG21 16 A4
Fletchers Fld GU30 39 B5
Fletchwood La SO40 15 A1
Fleuret Cl SO45 35 B6
Flexford Gdns PO9 30 C2
Flint St PO5 47 C4
Floating Bridge Rd SO14 51 G5
Florence Cl GU46 57 C2
Florence Rd GU52 26 C5
Florentine Way PO7 54 D1
Flowerdew Ct SP10 14 B4
Flushards SO41 41 E3
Foden Rd GU11 13 C2
Foldsgate Cl SO43 37 B4
Folly Cl GU52 26 C4
Folly Fld SO32 15 C6
Folly La GU31 46 C3
Fontwell Dr GU34 12 C4
Fordingbridge By-Pass SP6 27 F4
Fordington Rd SO22 56 A1
Forest Av PO8 21 A5
Forest Cl, Brockenhurst SO42 17 B3
Forest Cl, Southampton SO52 45 A2
Forest Cl, Tadley RG26 34 A1
Forest Cl, Waterlooville PO8 21 A5
Forest Cnr GU33 40 C1
Forest Ct BH25 44 C2
Forest Edge SO45 24 C2
Forest End, Fleet GU52 26 A5
Forest End, Waterlooville PO7 54 A2
Forest Front SO45 35 B6
Forest Gate SO45 24 B6
Forest Gate Gdns SO41 41 C4
Forest Gdns SO43 37 C5
Forest Glade Cl SO42 17 A3
Forest Hall SO42 17 D3
Forest Hill Way SO45 35 A5
Forest Hills Ct BH24 48 F4
Forest La GU35 19 F1
Forest Mead PO7 36 C6
Forest Park Rd SO42 17 B2
Forest Rd, Bordon GU35 18 C6
Forest Rd, Denmead PO7 36 A5
Forest Rd, Liss GU33 40 B1
Forest Rd, Waterlooville PO7 54 A3
Forest Rise GU33 40 C3
Forest Vw, Brockenhurst SO42 17 A3
Forest Vw, Southampton SO14 50 D4
Foresters Rd SO45 24 A3
Forestlake Av BH24 48 F4
Forestside Av PO9 30 C1
Forestside Gdns BH24 48 E1
Forge Ct GU46 57 D2
Forge Fld SP10 14 C2
Forge Rd SO45 24 A6
Forsythia Cl PO9 30 D2
Fort Blockhouse PO12 29 E6
Fort Rd PO12 29 A7
Fort Wallington Ind Est PO16 23 F1
Forth Ct SP10 14 D1
Forton Rd PO12 28 A2
Forward Dr SO41 41 B4
Foster Rd PO12 29 A5
Fountain St PO1 47 D2
Four Acre Coppice RG27 32 D5
Fourposts Hill SO15 50 B2
Fourshells Cl SO45 24 A3
Fourth Av, Havant PO9 30 C4
Fourth Av, Portsmouth PO6 20 B3
Fourth St SO45 24 A2
Fowey Ct PO12 28 C1
Fox Dr GU46 57 D1
Fox La RG23 45 D4
Fox Pond La SO41 41 C4
Foxbury Cl SO45 35 B5
Foxcote Gdns BH25 44 A2
Foxcott Gro PO9 30 A1
Foxcroft GU52 26 C6
Foxes Cl PO7 54 A3
Foxglade SO45 24 A6
Foxglove Dr GU35 18 D4
Foxhayes La SO45 24 A6

Foxhills Cl SO40 15 B1
Foxlands SO45 24 A6
Foxlea Gdns PO12 28 B1
Foxlease Ter SO43 37 C6
Foxs La RG20 37 A3
Foxs Walk SO45 24 A6
Foxtail Dr SO45 35 A5
Foxy Pad SO45 24 A6
Foye La GU52 26 D6
Frampton Pl BH24 48 B3
Frampton Way SO40 53 A5
Frances Rd RG21 16 B4
Francis Cl PO13 38 D5
Frank Judd Ct*, Kent St PO1 47 C2
Frankland Ter PO10 31 H5
Franklin Av, Hook RG27 32 B2
Franklin Av, Tadley RG26 34 C2
Franklin Rd BH25 44 D1
Fraynes Cft GU51 26 A3
Frayslea SO45 35 B5
Frederick St, Aldershot GU11 13 C2
Frederick St, Portsmouth PO1 47 D1
Free St SO32 15 C5
Freemantle Rd PO12 28 B2
French St, Portsmouth PO1 47 B4
French St, Southampton SO14 50 D5
Frenchies Vw PO7 36 B5
Frenchmans Rd GU31 46 B3
Frendstaple Rd PO7 54 C2
Frensham Av GU51 26 D2
Frensham Cl GU46 57 B2
Frensham La GU35 33 A2
Freshfield Gdns PO7 54 B1
Freshwater Rd PO6 20 B3
Freshwood Dr GU46 57 C4
Friars Rd SO50 22 B6
Friars Walk BH25 44 B4
Friarsgate SO23 56 D2
Frobisher Cl BH24 48 E2
Frobisher Gdns*, School La PO10 31 H6
Froghall SO45 35 B5
Frogmore La PO8 21 A3
Frogs Hole RG20 37 A2
Frome Cl RG23 45 D5
Frost La SO45 35 B6
Frouds Cl RG27 32 A6
Fry Cl SO45 24 B3
Fry's La GU46 57 E1
Fugelmere Rd GU51 26 D1
Fugelmere Walk GU51 26 D1
Fullers Vale GU35 33 B3
Fullerton Rd SO41 41 B2
Fullerton Way RG26 34 E3
Fulmar Dr SO45 35 C4
Furdies PO7 36 B5
Furniss Way PO11 52 A3
Furze Cft BH25 44 B3
Furze Hill Rd GU35 33 D4
Furze Rd RG26 34 C1
Furze Vale Rd GU35 33 E3
Furze Way PO8 21 C4
Furzedale Gdns SO45 35 C5
Furzedale Pk SO45 35 C5
Furzedown Mws SO45 35 C5
Furzeley Rd PO7 36 C6
Furzey Av SO45 35 C4
Furzey Cl SO45 24 A4
Fushia Cl PO9 30 D2

Gainsborough Cl GU14 25 C4
Gainsborough Ct, Andover SP10 14 A1
Gainsborough Ct, Lymington SO41 41 C4
Galaxie Rd PO8 21 B5
Gally Hill Rd GU52 26 A6
Galway Rd GU46 57 C4
Gannet Cl SO45 35 C4
Gar St SO23 56 C3
Garden Cl, Andover SP10 14 C3
Garden Cl, Hayling Island PO11 52 B4
Garden Cl, Hook RG27 32 A5
Garden Cl, Lyndhurst SO43 37 A5
Garden Cl, New Milton BH25 44 C3
Garden Cl, Newbury RG20 37 B2
Garden La, Southsea PO5 47 D4
Garden La, Winchester SO23 56 E2
Garden Mws GU31 46 C3
Gardner Rd BH24 48 D4
Garendon Ct SP6 27 E2
Garfield Cl SO32 15 C4
Garfield Rd SO32 15 C4
Garland Av PO10 31 G3
Garland Ct PO12 28 B3
Garnet Fld GU46 57 A3
Garnet Rd GU35 18 D5
Garnier Pk PO17 54 C4
Garrett Cl RG20 37 A1
Garrow Dr SO41 41 D1
Garth Cl GU35 18 C3
Gaston Gdns SO51 49 C2
Gaulter Cl PO9 30 C3
Gauvain Cl GU34 12 D4
Geales Cres GU34 12 D1
Geddes Way GU31 46 F2
Geffreys Flds RG21 16 E3
Genoa Cl SO41 41 B4
Gentles La GU35 33 C4
Geoffrey Av PO7 20 D1
George Rd, Fleet GU51 26 C2
George Rd, Lymington SO41 42 D2
George St, Basingstoke RG21 16 A3
George St, Eastleigh SO50 22 D3
George St, Gosport PO12 28 C3
George St, Newbury RG20 37 B2
George St, Southampton SO45 24 A5
George Yd SP10 14 B3
Georgia Cl PO13 38 D3
Georgian Cl BH24 48 C2
Giants Av SO40 53 B4
Gibbs Rd SO14 50 D2
Gibbs Way GU46 57 B4
Gibson Cl PO13 38 D4
Gilbert Cl SO41 41 C4
Gilbert Mead PO11 52 B3
Gilbert White Way GU34 12 B1
Giles Cl PO12 28 A2
Giles Ct RG26 34 F3
Giles Rd RG26 34 F3
Gilkicker Rd PO12 29 C6
Gillingham Rd SO41 42 E4
Gipsy La BH24 48 D2
Gladstone Rd PO12 28 A2
Gladstone St SO23 56 B1
Gladys Av PO8 21 A5
Glamis Cl, Basingstoke RG23 45 C4
Glamis Cl, Waterlooville PO7 54 C2
Glasspool PO7 36 A4
Glayshers Hill GU35 33 D2
Glebe Cl, Hayling Island PO11 52 A2
Glebe Cl, Tadley RG26 34 F4
Glebe Cnr PO17 54 C5
Glebe Ct GU51 26 A2
Glebe La RG27 32 C3
Glebe Rd GU35 33 A3
Glebefield Gdns PO6 20 A3
Glebefields SO41 42 D3
Glen Rd, Fleet GU51 26 A3
Glen Rd, Southampton SO40 53 B4
Glenavon BH25 44 D2
Glenavon Gdns GU46 57 D4
Glendale Rd RG26 34 D2
Gleneagles Dr PO7 21 C6
Glengarry BH25 44 D3
Glenleigh Av PO6 20 C3
Glenleigh Pk PO9 30 D4
Glenside SO45 35 A4
Glenthorne Cl PO13 38 A1
Glorney Mead GU9 13 C5
Gloucester Cl GU31 46 A3
Gloucester Mws PO5 47 D3
Gloucester Pl*, Kings Rd PO5 47 D4
Gloucester Rd, Aldershot GU11 13 D4
Gloucester Rd, Portsmouth PO1 47 B1
Gloucester Sq SO14 50 D5
Gloucester Ter PO5 47 D4
Gloucester Vw PO5 47 D3
Glyn Jones Cl SO45 24 B3
Goat La RG21 16 D3
Goddards Firs RG23 45 D6
Godfrey Pink Way SO32 15 D6
Godson Ho SO23 56 E2
Godwin Cl PO10 31 G2
Godwit Cl PO12 28 B1
Gofton Av PO6 20 D4
Gold Mead Cl SO41 41 D3
Gold St PO5 47 C4
Goldcrest Cl, Waterlooville PO8 21 A1
Goldcrest Cl, Yateley GU46 57 B2
Golden Gro SO14 51 F3
Golden Hind Pk SO45 35 A4
Goldenfields GU30 39 C5
Goldenfields Cl GU30 39 C5
Goldfinch Cl, Aldershot GU11 13 B4
Goldfinch Cl, New Milton BH25 44 A2
Goldfinch La PO13 38 D3
Goldring Cl PO11 52 D4
Goldsmith Rd SO50 22 C5
Golf La GU35 18 A5
Goodwood Cl, Alton GU34 12 C4
Goodwood Cl, Gosport PO12 28 B1
Goodwood Pl GU14 25 D3
Goodwood Rd, Eastleigh SO50 22 B2
Goodwood Rd, Gosport PO12 28 B1
Goodyers GU34 12 D3
Goose Grn, Hook RG27 32 A5
Goose Grn, Lyndhurst SO43 37 C6
Goose La RG27 32 B4
Gooseberry La BH24 48 B3
Gooserye Ct GU30 39 B5
Gordon Av GU52 26 C5
Gordon Rd, Aldershot GU11 13 C2
Gordon Rd, Fareham PO16 23 A2
Gordon Rd, Farnborough GU14 25 C6
Gordon Rd, Gosport PO12 28 A4
Gordon Rd, Lymington SO41 41 B3
Gordon Rd, Portsmouth PO1 47 C4
Gordon Rd, Winchester SO23 56 D1
Gordon Walk GU46 57 F3
Gore Grange BH25 44 B3
Gore Rd BH25 44 A3
Gore Rd Ind Est BH25 44 A2
Gorley Rd BH24 48 D2
Gorse Rd GU31 46 F3
Gorsedown Cl GU35 18 A5
Gorselands, Tadley RG26 34 E2
Gorselands, Yateley GU46 57 C4
Gorselands Cl GU35 33 E4
Gorseway GU52 26 C4
Gosport La SO43 37 C6
Gosport Rd, Fareham PO16 23 C4
Gosport Rd, Lee-on-the-Solent PO13 38 C6
Gosport St SO41 41 E1
Gough Rd GU51 26 A1
Gover Rd SO16 53 D3
Gower Cres RG27 32 C5
Grafton Cl, Bordon GU35 18 D5
Grafton Cl, Gosport PO12 28 C2
Graham Rd, Gosport PO12 28 A2
Graham Rd, Southampton SO14 51 E1
Graham St SO14 51 H1
Granada Cl PO8 21 B4
Granada Pl SP10 14 D2
Grand Par, Hayling Island PO11 52 C5
Grand Par, Hook RG27 32 B5
Grand Par, Portsmouth PO1 47 B4
Grange Cl, Alresford SO24 43 B5
Grange Cl, Havant PO9 30 C4
Grange La RG27 32 B3
Grange Mws SO51 49 F1
Grange Rd, Alresford SO24 43 B5
Grange Rd, Fleet GU52 26 A6
Grange Rd, Petersfield GU31 46 B4
Grantham Rd SO50 22 B5
Grantley Dr GU52 26 A3
Granville Cl PO9 30 C5
Granville Pl SO23 56 E4
Granville St SO14 51 G4
Grasmere SO50 22 C4
Grasmere Cl GU35 18 C1
Gravel La BH24 48 B2
Gravel Rd, Farnborough GU14 25 C5
Gravel Rd, Fleet GU52 26 C5
Gravelly Cl RG26 34 E4
Grayland Cl PO11 52 A3
Grayling Mead SO51 49 B2
Grays Av SO45 35 C3
Grays Cl SO51 49 D4
Grays Ct PO1 47 B3
Grayshott Laurels GU35 19 F1
Grayshott Rd GU35 33 D2
Great Hanger GU31 46 E3
Great La RG28 55 B3
Great Mead, Lyndhurst SO43 37 C6
Great Mead, Waterlooville PO7 36 D6
Great Minster St SO23 56 D3
Great Sheldons Coppice RG27 32 A5
Great Weir SO24 43 D3
Great Well Dr SO51 49 C2
Greatbridge Rd SO51 49 B2
Greatwood Cl SO45 35 B4
Grebe Cl SO41 42 E4
Green Acre, Aldershot GU11 13 B2
Green Acre, New Milton BH25 44 C5
Green Cl, Alresford SO24 43 D1
Green Cl, Southampton SO45 35 B3
Green End GU46 57 D1
Green Glades GU52 26 A6
Green Hill Vw SO51 49 A3
Green La, Alverstoke PO12 29 A5
Green La, Bishops Waltham SO32 15 C5
Green La, Blackfield SO45 24 B5
Green La, Farnham GU9 13 B6
Green La, Fordingbridge SP6 27 E3
Green La, Gosport PO12 28 B1
Green La, Hayling Island PO11 52 A5
Green La, Hook RG27 32 C3
Green La, New Milton BH25 44 C4
Green La, Ringwood BH24 48 C3
Green La, Waterlooville PO7 36 B4
Green La, Yateley GU46 57 B2
Green Link PO13 38 C5
Green Rd, Gosport PO12 29 A6
Green Rd, Southsea PO5 47 D4
Greenacre RG20 37 B2
Greenacres, Bordon GU35 19 E3
Greenacres, Southampton SO45 35 A5
Greenaways RG23 45 D5
Greenbanks Cl SO41 42 E3
Greenbanks Gdns PO16 23 F2
Greencroft GU14 25 A1
Greendale Cl SO53 22 B1
Greenfield Cl GU30 39 B3
Greenfield Cres PO8 21 B5
Greenfield Ct PO10 31 G2
Greenfield Gdns BH25 44 C4
Greenfield Rise PO8 21 B5
Greenfields GU33 40 C5
Greenfields Av, Alton GU34 12 A2
Greenfields Av, Southampton SO40 53 A2
Greenfields Cl SO40 53 A3
Greenfinch Cl SO50 22 A5
Greenfinch Walk BH24 48 E4
Greenhaven GU46 57 B3
Greenhaven Cl SP10 14 C4
Greenhill Rd SO22 56 A2
Greenlands Rd RG20 37 B2
Greenlea Cl PO7 20 D1
Greenleas Cl GU46 57 C1
Greens Cl SO32 15 B5
Greenside Ct BH25 44 C6
Greenway Cl SO41 41 B2
Greenway Rd PO12 28 B2
Greenways, Fleet GU52 26 A5
Greenways, Lymington SO41 42 D2
Greenways Rd SO42 17 D3
Greenwood Av PO6 20 A3
Greenwood Cl, Eastleigh SO50 22 B5
Greenwood Cl, Romsey SO51 49 C3
Greenwoods, New Milton BH25 44 D3
Greenwoods, Whitchurch RG28 55 B1
Greetham St PO5 47 D2
Gregan Ct GU11 13 B2
Grenehurst Way GU31 46 D3
Grenville Cl, Liphook GU30 39 C4
Grenville Cl, Ringwood BH24
Grenville Gdns SO45
Grenville Rd PO13
Gresham Ct GU14
Gresley Rd RG21
Greville Cl GU11
Greville Grn PO10
Greys Ct GU11
Greywell Rd, Havant PO9
Greywell Rd, Tadley RG26
Griffin Way North RG2
Griffin Way South RG2
Grigg La SO42
Grosvenor Mws SO41
Grosvenor Rd GU11
Grosvenor Sq SO15
Grosvenor St PO5
Grove Av PO12
Grove Pastures SO41
Grove Pk Ind Est GU34
Grove Pl SO41
Grove Rd, Alton GU34
Grove Rd, Fareham PO16
Grove Rd, Fleet GU52
Grove Rd, Gosport PO12
Grove Rd, Havant PO9
Grove Rd, Lee-on-the-PO13
Grove Rd, Lymington SO41
Grove Rd, New Milton BH25
Grove Rd South PO5
Grove St SO14
Guildford Rd GU51
Guildford Rd East GU1
Guildford Rd West GU14
Guildford St SO14
Guildhall Sq, Portsmouth PO1
Guildhall Sq, Southampton SO14
Guildhall Walk PO1
Guillemot Cl SO45
Gun Hill GU11
Gunners Pk SO32
Gunns Fm GU30
Gunwharf Quays Re & Leisure Pk PO1
Gunwharf Rd PO1
Gurkha Sq GU51
Gurnard Rd PO6
Gutteridge La RG26
Guys Cl BH24
Gypsy La PO8

Hackwood Rd RG21
Haddon Dr SO50
Hadleigh Gdns SO50
Hadleigh Pl RG21
Hadleigh Rd PO6
Haglane Copse SO41
Haig La GU52
Haig Rd SO24
Halden Cl SO51
Hale Av BH25
Hale Gdns BH25
Half Moon St PO1
Halfpenny La PO1
Halifax Cl SP10
Halifax Rise PO7
Halimote Rd GU11
Hall Cl SO32
Hall Farm Cres GU46
Hall La GU46
Hall Rd GU14
Hallett Rd PO9
Halliday Cl PO12
Halstead Rd PO6
Halterworth Cl SO51
Halterworth La SO51
Hamble Cl RG23
Hamble Ct SP10
Hamble Springs SO32
Hambledon Rd, Denmead PO7
Hambledon Rd, Waterlooville PO7
Hambrook Rd PO12
Hambrook St PO5
Hamelyn Cl RG21
Hamelyn Rd RG21
Hamesmoor Rd GU16
Hamesmoor Way GU1
Hamfield Dr PO11
Hamilton Cl, Bordon GU35
Hamilton Cl, Havant PO9

n Ct SO41 42 C3
n Mws SO45 35 C5
n Pl GU11 13 B3
n Rd GU52 26 C5
n Way BH25 44 A2
nds La SO40 53 A3
ire Rd GU35 18 C2
ire Ter PO1 47 C3
ead Ho RG21 16 C2
n Cl,
mpton SO45 24 A5
n Cl,
oville PO7 54 C2
n Dr BH24 48 C1
n La SO45 24 A4
Cres SO40 53 A2
St SO14 50 D4
Rd SO15 50 C1
Ter SO15 50 C1
d La GU46 57 C3
Ct BH24 48 A3
Rd RG26 34 C1
Way GU31 46 E3
ield Cl GU46 57 C3
Gdns PO7 54 B1
Way SO50 22 D4
Bldgs SO14 50 D3
Cl GU46 57 D2
Ct,
k GU30 39 B3
Ct,
outh PO1 47 B4
St PO1 47 B2
Ct BH25 44 A6
Par SO15 50 C3
Rd PO12 28 D3
Way PO10 31 H6
Cl PO8 21 A4
Rd PO12 28 A3
s La RG27 32 C2
GU46 57 C4
BH25 44 B2
r SO45 35 C5
d SO50 22 C5
Fld RG20 37 A1
Cl RG27 32 C2
Gdns RG27 32 C2
d Ct SO51 49 E2
RG27 32 C2
od Cl SO50 22 C1
Cl RG27 32 B5
Cl SO41 41 B4
s Dr PO7 54 D1
n Cl SO50 22 B1
n Rd PO6 20 A2
on Way GU51 26 A2
orth Rd RG26 34 E3
dns GU34 12 D1
ackson Ter
16 E4
d PO11 52 D5
Cl GU46 57 D1
Par GU46 57 D2
l, Lee-on-the-Solent
38 D4
l,
oville PO8 21 A1
Cut SO14 51 F3
Rd PO16 23 C1
La GU31 46 C1
Way RG23 45 A4
rrows Cl BH24 48 B3
SO45 35 D5
Av PO8 21 A6
Ct RG27 32 C2
Rd RG27 32 B2
Ter RG27 32 C2
Down GU31 46 E3
on Rd SO14 51 G1
s Rd PO16 23 C3
l SO45 35 B6
dns RG26 34 E4
Mdw RG28 55 B3
Walk SO45 35 B5
ve Av SO45 24 A5
ve Cl SO45 24 A4
Rd RG26 34 C2
Cl GU51 26 B3
Cl GU46 57 B4
Rd PO7 36 A4
dns SO45 35 C3
d PO6 20 B2
Rd PO6 20 A2
Ct BH25 44 B2
y Rd SO40 53 A4
Cl SO43 37 B6
d PO12 29 C6
ea Wall PO12 29 D7
re Rd GU30 39 B4
r SO24 43 C6
GU33 40 D4
Ct BH25 44 A1
Gdns GU14 25 C3
y Cl SO50 22 D3
ood GU46 57 F3
y-Pass PO9 30 A5

Havant Farm Cl PO9 30 B3
Havant Rd,
Emsworth PO10 30 D5
Havant Rd,
Hayling Island PO11 52 C1
Havant Rd,
Portsmouth PO6 20 C3
Havant Rd,
Waterlooville PO8 21 D1
Havant St PO1 47 B2
Havelock Rd SO14 50 C2
Haven Ct SO41 42 C3
Haven Gdns BH25 44 C3
Haweswater Cl GU35 18 C2
Hawke St PO1 47 B2
Hawkes Cl RG27 32 B2
Hawkins Cl,
Ringwood BH24 48 E2
Hawkins Cl,
Yateley GU46 57 B3
Hawkins Way GU52 26 D3
Hawkley Dr RG26 34 E4
Hawkley Rd GU33 40 A3
Hawks Mead GU33 40 B3
Hawkshaw Cl GU30 39 D4
Hawthorn Cl SO24 43 C5
Hawthorn Cres PO6 20 C4
Hawthorn Ct GU31 46 F3
Hawthorn Rd,
Southampton SO45 35 A3
Hawthorn Rd,
Waterlooville PO7 36 A4
Hawthorn Rise RG27 32 C4
Hawthorn Walk PO13 38 D4
Hawthorne Gro PO11 52 C3
Hawthorns GU34 12 B1
Haydens Ct SO41 41 E2
Haydock Cl GU34 12 C4
Haydon Pl GU46 57 E2
Hayley Cl SO45 35 B6
Haysoms Cl BH25 44 C4
Hayter Gdns SO51 49 D3
Hayward Bsns Centre
PO9 30 C2
Haywarden Pl RG27 32 C1
Haywood Dr GU52 26 B4
Hazel Cl RG23 45 D6
Hazel Coppice RG27 32 B4
Hazel Grn RG26 34 A2
Hazelbank Cl GU31 46 E2
Hazeley Cl RG27 32 B2
Hazeley Grn PO9 30 D1
Hazelton Way PO8 21 B3
Hazelwood Av BH25 44 A1
Hazlebank Cl GU30 39 D4
Hazlebank Mws GU30 39 C4
Head Down GU31 46 E3
Headley Cl,
Alresford SO24 43 D6
Headley Cl,
Lee-on-the-Solent
PO13 38 D4
Headley Flds GU35 33 A3
Headley Hill Rd GU35 33 C2
Headley Rd,
Bordon GU35 19 F1
Headley Rd,
Liphook GU30 39 A2
Hearmon Cl GU46 57 D2
Hearn Vale GU35 33 D1
Hearts of Oak Mws
SO41 41 C2
Heath Cl PO8 21 B1
Heath Ct RG26 34 B1
Heath End Fm RG26 34 B2
Heath End Rd RG26 34 A2
Heath Rd,
Lymington SO41 36 A2
Heath Rd,
Petersfield GU31 46 D3
Heath Rd,
Southampton SO52 45 C3
Heath Rd East GU31 46 E4
Heath Rd West GU31 46 D4
Heath Vale SP10 14 C4
Heathcote Rd GU35 18 D4
Heather Cl,
Aldershot GU11 13 A2
Heather Cl,
Bordon GU35 18 B6
Heather Cl,
Lymington SO41 36 B2
Heather Cl,
Waterlooville PO7 54 C3
Heather Dr,
Andover SP10 14 A2
Heather Dr,
Bordon GU35 19 E2
Heather Dr, Fleet GU52 26 B6
Heather Dr,
Tadley RG26 34 C1
Heather Gro RG27 32 B1
Heather Rd,
Petersfield GU31 46 F3
Heather Rd,
Southampton SO45 24 A3

Heatherbrae Gdns
SO52 45 B2
Heatherstone Av SO45 35 A6
Heatherton Mws PO10 31 G3
Heatherview Cl SO52 45 B1
Heathfield SO45 35 A4
Heathfield Rd GU31 46 F3
Heathland St GU11 13 C2
Heathlands RG26 34 A2
Heathlands Ct GU46 57 E4
Heathrow Copse RG26 34 A2
Heathside Way RG27 32 C2
Heathview RG27 32 D5
Heathwood Av BH25 44 A4
Heathwood Cl GU46 57 D1
Heathy Cl BH25 44 B5
Hedge End RG26 34 F4
Hedge End Rd SP10 14 C5
Hedgecroft GU46 57 B2
Hedgerley BH25 44 C5
Hedgerow Gdns PO10 31 G2
Hedley Cl SO45 24 A4
Helen Ct GU14 25 A1
Helston Dr PO10 31 G3
Hemming Cl SO40 53 A5
Hemsley Walk PO8 21 A4
Hendon Rd GU35 18 D5
Hengistbury Rd BH25 44 A5
Henley Gdns GU46 57 D3
Henry St PO12 28 C4
Henwood Down GU31 46 D3
Hepplewhite Cl RG26 34 B2
Hepworth Cl SP10 14 B1
Herald Ct GU12 13 C2
Herbert Rd BH25 44 C2
Herbert Walker Av,
Southampton SO15 50 A3
Herbert Walker Av,
Southampton SO15 50 B4
Herbert Walker Av,
Southampton SO15 50 C5
Hereward Cl SO51 49 E3
Hermes Ct PO12 28 C1
Hermitage Cl,
Farnborough GU14 25 C5
Hermitage Cl,
Havant PO9 30 A2
Hermitage Cl,
Southampton SO32 15 A4
Hermitage Ct SO23 56 D2
Hermitage Gdns PO7 54 C2
Herne Ct GU31 46 D3
Herne Rd,
Petersfield GU31 46 D3
Herne Rd,
Portsmouth PO6 20 A3
Heron Cl GU52 26 D5
Heron Sq SO50 22 A5
Herons Rise SP10 14 C5
Herriard Way RG26 34 E3
Herriot Ct GU46 57 C4
Herriott Cl PO8 21 A3
Hertford Cl SP6 27 E2
Hestia Cl SO51 49 F2
Hewitt Cl PO12 28 A2
Hewitts Rd SO15 50 A2
Hewshott La GU30 39 C2
Hibiscus Gro GU35 18 D4
Hickley Path PO16 23 E1
Hicks Cl RG26 34 F3
Hides Cl RG28 55 B3
High Firs Gdns SO51 49 E3
High Firs Rd SO51 49 F3
High Lawn Way PO9 30 A1
High Ridge Cres BH25 44 D2
High St, Aldershot GU11 13 B1
High St, Alton GU34 12 C3
High St, Andover SP10 14 B3
High St,
Bishops Waltham SO32 15 C5
High St, Bordon GU35 18 C5
High St, Cosham PO6 20 B4
High St, Eastleigh SO50 22 C6
High St, Eastleigh SO50 22 D4
High St,
Emsworth PO10 31 H5
High St, Fareham PO16 23 D1
High St,
Farnborough GU14 25 B5
High St,
Fordingbridge SP6 27 E4
High St, Gosport PO12 28 D4
High St, Headley GU35 33 A3
High St, Hook RG27 32 C3
High St, Hythe SO45 35 B2
High St,
Lee-on-the-Solent
PO13 38 B4
High St,
Lymington SO41 41 D2
High St,
Lyndhurst SO43 37 B5
High St,
Milford on Sea SO41 42 E3
High St,
Petersfield GU31 46 C3

High St,
Portsmouth PO1 47 B4
High St,
Ringwood BH24 48 A3
High St,
Sandhurst GU47 57 F1
High St,
Southampton SO14 50 D4
High St, Totton SO40 53 B5
High St,
Winchester SO23 56 C2
High Trees PO7 54 B1
High View Rd GU14 25 A1
Highams Cl RG20 37 C2
Highbank Gdns SP6 27 E4
Highbury Cl BH25 44 D2
Highbury Gro PO6 20 C5
Highbury St PO1 47 B3
Highbury Way PO6 20 B5
Highclere Av PO9 30 A1
Highcliffe Rd SO23 56 F4
Highcroft La PO8 21 C1
Highdown GU51 26 B1
Highfield SO41 41 C3
Highfield Av,
Aldershot GU11 13 C4
Highfield Av,
Lymington SO41 41 B3
Highfield Av,
Ringwood BH24 48 B2
Highfield Av,
Waterlooville PO7 54 C1
Highfield Cl,
Aldershot GU11 13 C3
Highfield Cl,
Eastleigh SO53 22 A1
Highfield Dr BH24 48 C1
Highfield Gdns,
Aldershot GU11 13 C3
Highfield Gdns,
Liss GU33 40 D5
Highfield La GU30 39 C6
Highfield Par PO7 54 C1
Highfield Rd,
Eastleigh SO53 22 A1
Highfield Rd,
Lymington SO41 41 B2
Highfield Rd,
Petersfield GU31 46 C2
Highfield Rd,
Ringwood BH24 48 C2
Highfield Ter SO22 56 B3
Highgate La GU14 25 B1
Highland Cl PO10 31 G5
Highland Dr RG23 45 C4
Highland Rd PO10 31 G5
Highlands Cl,
North Baddesley SO52 45 A1
Highlands Cl,
Southampton SO45 35 B5
Highlands Rd,
Andover SP10 14 D3
Highlands Rd,
New Milton BH25 44 B5
Highlands Way SO45 35 B4
Highridge GU34 12 A3
Hightown Gdns BH24 48 D4
Hightown Hill BH24 48 F4
Hightown Ind Est
BH24 48 C4
Hightown Rd BH24 48 B4
Highwood Cl GU46 57 C4
Highwood La SO51 49 F2
Highwood Rd SO42 17 C4
Highworth La PO11 52 B2
Hilary Av PO6 20 C4
Hilda Gdns PO7 36 C5
Hilder Gdns GU14 25 C3
Hill Brow Rd GU33 40 B5
Hill House Hill GU30 39 A2
Hill La SO15 50 B1
Hill Rd RG23 45 C6
Hilland Rise GU35 33 B3
Hillcrest RG26 34 E2
Hillcrest Av SO53 22 A1
Hillcrest Cl SO52 45 A1
Hiller Walk PO13 38 D4
Hillfield GU46 57 F3
Hillside RG28 55 C3
Hillside Av,
Romsey SO51 49 D3
Hillside Av,
Waterlooville PO7 20 D1
Hillside Cl, Alton GU34 12 C1
Hillside Cl,
Bordon GU35 33 D2
Hillside Ct SP10 14 A3
Hillside Rd,
Aldershot GU11 13 B3
Hillside Rd,
Farnham GU9 13 A5
Hillside Rd,
Lymington SO41 41 B3
Hilltop Vw GU46 57 B3
Hillview PO8 21 C3
Hillview Rd SO45 35 A3

Hilsea Cres PO6 20 A6
Hiltom Rd BH24 48 D3
Hilton Rd PO12 29 C5
Hinton Cl RG26 34 E3
Hipley Rd PO9 30 B3
Hirst Rd SO45 35 C4
Hoadlands GU31 46 E2
Hoads Hill PO17 54 C6
Hobart Dr SO45 35 C3
Hobart Rd BH25 44 B3
Hobbs Pass PO12 28 E4
Hockley Cl PO6 20 A3
Hodges Cl PO9 30 C3
Hoe La SO52 45 A3
Hoe Rd SO32 15 D5
Hogarth Cl SO51 49 E1
Hogarth Ct SP10 14 A1
Hoggarth Cl GU31 46 D2
Hogmoor Rd GU35 18 A4
Holbeach Cl PO6 20 A2
Holbeche Cl GU46 57 A3
Holbrook Cl GU9 13 B4
Holbrook Rd PO16 23 C4
Holbrook Way GU11 13 C4
Holes Cl SO41 36 A1
Holland Gdns GU51 26 B3
Hollins Walk RG21 16 D2
Hollman Dr SO51 49 A2
Hollow La PO11 52 B4
Hollowshot La RG20 37 A3
Holly Acre GU46 57 D3
Holly Bush La GU11 25 D6
Holly Cl GU35 33 F3
Holly Dr PO7 54 C3
Holly Gdns SO41 42 C3
Holly Rd, Ashurst SO40 15 A2
Holly Rd,
Blackfield SO45 24 A5
Holly St PO12 28 C4
Hollybank PO13 38 C5
Hollybank Cl,
Southampton SO45 35 B3
Hollybank Cl,
Waterlooville PO8 21 C4
Hollybank Cres SO45 35 B2
Hollybank La PO10 31 G1
Hollybank Rd SO45 35 A3
Hollybrook Ct GU35 18 D3
Hollybrook Pk GU35 18 D4
Hollycombe Cl GU30 39 C6
Hollywater Rd GU35 19 E6
Hollywood Cl SO52 45 A2
Hollywood La SO41 41 C1
Holm Cl BH24 48 E1
Holm Ct PO11 52 B5
Holman Cl PO8 21 A6
Holme Cl SO41 41 B3
Holmsley Cl SO41 41 A4
Holmwood Garth BH24 48 E4
Holmwood Ter RG27 32 B3
Holt Cl PO17 54 B5
Holt Down GU31 46 E3
Holt La RG27 32 D5
Holt Way RG27 32 D4
Holyborne Rd SO51 49 E3
Holybourne Rd PO9 30 A3
Holyrood Cl PO7 54 C2
Holyrood Pl SO14 50 D5
Home Farm Cl SO45 35 C4
Home Fld SO51 49 D1
Home Mead PO7 36 B6
Home Park Dr GU46 57 D3
Home Way GU31 46 F3
Homefield SO43 37 C5
Homefield Cotts GU33 40 A3
Homegrange Ho SO41 42 D4
Homerise Ho SO23 56 C1
Homewell PO9 30 B5
Homewood Cl BH25 44 D1
Honeybottom Rd RG26 34 E2
Honeysuckle Cl GU46 57 A2
Honeysuckle La GU35 33 D3
Honister Gdns GU51 26 D1
Hook Rd RG20 37 C2
Hoopers Way RG23 45 C5
Hop Garden Rd RG27 32 A6
Hope Cl PO10 31 H3
Hope St PO1 47 D1
Hope Way GU11 13 B1
Hopfield Cl PO7 54 B3
Hopfield Mws PO7 54 B3
Hordle La SO41 36 B3
Horlock Rd SO42 17 C3
Hornbeam Pl RG27 32 C4
Hornbeam Rd PO9 30 D3
Horndean Rd PO10 31 F1
Hornet Cl PO12 29 C5
Horsea La PO6 20 A6
Horsea Rd PO6 20 B6
Horsebridge Rd PO9 30 C2
Horsecroft SO51 49 C2
Horsefair Ct SO51 49 B3
Horsefair Mws SO51 49 B3
Horseshoe Cres GU35 18 D4
Horseshoe Dr SO51 49 E1
Hospital Hill GU11 13 B1

Hostel Rd GU14 25 A5
Hotspur Cl SO45 35 A2
Houchin St SO32 15 C5
Houndwell Pl SO14 51 E4
Hounsdown Av SO40 53 A6
Hounsdown Cl SO40 53 A6
Howard Cl, Eastleigh SO53 22 A2
Howard Cl, Fleet GU51 26 D2
Howard Cole Way GU11 13 A2
Howard Rd PO6 20 A6
Howards Mead SO41 41 A3
Howe Cl BH25 44 B1
Howes Gdns GU51 26 A4
Howlett Cl SO41 41 B1
Huddington Glade GU46 57 A3
Hudson Cl, Liphook GU30 39 C5
Hudson Cl, Ringwood BH24 48 E2
Hulbert Rd PO7 54 B2
Hulles Way SO52 45 B3
Humberstone Rd SP10 14 B5
Hunter Rd PO6 20 B2
Hunters Chase GU30 39 B2
Hunters Cl RG23 45 C4
Hunters Cres SO51 49 F1
Hunters Hill SO40 15 D1
Hunters Mws GU11 13 B1
Hunters Ride PO7 54 A3
Hunts Cl RG27 32 C6
Hunts Cotts RG27 32 C1
Huntsbottom La GU33 40 D5
Huntsmead GU34 12 D3
Huntsmoor Rd RG26 34 B2
Hurdles Mead SO41 42 E4
Hurland La GU35 33 B4
Huron Dr GU30 39 C5
Hursley Dr SO45 24 A6
Hursley Rd PO9 30 A1
Hurst Cl, Liphook GU30 39 A3
Hurst Cl, Southampton SO40 53 B3
Hurst Ct SO41 42 C3
Hurst Green Cl PO8 21 B6
Hurst Rd, Lymington SO41 42 E4
Hurst Rd, Ringwood BH24 48 B1
Hurstville Dr PO7 54 B3
Hussar Ct GU11 13 A2
Hyde Abbey Rd SO23 56 D1
Hyde Cl SO23 56 C1
Hyde Gate SO23 56 D1
Hyde Park Rd PO5 47 D2
Hyde St, Southsea PO5 47 D4
Hyde St, Winchester SO23 56 D1
Hylton Ct RG26 34 F3
Hylton Rd GU31 46 C3
Hyman Way SO40 53 A4
Hythe Cl RG26 34 D3
Hythe Marina SO45 35 B1
Hythe Rd PO6 20 A2

Idsworth Rd PO8 21 B6
Ilex Cl GU46 57 B2
Imadene Cl GU35 19 E2
Imadene Cres GU35 19 E2
Imjin Cl GU11 13 D1
Imran Ct GU12 13 D3
Ingle Glen SO45 35 B5
Ingledene Cl PO12 28 B4
Inglegreen Cl BH25 44 A4
Inglewood Dr BH25 44 D3
Ings Cl GU34 12 C4
Inhams La PO7 36 A5
Inhurst Av PO7 54 C1
Inhurst Way RG26 34 B2
Inmans La GU31 46 E1
Inner By-Pass PO10 31 H5
Innisfail Gdns GU11 13 A3
Institute Rd GU11 25 B6
Inverkip Cl PO13 38 B3
Inverness Rd PO12 28 A3
Inwood Rd GU33 40 C5
Iona Cl SO14 51 G4
Ipley Way SO45 35 B5
Irwell Cl RG21 16 F3
Isambard Brunel Rd PO1 47 D2
Island View Cl SO41 42 E4
Island View Ct BH25 44 B5
Islay Gdns PO6 20 C2
Itchen Bri SO14 51 G5
Itchen Cl, Basingstoke RG23 45 D5
Itchen Cl, Petersfield GU31 46 B4
Itchen Ct SO23 56 E3
Itchen Way SO24 43 A6
Itchia Cl PO11 52 C3
Ives Cl GU46 57 B1
Ivy Down La RG23 45 A4
Ivy La PO1 47 B1
Ivydene Gdns PO8 21 A5

Jacaranda Rd GU35 18 C4
Jackie Wigg Gdns SO40 53 B5
Jacklyns Cl SO24 43 C5
Jacklyns La SO24 43 C4
Jacobs Alley RG21 16 D4
Jacobs Cl SO51 49 D3
Jacobs St PO1 47 D1
Jacobs Yd RG21 16 D4
Jago Rd PO1 47 B1
Jaguar Rd GU14 25 A3
Jamaica Pl PO12 28 C4
James Callaghan Way PO6 20 A1
James Cl PO11 52 A3
James Ct SO51 49 D4
James Howell Ct PO7 36 C5
James Rd GU11 25 C6
James St SO14 51 F3
Janes Cl SO45 24 A5
Janred Ct BH25 44 A6
Japonica Way PO9 30 D2
Jasmine Ct SO41 41 D2
Jasmine Way GU35 18 D5
Jasmond Rd PO6 20 C5
Jaundrells Cl BH25 44 D2
Jay Cl PO8 21 B1
Jean Orr Ct GU52 26 B6
Jenner Rd PO6 20 B2
Jenner Way SO51 49 F2
Jennings Rd SO40 53 B4
Jenny's Walk GU46 57 E2
Jersey Cl PO13 38 A1
Jervis Ct SP10 14 D2
Jervis Dr PO12 28 B3
Jesse Cl GU46 57 F3
Jessica Cl PO7 54 D1
Jessie Rd PO12 28 A4
Jessie Ter SO14 51 E5
Jessop Cl SO45 35 B1
Jessop Walk SO45 35 A1
Jesty Rd SO24 43 B5
Jewry St SO23 56 C2
Jobson Cl RG28 55 B2
Jodrell Cl PO8 21 C1
John Eggars Sq GU34 12 D1
John King Shipyard PO10 31 H6
John Morgan Cl RG27 32 B4
John Pounds Ho GU35 18 C5
John St SO14 51 E5
Johnson St SO14 51 E3
Johnson Way GU52 26 B5
Joices Yd RG21 16 C3
Jonas Nichols Sq SO14 51 F3
Jonathan Cl SO41 41 D1
Jones La SO45 35 B2
Joseph St PO12 28 C4
Josian Walk SO14 51 F2
Jowitt Dr BH25 44 A2
Joyce Dickson Cl BH24 48 D4
Jubilee Bsns Centre PO7 54 A1
Jubilee Cl, Eastleigh SO50 22 C5
Jubilee Cl, Fordingbridge SP6 27 C3
Jubilee Cl, Ringwood BH24 48 D2
Jubilee Hall Rd GU14 25 B1
Jubilee Ho GU35 18 D3
Jubilee Rd, Aldershot GU11 13 D4
Jubilee Rd, Basingstoke RG21 16 D4
Jubilee Rd, Fordingbridge SP6 27 B3
Jubilee Rd, Gosport PO12 28 B3
Jubilee Rd, Romsey SO51 49 B3
Jubilee Rd, Waterlooville PO7 54 A1
Jubilee Ter PO5 47 C4
Juliet Ct PO7 54 D1
Junction Rd, Andover SP10 14 A2
Junction Rd, Southampton SO40 53 B4
Juniper Cl, Bordon GU35 18 A4
Juniper Cl, Lymington SO41 41 A4
Juniper Cl, Southampton SO52 45 B1
Juniper Sq PO9 30 B5
Jupiter Ct PO1 47 B3
Jura Cl PO6 20 C2
Juventu Cl PO9 30 B2

Kashmir Ct GU14 25 B5
Katrina Gdns PO11 52 C2
Kay Cres GU35 33 D2
Kealy Rd PO12 28 B2
Keats Av SO41 42 D3
Keats Cl PO8 21 A4
Keats Gdns GU51 26 C2
Keats Way GU46 57 B4
Keeps Mead RG20 37 A1
Kefford Cl PO8 21 B2
Keith Cl PO12 28 B2
Kellynch Cl GU34 12 B1
Kelsall Gdns BH25 44 B2
Kelsey Cl GU33 40 C4
Kelsey Gro GU46 57 E3
Kelvin Cl SO45 35 B3
Kelvin Rd SO50 22 B4
Kempton Cl GU34 12 C4
Kendal Cl PO8 21 B4
Kenilworth Cl, Lee-on-the-Solent PO13 38 C3
Kenilworth Cl, New Milton BH25 44 D2
Kenilworth Cres GU51 26 D1
Kenilworth Rd GU51 26 C2
Kenley Rd GU35 33 E3
Kenmore Cl GU52 26 C6
Kennard Ct BH25 44 B1
Kennard Rd BH25 44 B1
Kennet Cl PO12 29 B6
Kennet Rd GU31 46 B4
Kennet Way RG23 45 C5
Kennett Cl SO51 49 F3
Kennett Rd SO51 49 F3
Kensington Pk SO41 42 D3
Kensington Rd PO12 29 C5
Kent La GU34 12 C3
Kent Rd, Bordon GU35 18 C5
Kent Rd, Fleet GU51 26 C2
Kent Rd, Southsea PO5 47 D4
Kent St, Portsmouth PO1 47 B2
Kent St, Southampton SO14 51 G1
Keppel Cl BH24 48 D3
Kerfield Way RG27 32 C5
Kerry Cl SO41 41 B3
Kerry Gdns SP6 27 A3
Kestrel Cl SO32 15 A4
Kestrel Ct, Alton GU34 12 C1
Kestrel Ct, Ringwood BH24 48 B2
Kestrel Rd, Eastleigh SO50 22 A4
Kestrel Rd, Farnborough GU14 25 A3
Kevin Cl RG20 37 D2
Kevins Dr GU46 57 E2
Kevins Gro GU51 26 C2
Keydell Av PO8 21 B3
Keydell Cl PO8 21 A4
Keyhaven Rd SO41 42 F3
Keysworth Av BH25 44 A4
Kidmore La PO7 36 C4
Kildare Cl GU35 18 C2
Kildare Rd GU35 18 C2
Kiln Cl SO45 35 A4
Kiln Fld GU33 40 B3
Kiln Gdns RG27 32 B3
Kiln La SO24 43 D1
Kiln Way GU11 13 C4
Kilnside PO7 36 C6
Kimbers GU31 46 C2
Kimpton Cl PO13 38 D4
King Alfred Pl SO23 56 D1
King Alfred Ter SO23 56 D1
King Charles St PO1 47 B3
King Edward Ct*, White Hart Rd PO1 47 B4
King George Av GU31 46 C2
King George Cl GU14 25 A5
King George Mobile Home Pk BH25 44 B3
King George Mws*, King George Av GU31 46 C2
King Henry I St PO1 47 C2
King John Rd RG20 37 B2
King Richard Rd PO1 47 C2
King St, Emsworth PO10 31 H6
King St, Gosport PO12 28 D3
King St, Southampton SO14 51 E5
King St, Southsea PO5 47 D3
King William St PO1 47 B1
Kingdom Yd SO23 56 D2
Kingdons Mws GU34 12 C2
Kingfisher Cl, Bordon GU35 18 D5
Kingfisher Cl, Fleet GU52 26 C6
Kingfisher Cl, Whitchurch RG28 55 B3
Kingfisher Dr GU46 57 B2
Kingfisher Rd SO50 22 A4
Kingfisher Way, Ringwood BH24 48 D1
Kingfisher Way, Romsey SO51 49 C2
Kings Arms La BH24 48 A3
Kings Arms Row BH24 48 A3
Kings Bench Alley PO1 47 B2
Kings Cl, Lymington SO41 41 C2
Kings Cl, Lyndhurst SO43 37 C5
Kings Cres SO41 41 C1
Kings Ct GU14 25 B6
Kings Farm La SO41 36 C3
Kings Head Yd SO23 56 C3
Kings Keep GU52 26 B5
Kings Mdw SP10 14 C3
Kings Mede PO8 21 B3
Kings Orch RG23 45 C6
Kings Park Rd SO15 51 E1
Kings Rd, Aldershot GU11 13 A2
Kings Rd, Alton GU34 12 A3
Kings Rd, Emsworth PO10 31 F6
Kings Rd, Fareham PO16 23 C3
Kings Rd, Fleet GU51 26 B1
Kings Rd, Gosport PO12 28 B4
Kings Rd, Hayling Island PO11 52 C2
Kings Rd, Lee-on-the-Solent PO13 38 B4
Kings Rd, Lymington SO41 41 C2
Kings Rd, Petersfield GU31 46 A2
Kings Rd, Portsmouth PO1 47 B1
Kings Rd, Southsea PO5 47 C4
Kings Rd, Waterlooville PO8 21 A6
Kings Ride SO45 24 A6
Kings Saltern Rd SO41 41 E4
Kings Ter, Emsworth PO10 31 H5
Kings Ter, Southsea PO5 47 C4
Kings Walk, Whitchurch RG28 55 B2
Kings Walk, Winchester SO23 56 E3
Kings Yd SP10 14 B3
Kingsbridge La SO15 50 C2
Kingsbury La BH24 48 A3
Kingsclere By-Pass RG20 37 B1
Kingsclere Pk Ind Est RG20 37 A1
Kingsclere Rd RG21 16 B1
Kingscroft GU51 26 B3
Kingsdale Ct SO23 56 C1
Kingsfernsden La GU31 46 D1
Kingsfield, Lymington SO41 41 F4
Kingsfield, Ringwood BH24 48 C4
Kingsgate St SO23 56 D4
Kingsland Ct SO14 51 E3
Kingsland Rd GU34 12 B3
Kingsland Sq SO14 51 F3
Kingsley Av PO10 31 F6
Kingsley Bungalows SO24 43 B6
Kingsley Pk RG28 55 B2
Kingsmead, Alton GU34 12 C2
Kingsmead, Farnborough GU14 25 A2
Kingsmead Av PO13 38 A1
Kingsmead Centre GU14 25 A2
Kingston Pk SO41 41 C4
Kingsway, Aldershot GU11 13 A2
Kingsway, Southampton SO14 51 E2
Kingswell St PO1 47 D1
Kingsworthy Rd PO9 30 A2
Kinnell Cl PO10 31 G5
Kinross Cres PO6 20 D4
Kinross Rd SO40 53 A5
Kintyre Cl RG23 45 C4
Kintyre Rd PO6 20 C2
Kinver Cl SO51 49 D1
Kipling Cl GU46 57 C4
Kipling Rd SO50 22 B3
Kirk Knoll GU35 33 B2
Kitwalls La SO41 42 D2
Kitwood Grn PO9 30 C1
Kivernell Rd SO41 42 C3
Knatchbull Cl SO51 49 C3
Knighton Cnr PO8 21 C1
Knights Way GU34 12 A3
Knightstone Grange SO45 35 B4
Knightwood Av, Havant PO9 30 C1
Knightwood Av, Lyndhurst SO43 37 B5
Knightwood Cl, Lyndhurst SO43
Knightwood Cl, Southampton SO40
Knightwood Rd SO45
Knoll Cl GU51
Knoll Rd GU51
Knowland Dr SO41
Knowle Cres RG20
Knowle Rd SO42
Knowles Cl SO35
Knowsley Cres PO6
Knowsley Rd PO6
Knox Ter*, Orchard La GU34
Knyght Cl SO51
Kohat Ct GU11
Kohima Cl GU11

Laburnam Gro PO11
Laburnum Cl, Aldershot GU11
Laburnum Cl, Southampton SO52
Laburnum Gdns GU52
Laburnum Gro SO50
Laburnum Rd, Aldershot GU11
Laburnum Rd, Waterlooville PO7
Lackford Av SO40
Ladies Mile PO5
Ladycross Rd SO45
Ladysmith Pl GU35
Ladywell La SO24
Lake Dr GU35
Lake Grove Rd BH25
Lakeside, Lee-on-the-So PO13
Lakeside, Ringwood BH24
Lakeside Gdns PO9
Lakesmere Rd PO8
Lakeview Dr BH24
Lakewood Rd SO40
Lamb Cl SP10
Lambourne Cl SO45
Lamdens Walk RG26
Lamerton Cl GU35
Lamerton Rd GU35
Lammas Rd SO45
Lampeter Av PO6
Lancaster Cl SP10
Lancaster Rd GU14
Lancaster Way PO7
Lancer Ct GU11
Landon Ct PO12
Landport St PO5
Landport Ter PO1
Landport Vw PO1
Lands End La GU35
Landseer Ct SP10
Lane End Dr PO10
Lanehays Rd SO45
Langbrook Cl PO9
Langdale Av PO6
Langdown Firs SO45
Langdown Lawn SO45
Langdown Lawn Cl SO45
Langdown Rd SO45
Langham Cl SO52
Langham Rd GU34
Langley Cl GU52
Langley Dr GU11
Langley Gdn SP6
Langley Lodge Gdns SO45
Langstone Rd PO9
Langton Cl BH25
Langton Dr GU35
Langton Rd SO32
Langtons Ct SO24
Lansdowne Cl SO51
Lansdowne Gdns SO51
Lansdowne Hill SO14
Lansdowne Rd, Aldershot GU11
Lansdowne Rd, Alton GU34
Lansdowne St PO5
Lantana Cl PO7
Lapwing Cl, Gosport PO12
Lapwing Cl, Waterlooville PO8
Lapwing Rise RG28
Larch Cl, Lee-on-the-Sol PO13
Larch Cl, Liphook GU30
Larch Cl, Lymington SO41
Larch Dr RG20
Larch Rd GU35
Larchfield Rd GU52
Larchfield Way PO8

be Rd GU31 46 B4
se GU30 39 A3
r Cl GU11 13 C4
ore Forest Gro 21 A5
Rd SO51 49 C3
St,
ey SO51 49 B3
St,
ampton SO14 51 E5
yn Cl SO52 45 B3
ston Cl PO12 28 C1
ston Dr SO50 22 B1
La SO41 42 F3
Yd RG28 55 B3
l, Gosport PO12 28 C1
l,
gton SO41 36 A1
l,
ampton SO45 35 A3
dns GU11 13 C4
d PO8 21 C4
e Grn PO10 31 H2
Walk PO13 38 D4
Ct GU31 46 B2
Dr PO9 30 B3
St GU31 46 C3
er Gdns GU35 18 C4
er Rd,
gton SO41 36 A2
er Rd,
oville PO7 54 C3
on Gdns SO52 45 B3
Rd PO12 28 A4
Cres GU46 57 D2
SO41 42 F3
SO23 56 E2
d,
gh SO50 22 D2
d,
gton SO41 41 A3
d,
d on Sea SO41 42 F3
SO23 56 E2
ce Cl SP10 14 A1
ce Rd,
U52 26 A3
ce Rd,
ood BH24 48 E1
GU11 13 D1
RG27 32 A5
U9 13 C5
U9 13 B4
gton Cres PO13 38 C4
Cl SO50 22 C1
Dr PO12 28 C1
PO12 28 B3
Rd SO15 53 D4
U11 13 D3
PO12 28 A2
s SO41 41 C4
PO12 29 B6
PO12 28 B3
w RG27 32 D5
d Rd PO12 28 A3
k GU51 26 A2
res GU11 13 A2
d PO11 52 C3
Pl SP10 14 B4
SP10 14 C4
dns SP10 14 C4
SO41 41 B2
l, Andover SP10 14 C4
l,
gh SO50 22 A3
l,
m PO16 23 B2
l, Havant PO9 30 B4
l,
ilton BH25 44 C1
GU11 13 B1
Gro GU35 18 C6
er Av PO6 20 D3
dns GU52 26 D5
Cl PO12 29 B7
Lodge PO11 52 A4
Row PO1 47 C1
Gdns PO8 21 A2
t GU34 12 B3
Way SO41 41 C3
Rd PO12 28 C3
Dr SO32 15 A5
SO45 24 A6
l SO15 50 C1
Way GU51 26 D1
orpe Ct PO12 28 C4
l PO10 31 H3
d SO40 53 B6
Gdns PO11 52 B3
Cl PO12 29 B5
PO9 30 B1
d SO40 53 B4
Dr PO12 28 C2
Cl SO45 24 B3
d RG23 45 C4
Bordon GU35 18 C4

Lilac Cl, Havant PO9 30 D2
Lilac Cl,
Ringwood BH24 48 C2
Limberline Rd PO6 20 C6
Limberline Spur PO6 20 C6
Lime Av GU34 12 B1
Lime Gro GU34 12 B1
Lime Rd SO24 43 D5
Lime St,
Aldershot GU11 13 B2
Lime St,
Southampton SO14 51 E4
Lime Walk SO45 35 A4
Limecroft GU46 57 C3
Limes Cl,
Liphook GU30 39 B1
Limes Cl, Liss GU33 40 B5
Linbrook Ct BH24 48 B1
Lincoln Cl SO51 49 E1
Lincoln Grn GU34 12 B4
Lincoln Rise PO8 21 B4
Lind Rd PO12 29 C7
Linda Gro PO8 21 A5
Linda Rd SO45 24 C2
Linden Dr GU33 40 B5
Linden Gdns BH24 48 B2
Linden Gro,
Gosport PO12 29 B5
Linden Gro,
Hayling Island PO11 52 C4
Linden Rd,
Bordon GU35 33 E3
Linden Rd,
Romsey SO51 49 B3
Linden Walk SO52 45 B1
Linden Way,
Havant PO9 30 B2
Linden Way,
Lymington SO41 41 B2
Linden Way,
Waterlooville PO8 21 C3
Lindens Cl PO10 31 G3
Lindford Chase GU35 19 E2
Lindford Rd GU35 18 D1
Lindford Wey GU35 19 E2
Lindisfarne Cl PO6 20 C3
Lindley Gdns SO24 43 C6
Lindum Cl GU11 13 C3
Lindum Dene GU11 13 B3
Linford Rd BH24 48 E1
Ling Cres GU35 33 D2
Lingfield Cl GU34 12 C4
Lingmala Gro GU52 26 C6
Link Rd, Newbury RG20 37 C2
Link Rd,
Ringwood BH24 48 D2
Link Way,
Basingstoke RG23 45 D6
Link Way, Lee-on-the-Solent
PO13 38 A1
Linkway GU52 26 B4
Linkway Par GU52 26 B5
Linnet Cl BH24 48 E4
Linnet Ct BH25 44 B2
Linnet Sq SO50 22 A5
Linnets Rd SO24 43 C6
Linnets Way GU34 12 C1
Linsted La GU35 33 A1
Linton Cl RG26 34 F4
Linton Dr SP10 14 A1
Linwood Cl SO45 35 B5
Lion Rd GU14 25 A3
Lion St PO1 47 C2
Lion Ter PO1 47 C2
Lion Way GU52 26 D6
Lions Hall SO23 56 C3
Liphook By-Pass GU30 39 A3
Liphook Rd,
Bordon GU35 18 B6
Liphook Rd,
Headley GU35 19 H4
Liphook Rd,
Headley GU35 33 B3
Liphook Rd,
Lindford GU35 19 F1
Liphook Rd,
Passfield GU30 19 H4
Lipscombe Rise GU34 12 C1
Lisa Ct RG21 16 A3
Lisle Cl SO41 41 C3
Lisle Way PO10 31 F2
Lismoyne Cl GU51 26 A1
Lister Rd PO6 20 B2
Lit Copse GU46 57 D1
Litchfield Ho RG26 34 D2
Litchford Rd BH25 44 D1
Little Anglesey Rd PO12 29 A6
Little Barn Pl GU33 40 D5
Little Barrs Dr BH25 44 C1
Little Britain St PO1 47 B2
Little Cft GU46 57 D4
Little Chilworth PO12 28 A3
Little Cnr PO7 36 C6
Little Copse GU52 26 B4
Little Dene Copse SO41 41 A4
Little Green Orch PO12 29 A6

Little Grn PO12 29 A6
Little La PO12 29 A6
Little Mead PO7 36 C6
Little Meads SO51 49 A3
Little Minster St SO23 56 D3
Little Sheldons RG27 32 A5
Little Shore La SO32 15 C5
Little South Sea PO5 47 D4
Little Vigo GU46 57 B4
Little Wellington St
GU11 13 C1
Littlefield Rd GU34 12 D2
Littlegreen Av PO9 30 C2
Littleton Gro PO9 30 B1
Litton Gdns RG23 45 C5
Locke Rd GU30 39 C4
Lockerley Cl SO41 41 D3
Lockerley Rd PO9 30 B2
Locksley Rd SO50 22 B5
Loddon Dr RG21 16 F3
Loddon Mall RG21 16 C2
Lodge Av PO6 20 D3
Lodge Cl GU11 13 D3
Lodge Dr SO45 35 B5
Lodge Gdns PO12 29 A5
Lodge Gro GU46 57 F2
Lodge Rd SO41 41 A3
Lombard St PO1 47 B3
Lomond Cl RG23 45 B5
London Rd,
Andover SP10 14 C3
London Rd,
Basingstoke RG21 16 E4
London Rd,
Clanfield PO8 21 D1
London Rd,
Cosham PO6 20 B5
London Rd,
Cowplain PO8 21 A6
London Rd,
Hartley Wintney RG27 32 B3
London Rd, Hook RG27 32 A6
London Rd,
Liphook GU30 39 B4
London Rd,
Petersfield GU31 46 F1
London Rd,
Portsmouth PO6 20 C3
London Rd,
Southampton SO15 50 D1
London Rd,
Waterlooville PO7 54 A3
London Rd,
Whitchurch RG28 55 C3
London St,
Andover SP10 14 B3
London St,
Basingstoke RG21 16 D4
London St,
Whitchurch RG28 55 B3
Long Copse La PO10 31 G1
Long Cross Hill GU35 33 A2
Long Curtain Rd PO5 47 B4
Long Down GU31 46 E2
Long Gro RG26 34 A1
Long Rd GU31 46 D1
Long Water Dr PO12 29 C7
Longacre Cl GU33 40 D4
Longbridge Ind Est
SO14 51 G5
Longcroft Cl RG21 16 A4
Longcroft Rd RG20 37 A1
Longcroft St SO14 51 G3
Longdown GU52 26 A5
Longfield Rd SO41 36 C3
Longfields RG23 45 C4
Longfld Rd PO10 31 G2
Longford Pl SO41 41 C4
Longleat Gdns BH25 44 A1
Longleat Sq GU14 25 C2
Longmead, Fleet GU52 26 B4
Longmead, Liss GU33 40 B5
Longmead Gdns PO9 30 B6
Longmeadow Gdns
SO45 35 B3
Longmoor Cl RG21 16 A4
Longmoor Rd GU30 39 A4
Longs Ct RG28 55 B3
Longwood Av PO8 21 A5
Lonsdale Av PO6 20 C4
Lord Montgomery Way
PO1 47 C3
Lortemore Pl SO51 49 B3
Loughwood Cl SO50 22 C1
Louisburg Rd GU35 18 C1
Louise Margaret Rd
GU11 13 D1
Love La, Andover SP10 14 C4
Love La,
Lymington SO41 42 E3
Love La,
Newbury RG20 37 B2
Love La,
Petersfield GU31 46 D2
Love La, Romsey SO51 49 B3
Love La, Yateley GU46 57 A2

Lovedean La PO8 21 A3
Lovells Walk SO24 43 C5
Low La GU9 13 C5
Lower Bartons SP6 27 E3
Lower Bere Wood PO7 54 B3
Lower Brook St,
Basingstoke RG21 16 A2
Lower Brook St,
Winchester SO23 56 E2
Lower Brownhill Rd
SO16 53 D2
Lower Buckland Rd
SO41 41 C1
Lower Canal Walk SO14 51 E6
Lower Canes GU46 57 A2
Lower Church Path PO1 47 D2
Lower Evingar Rd RG28 55 B3
Lower Farnham Rd
GU11 13 D5
Lower Grove Rd PO9 30 B5
Lower Heyshott GU31 46 D2
Lower La SO32 15 C5
Lower Mead GU31 46 E3
Lower Moor GU46 57 D3
Lower Mullins La SO45 35 A3
Lower Nelson St GU11 13 C1
Lower Pennington La
SO41 41 C4
Lower Quay PO16 23 D4
Lower Quay Cl PO16 23 C4
Lower Turk St GU34 12 C3
Lower Wardown GU31 46 E2
Lower Weybourne La
GU9 13 A5
Lower Wote St RG21 16 D2
Lowestoft Rd PO6 20 A2
Loweswater Gdns
GU35 18 C1
Lowland Rd PO7 36 B5
Lowry Ct SP10 14 A1
Loxwood Rd PO8 21 A2
Luard Ct PO9 30 D5
Lucas Cl GU46 57 D3
Lucerne Rd SO41 42 E3
Ludcombe PO7 36 C4
Ludlow Rd PO6 20 A2
Ludshott Gro GU35 33 E3
Luke Rd GU11 13 A3
Luke Rd East GU11 13 A3
Lulworth Cl PO11 52 C2
Lulworth Rd PO13 38 C5
Lumby Dr BH24 48 D2
Lumby Drive Caravan Pk
BH24 48 D2
Lumley Gdns PO10 31 H5
Lumley Path PO10 31 H5
Lumley Rd PO10 31 H5
Lutman St PO10 31 F2
Lych Gate Ct BH24 48 E4
Lychgate Dr PO8 21 B1
Lyde Cl RG23 45 C5
Lydiard Cl SO50 22 C1
Lydlynch Rd SO40 53 A4
Lymbourn Rd PO9 30 C5
Lyme Cl SO50 22 B1
Lymefields SO41 42 E2
Lymington Av GU46 57 B3
Lymington Rd,
Brockenhurst SO42 17 D6
Lymington Rd,
Lymington SO41 42 E2
Lymington Rd,
New Milton BH25 44 B4
Lymore La SO41 42 F1
Lymore Valley SO41 42 F1
Lynch Hill RG28 55 B3
Lynch Hill Pk RG28 55 C2
Lynchford La GU14 25 D5
Lynchford Rd GU14 25 A6
Lyndale Cl SO41 42 E3
Lyndford Ter GU52 26 B4
Lyndhurst Av GU11 13 D5
Lyndhurst Cl PO11 52 C5
Lyndhurst Rd,
Brockenhurst SO42 17 D1
Lyndhurst Rd,
Gosport PO12 28 A4
Lyndhurst Rd,
Southampton SO40 15 A3
Lyndum Cl GU31 46 C2
Lyne Pl PO8 21 B2
Lynes La BH24 48 A3
Lynric Cl BH25 44 B6
Lynton Rd,
Bordon GU35 18 C4
Lynton Rd,
Petersfield GU31 46 B2
Lynwood Cl GU35 19 F1
Lynwood Gdns RG27 32 B5
Lyon Av BH25 44 C2
Lysander Ct PO1 47 B3
Lysander Way,
Farnborough GU14 25 A5
Lysander Way,
Waterlooville PO7 54 D2
Lyson's Rd GU11 13 B2

Lyss Ct GU33 40 B4
Lysses Ct PO16 23 E2
Lysses Path PO16 23 E2
Lyster Rd SP6 27 F3
Lyteltane Rd SO41 41 C3
Lytham Cl GU35 18 A5
Lytton Rd,
Basingstoke RG21 16 F3
Lytton Rd,
Southampton SO45 35 C4

Mabey Cl PO12 29 C6
Mablethorpe Rd PO6 20 A2
Macrae Rd GU46 57 C2
Maddison Ct PO16 23 E3
Maddison St SO14 50 D4
Madeira Walk SO41 41 E2
Madeley Rd GU52 26 C5
Madeline Rd GU31 46 D2
Madrid Rd SP10 14 D2
Magdala Rd,
Hayling Island PO11 52 A4
Magdala Rd,
Portsmouth PO6 20 C3
Magdalen Hill SO23 56 F3
Magdalen Mws SO23 56 F3
Magdalen Row GU31 46 B3
Magnolia Way,
Fleet GU52 26 B4
Magnolia Way,
Waterlooville PO8 21 C4
Magpie Cl GU35 18 D5
Magpie Gro BH25 44 B3
Magpie La,
Eastleigh SO50 22 A4
Magpie La, Lee-on-the-Solent
PO13 38 C3
Maidstone Cres PO6 20 A2
Main Gate Rd GU14 25 A4
Main Rd,
Portsmouth PO1 47 A1
Main Rd,
Portsmouth PO1 47 B1
Main Rd, Tadley RG26 34 F4
Mainstone SO51 49 A4
Maisemore Gdns PO10 31 F6
Maitland Rd GU14 25 A6
Maizemore Walk PO13 38 D4
Majorca Av SP10 14 C1
Maldon Rd PO6 20 A2
Mallard Cl,
Alresford SO24 43 C4
Mallard Cl,
Lymington SO41 36 C2
Mallard Cl,
Romsey SO51 49 C3
Mallard Cl,
Southampton SO32 15 A5
Mallard Way GU46 57 B3
Mallards GU34 12 B1
Mallow Cl,
Bordon GU35 19 F2
Mallow Cl,
Portsmouth PO6 20 C3
Mallow Cl,
Waterlooville PO7 54 C3
Malmesbury Rd SO51 49 B2
Malmsbury Rd GU35 18 C5
Malshanger La RG23 45 B4
Malt La SO32 15 C5
Malthouse Cl SO51 49 B2
Malthouse Ct GU30 39 C4
Malthouse La,
Fareham PO16 23 C3
Malthouse La,
Tadley RG26 34 F4
Malthouse Mdws
GU30 39 C4
Maltings Cl GU34 12 C3
Malvern Cl SO32 15 C5
Malvern Mws PO10 31 H5
Malwood Rd SO45 35 A2
Malwood Rd West
SO45 35 A3
Manchester St SO14 50 D3
Mandela Way SO15 50 B1
Manderley SO41 42 E4
Manica Cl GU35 18 C4
Mann Cl RG28 55 C4
Manor Cl,
Fareham PO17 54 C6
Manor Cl,
Fordingbridge SP6 27 F3
Manor Cl, Havant PO9 30 B4
Manor Cl,
Lymington SO41 42 D2
Manor Ct BH24 48 B2
Manor Farm Cl BH25 44 A3
Manor Farm Rd SP6 27 B3
Manor Flds GU30 39 C4
Manor Gdns BH24 48 B3
Manor Park Dr GU46 57 D3
Manor Pk Ind Est
GU12 13 D2
Manor Rd,
Aldershot GU11 13 B3

Manor Rd, Andover SP10 14 A2
Manor Rd, Farnborough GU14 25 C2
Manor Rd, Hayling Island PO11 52 B3
Manor Rd, Lymington SO41 42 D2
Manor Rd, New Milton BH25 44 C1
Manor Rd, Ringwood BH24 48 C3
Manor Walk GU12 13 D2
Manor Way Hayling Island PO11 52 C5
Manor Way, Lee-on-the-Solent PO13 38 C4
Mansbridge Rd SO50 22 C6
Manse La RG26 34 F4
Mansfield Rd BH24 48 B3
Mansvid Av PO6 20 D4
Mants La SO23 56 E4
Maple Cl, Alresford SO24 43 C6
Maple Cl, Alton GU34 12 B1
Maple Cl, Emsworth PO10 31 H3
Maple Cl, Lee-on-the-Solent PO13 38 D5
Maple Cl, New Milton BH25 44 C6
Maple Cl, Romsey SO51 49 F4
Maple Dr PO7 36 D5
Maple Gdns GU46 57 D3
Maple Gro RG26 34 E3
Maple Leaf Dr GU35 18 C3
Maple Sq SO50 22 B5
Maple Way GU35 33 D2
Mapleleaf Gdns SO50 22 C5
Mapletree Av PO8 21 C4
Maralyn Av PO7 54 B3
Marbream Cl SP6 27 C3
March Cl SP10 14 C2
Marchwood By-Pass SO40 53 A6
Marden Way GU31 46 D3
Mareth Cl GU11 13 D1
Margerys Ct PO1 47 B2
Marina Cl PO10 31 H6
Marine Dr BH25 44 A6
Marine Dr East BH25 44 B6
Marine Par SO14 51 G4
Marine Par East PO13 38 B5
Marine Par West PO13 38 A3
Mariners Ct SO41 41 E3
Mariners Mws SO45 35 C3
Mariners Way PO12 29 D5
Maritime Walk SO14 51 F6
Maritime Way SO14 51 E6
Marjoram Cres PO8 21 B5
Mark Anthony Ct PO11 52 B4
Mark Ct PO7 54 B1
Mark La RG21 16 D4
Market La SO23 56 D3
Market Par PO9 30 B4
Market Pl, Basingstoke RG21 16 D4
Market Pl, Fordingbridge SP6 27 E4
Market Pl, Ringwood BH24 48 A3
Market Pl, Romsey SO51 49 B3
Market Pl, Southampton SO14 50 D5
Market Sq GU34 12 C3
Market St, Alton GU34 12 C3
Market St, Eastleigh SO50 22 D5
Market St, Eastleigh SO50 22 D4
Market St, Winchester SO23 56 D3
Marketway PO1 47 D1
Markway Cl PO10 31 F5
Marl La SP6 27 B2
Marlborough Ct SO45 35 A4
Marlborough Gdns RG23 45 C5
Marlborough Pk PO9 30 D3
Marlborough Pl SO41 41 C1
Marlborough Row PO1 47 B1
Marlborough St SP10 14 B2
Marley Av BH25 44 A1
Marley Cl BH25 44 A1
Marlow Rd SO32 15 A4
Marmion Rd PO5 47 D5
Marryat Ct BH25 44 B1
Marryat Rd BH25 44 B2
Marsh Cl GU35 19 E4
Marsh La, Fawley SO45 24 C1
Marsh La, Lymington SO41 41 D1
Marsh La, Southampton SO14 51 F4
Marsh Par SO45 35 B2
Marshal Cl GU34 12 B4
Marshwood Av PO7 54 D2
Marston Gate SO23 56 D1
Martells Ct PO1 47 B3
Martin Av PO7 36 C5
Martin Cl PO13 38 C3
Martin Rd PO9 30 B1
Martin St SO32 15 B5
Martingale Ct GU11 13 A2
Martins Rd SO42 17 D2
Mary Rose Mws GU34 12 D1
Maryfield SO14 51 F4
Maryland Ct SO41 42 B3
Maryland Gdns SO41 42 C3
Masefield Cl SO50 22 B3
Mason Cl GU46 57 E3
Mason Way GU11 13 C4
Mathews Cl GU14 25 C5
Mathews Ter GU11 13 D1
Matilda Pl SO23 56 D1
Matthews Way RG23 45 D5
Maturin Cl SO41 41 D3
Maurepas Way PO7 54 A2
Mavis Cres PO9 30 A4
May Av SO41 41 C1
May Cl GU35 33 B4
May Pl RG21 16 D3
May St RG21 16 A2
Mayfair Ho RG21 16 D3
Mayfield Av SO40 53 A4
Mayfield Cl GU9 13 C5
Mayfield Rd, Fordingbridge SP6 27 B3
Mayfield Rd, Gosport PO12 29 C5
Mayflower Cl, Lee-on-the-Solent PO13 38 A1
Mayflower Cl, Lymington SO41 41 F3
Mayflower Dr GU46 57 A1
Mayflower Rd GU35 18 B6
Mayfly Cl SP6 27 E2
Mayles Cl PO17 54 C6
Mayles La PO17 54 B6
Maynard Pl PO8 21 B1
Maynard Rd SO40 53 A4
Maytree Gdns PO16 23 A3
Maytree Rd PO16 23 B3
McFauld Way RG28 55 C3
Mead Cl, Alton GU34 12 D3
Mead Cl, Andover SP10 14 A4
Mead Cl, Romsey SO51 49 E3
Mead End Rd PO7 36 C6
Mead Hatchgate RG27 32 B4
Mead Hedges SP10 14 A4
Mead Rd, Andover SP10 14 A4
Mead Rd, Lymington SO41 41 A4
Meadow Av SP6 27 E3
Meadow Cl, Alresford SO24 43 D5
Meadow Cl, Fordingbridge SP6 27 E2
Meadow Cl, Liphook GU30 39 B3
Meadow Cl, North Baddesley SO52 45 C3
Meadow Cl, Ringwood BH24 48 C2
Meadow Cl, Totton SO40 53 A6
Meadow Ct, Emsworth PO10 31 H5
Meadow Ct, Fleet GU51 26 A2
Meadow Ct, Fordingbridge SP6 27 E3
Meadow Edge PO7 20 D1
Meadow End, Brockenhurst SO42 17 B3
Meadow End, Liphook GU30 39 B3
Meadow Heights SP10 14 C3
Meadow La RG27 32 B2
Meadow Rd, Lymington SO41 41 B4
Meadow Rd, New Milton BH25 44 D1
Meadow Rd, Ringwood BH24 48 C2
Meadow Rise PO8 21 B5
Meadow St PO5 47 D3
Meadow Vw, Bordon GU35 19 E3
Meadow Vw, Whitchurch RG28 55 A2
Meadow Walk GU33 40 C4
Meadow Way, New Milton BH25 44 C6
Meadow Way, Ringwood BH24 48 C2
Meadow Way, Southampton SO45 24 C2
Meadowlands, Havant PO9 30 C5
Meadowlands, Lymington SO41 41 B2
Meadowsweet Way PO6 20 A1
Meadway PO7 54 C1
Medina Cl SO53 22 A2
Medina Ct SP10 14 D1
Medina Gdns RG23 45 C6
Medina Rd PO6 20 A3
Medonte Cl GU51 26 C3
Medstead Rd PO9 30 A2
Medway Av RG23 45 C5
Meerut Rd SO42 17 C3
Meeting House La BH24 48 A3
Melbourne Pl PO5 47 D3
Melbourne St SO14 51 G4
Melbury Cl SO41 41 C2
Mellor Cl PO6 20 A3
Melrose Cl GU35 18 D5
Melville Rd PO12 28 A2
Memorial Rd RG27 32 B6
Mendip Cl BH25 44 D3
Mengham Av PO11 52 C5
Mengham Ct PO11 52 C4
Mengham La PO11 52 C4
Mengham Rd PO11 52 C4
Meon Cl, Petersfield GU31 46 B2
Meon Cl, Romsey SO51 49 F3
Meon Cl, Tadley RG26 34 D1
Meon Rd, Basingstoke RG23 45 C5
Meon Rd, Romsey SO51 49 F3
Meon Walk RG21 16 F2
Mercer Way SO51 49 C2
Merchants Pl SO23 56 D2
Merchants Walk SO14 50 D5
Merchistoun Rd PO8 21 B2
Mercury Cl GU35 19 E4
Merganser Cl PO12 28 B1
Meriden Rd PO5 47 D3
Meridian Centre PO9 30 B4
Meridian Ind Est RG27 32 C6
Meridian Ind Pk SP10 14 B1
Merlin Cl, Ringwood BH24 48 E4
Merlin Cl, Southampton SO32 15 B5
Merlin Rd GU14 25 A3
Mermaid Way SO14 51 F6
Merriemeade Cl SO45 35 A6
Merrivale Cl SO45 35 A3
Merron Cl GU46 57 C3
Merry Gdns SO52 45 B2
Merryfield Rd GU31 46 E2
Merryweather Est BH24 48 E2
Mersey Ct SP10 14 D1
Merton Cl SP6 27 E2
Merton Gro BH24 48 B2
Merton Rd PO5 47 D4
Meryon Rd SO24 43 B6
Meudon Av GU14 25 A3
Mews La SO22 56 A3
Mey Cl PO7 54 C2
Meynell Cl SO50 22 B3
Michaelmas Cl GU46 57 D4
Michaels Way SO45 35 A2
Micheldever Cl RG28 55 C5
Micheldever Rd, Andover SP10 14 C3
Micheldever Rd, Whitchurch RG28 55 B4
Middle Brook St SO23 56 E2
Middle Hill GU11 13 C1
Middle La BH24 48 B3
Middle Mdw GU33 40 C4
Middle Mead RG27 32 B5
Middle Rd, Lymington SO41 41 C2
Middle Rd, Southampton SO52 45 C1
Middle Rd, Winchester SO22 56 A2
Middle St, Southampton SO32 15 C5
Middle St, Southsea PO5 47 D3
Middle Vw SO22 56 A2
Middlebridge St SO51 49 A4
Middlebrook SO32 15 C5
Middleton Rd BH24 48 C2
Midhurst Rd GU30 39 B4
Midway SO45 35 A4
Midway Rd PO6 20 B6
Milbeck Cl PO8 21 A5
Mildmay Ct SO23 56 E3
Mildmay Ter RG27 32 C3
Milford Cres SO41 42 E3
Milford Ct SO41 42 E3
Milford Gdns SO53 22 B1
Milford Rd, Lymington SO41 41 B4
Milford Rd, New Milton BH25 44 C4
Milford Trading Est SO41 42 E3
Military Rd, Cosham PO6 20 B6
Military Rd, Fareham PO16 23 F1
Military Rd, Portsmouth PO1 47 C1
Mill Chase Rd GU35 19 E3
Mill Cl PO7 36 D5
Mill Ct SP6 27 E4
Mill Hill SO24 43 D3
Mill La, Alton GU34 12 D2
Mill La, Bordon GU35 19 F2
Mill La, Brockenhurst SO42 17 D4
Mill La, Emsworth PO10 31 H5
Mill La, Fareham PO17 54 C4
Mill La, Gosport PO12 28 B2
Mill La, Lymington SO41 41 E2
Mill La, Petersfield GU31 46 F1
Mill La, Romsey SO51 49 A3
Mill La, Waterlooville PO7 20 B1
Mill La, Yateley GU46 57 D1
Mill La Ind Est GU34 12 E2
Mill Mdw SO41 42 D3
Mill Pond Rd PO12 28 B2
Mill Rd, Denmead PO7 36 D5
Mill Rd, Fareham PO16 23 C4
Mill Rd, Gosport PO12 28 A2
Mill Rd, Liss GU33 40 C5
Mill Rd, Southampton SO40 53 B4
Mill Rd, Waterlooville PO7 54 A3
Mill St SO50 22 D3
Mill Stream GU9 13 A5
Millbank St SO14 51 H1
Millbridge Rd GU46 57 B1
Millbrook Cl GU33 40 C4
Millbrook Rd East SO15 50 A1
Miller Dr PO16 23 A1
Millers Rd RG26 34 E3
Millers Way SO45 35 A5
Millfield BH25 44 A2
Milliken Cl SO45 24 B3
Millmere GU46 57 D1
Millstream Cl SP10 14 A5
Millstream Rise SO51 49 A3
Milman Ct SO23 56 D2
Milnthorpe La SO22 56 A4
Milton Gro BH25 44 C3
Milton Mead BH25 44 A3
Milton Rd, Eastleigh SO50 22 D1
Milton Rd, Waterlooville PO8 21 A4
Milverton Cl SO40 53 B6
Milverton Rd SO40 53 B6
Milvil Rd PO13 38 B3
Mimosa Cl GU35 19 F2
Minehurst Rd GU16 25 D1
Minerva Cres PO1 47 B3
Minerva Dr PO12 28 C1
Minerva Rd GU14 25 A4
Minley Ct PO9 30 D1
Minnitt Rd PO12 28 E4
Minstead Cl RG26 34 E4
Minstead Dr GU46 57 C3
Minster La SO23 56 C3
Mint Rd GU33 40 D3
Mint Yd SO23 56 D3
Minter Ct RG26 34 C2
Mission La PO8 21 A5
Mistletoe Rd GU46 57 D4
Mitchell Cl BH25 44 B6
Mitchell Rd SO50 22 D4
Mitchell Way SO50 22 C6
Mitchells Cl SO51 49 C3
Mitford Rd SO24 43 B5
Moat La BH25 44 B4
Moggs Mead GU31 46 D3
Molefields SO41 42 E3
Molesworth Rd PO12 29 C5
Monachus La RG27 32 C2
Monarch Cl PO7 54 C2
Monckton Rd PO12 29 B7
Monks Cl GU14 25 B1
Monks Hill PO13 38 A3
Monks Orch GU31 46 C1
Monks Walk SO45 35 A6
Monks Way SO50 22 B6
Monks Wood GU31 46 D1
Monksbrook Cl SO50 22 B6
Monkswood Cres RG26 34 E4
Monkton La GU9 13 A6
Montacute Cl GU14 25 C2
Montague Gdns GU31 46 F3
Montague Wallis Ct PO1
Monteagle La GU46
Monteray Dr SO41
Monterey Dr PO9
Montford Rd SO51
Montfort Cl SO51
Montfort Heights SO51
Montgomery Rd PO9
Montreal Walk GU30
Montrose Cl, Bordon GU35
Montrose Cl, Fleet GU51
Montserrat Rd PO13
Monument Chase GU35
Monument La SO41
Moody Rd PO13
Moor Cl GU35
Moore Cl, Andover SP10
Moore Cl, Fleet GU52
Moore Cl, New Milton BH25
Moore Rd GU52
Moorgreen Rd PO9
Moorhead Ct SO14
Moorland Av BH25
Moorlands Cl, Brockenhurst SO42
Moorlands Cl, Fleet GU51
Moorside SO23
Mopley SO45
Mopley Cl SO45
Morant Rd BH24
Moreland Cl GU34
Moreland Rd PO12
Morland Rd GU11
Morley Cl GU46
Morley Cres PO8
Morley Dr SO32
Mornington Cl, Andover SP10
Mornington Cl, Tadley RG26
Mornington Rd GU35
Morpeth Av SO40
Morris Rd, Farnborough GU14
Morris Rd, Southampton SO15
Morris St RG27
Mortimer Gdns RG26
Mortimer La RG21
Mortimer Way SO52
Moss Cl GU33
Mottisfont Ct SO23
Mottisfont Rd SO50
Moulsham Copse La GU46
Moulsham La GU46
Mound Cl PO12
Mount Av BH25
Mount Cl BH25
Mount Dr SO53
Mount House Cl SO45
Mount Pleasant, Hook RG27
Mount Pleasant, Tadley RG26
Mount Pleasant Dr RG26
Mount Pleasant La BH24
Mount Pleasant Rd, Aldershot GU12
Mount Pleasant Rd, Alton GU34
Mount Pleasant Rd, Bordon GU35
Mount Pleasant Rd, Gosport PO12
Mount Vw, Aldershot GU11
Mount Vw, Eastleigh SO50
Mountbatten Av SO51
Mountbatten Bsns Ce SO15
Mountbatten Ct SP10
Mountbatten Rd SO50
Mountbatten Way SO15
Mountfield SO45
Mounttemple SO51
Mousehole La SO45
Moxhams SP6
Muccleshell Cl PO9
Mulberry Av, Lee-on-the-Solent PO13
Mulberry Av, Portsmouth PO6
Mulberry Cl PO12
Mulberry Gdns SP6
Mulberry La PO6

erry Path PO6 20 D3
ords Hill RG26 34 D1
Cl RG23 45 B5
by Rd PO12 28 D3
nings Ct SP10 14 A1
el Rd PO7 54 B1
ay Cl SP10 14 A6
ay Rd PO8 21 B2
ays La PO1 47 B1
eum Rd PO1 47 C3
grove Gdns GU34 12 B2
ords La PO11 52 D4
e Cl SO41 36 A1

er Rd PO8 21 C2
ow La,
gwood BH24 48 E1
ow La,
nsey SO51 49 A3
Rd PO1 47 B1
lles Ct SO41 42 C3
les Point SO41 42 D4
em Ct GU14 25 B5
on Cl,
Milton BH25 44 B2
on Cl,
nsey SO51 49 C2
on Cres PO8 21 C1
on Ct SO45 35 C5
on Gate SO15 50 B2
on Hill SO15 50 B2
on Pl SO41 41 E2
on Rd,
port PO12 28 B4
n Rd,
thsea PO5 47 D4
n St GU11 13 B1
an Cl PO12 29 B7
une Ct PO1 47 B3
une Rd GU35 18 D4
une Way SO14 51 F6
sa Cl PO7 54 D1
uis Cl SO51 49 D2
er St GU34 12 C2
erfield Cl,
n GU34 12 B2
erfield Cl,
ant PO9 30 C5
Rd PO5 47 D5
St GU14 25 A6
Ter PO5 47 D5
c Way RG28 55 C4
e Cl,
over SP10 14 C5
e Cl,
sey SO51 49 C2
e Ct PO12 28 B4
e Gdns PO10 31 F2
Alresford By-Pass
4 43 A6
Barn La GU34 12 C3
Brighton Rd
) 31 H4
Cotts SO16 53 D1
Ct BH24 48 A3
Down La PO7 20 D1
Farm Rd SO24 43 B5
Forest Dr SO42 17 A2
La, Havant PO9 30 C3
La,
ngton SO41 42 F4
Market Sq RG21 16 D2
Odiham Rd GU34 12 A1
Rd, Ashurst SO40 15 B2
Rd,
ngstoke RG21 16 D3
Rd,
field SO45 24 A4
Rd, Bordon GU35 18 C6
Rd, Fareham PO16 23 B2
Rd, Fleet GU52 26 C5
Rd,
ey Wintney RG27 32 C3
Rd, Havant PO9 30 A3
Rd, Hook RG27 32 B6
Rd, Hythe SO45 35 B2
Rd, Romsey SO51 49 C2
Rd,
hampton SO14 50 D2
Rd, Tadley RG26 34 C4
t, Andover SP10 14 C1
t,
ngstoke RG21 16 C3
t,
ngton SO41 41 D2
t,
wood BH24 48 B4
treet Mws SO41 41 D2
alley Rd SO41 42 D3
rgh St SO23 56 B2
ury Rd,
bury RG20 37 A1
bury Rd,
bury RG20 37 A2
ury Rd,
hurch RG28 55 B2

Newbury St,
Andover SP10 14 B3
Newbury St,
Whitchurch RG28 55 B3
Newchurch Rd RG26 34 C2
Newcomb Cl SP10 14 A5
Newcombe Rd SO15 50 C1
Newcome Rd GU9 13 A5
Newenham Rd SO41 41 D4
Newfield Rd GU33 40 C2
Newlands GU52 26 B4
Newlands Av PO12 28 A4
Newlands Cl,
Southampton SO45 24 A5
Newlands Cl,
Yateley GU46 57 D4
Newlands Copse SO45 24 A4
Newlands Rd,
New Milton BH25 44 C3
Newlands Rd,
Southampton SO45 24 A3
Newlyn Walk SO51 49 D2
Newman La GU34 12 E1
Newnham Pk RG27 32 A6
Newnham Rd RG27 32 A6
Newport Cl SO50 22 B4
Newton La SO51 49 B4
Newton Pl PO13 38 B3
Newton Rd BH25 44 D4
Newtown RG26 34 D2
Newtown La PO11 52 A3
Newtown Rd,
Eastleigh SO50 22 D3
Newtown Rd,
Liphook GU30 39 B5
Nicholas Ct PO11 52 A4
Nicholas Rd SO45 24 A6
Nichols Rd SO14 51 F2
Nicholson Pl SO24 43 B5
Nicholson Way PO9 30 A3
Nickel Cl SO23 56 F1
Nickel St PO5 47 C4
Nightingale Av SO50 22 A5
Nightingale Cl,
Bordon GU35 18 D5
Nightingale Cl,
Romsey SO51 49 D3
Nightingale Gdns RG27 32 B5
Nightingale Pk PO9 30 D5
Nightingale Rd,
Petersfield GU31 46 B4
Nightingale Rd,
Southsea PO5 47 D5
Nightjar Cl PO8 21 A2
Nile St PO10 31 H6
Noads Cl SO45 35 A5
Noads Way SO45 35 A5
Nobbs La PO1 47 C3
Noel Cl SO42 17 D3
Nore Cres PO10 31 E5
Nore Farm Av PO10 31 F5
Noreuil Rd GU31 46 A3
Norfolk Cres PO11 52 A5
Norfolk St PO5 47 D4
Norley Cl PO9 30 A1
Norman Cl GU35 19 E4
Norman Ct La SP11 14 A6
Norman Rd,
Gosport PO12 28 A3
Norman Rd,
Hayling Island PO11 52 D5
Norman Rd,
Southampton SO45 24 A5
Normandy Ct PO17 54 C5
Normandy La SO41 41 E4
Normandy St GU34 12 C2
Normandy Way SP6 27 E3
Norn Hill RG21 16 E1
Norris Cl, Bordon GU35 18 A6
Norris Cl, Romsey SO51 49 F1
Norris Gdns,
Havant PO9 30 C5
Norris Gdns,
New Milton BH25 44 C3
Norris Hill Rd GU52 26 D3
North Av PO6 20 B6
North Cl, Havant PO9 30 C5
North Cl,
Lymington SO41 41 D1
North Cl, Romsey SO51 49 F1
North Cres PO11 52 D5
North Cross St PO12 28 D4
North Front SO14 51 E2
North Fryerne GU46 57 D1
North Gate Rd GU14 25 B3
North Greenlands SO41 41 C4
North Head SO41 42 B3
North Mall GU51 26 B2
North Par GU35 18 C1
North Poulner Rd BH24 48 C1
North Rd,
Aldershot GU11 25 B6
North Rd,
Brockenhurst SO42 17 D3
North Rd,
Petersfield GU31 46 C2

North St,
Emsworth PO10 31 H4
North St, Gosport PO12 28 D4
North St, Havant PO9 30 B4
North St,
Lymington SO41 41 B3
North St,
Newbury RG20 37 B2
North St,
Portsmouth PO1 47 C1
North Street Arc PO9 30 B4
North View Rd RG26 34 F4
North Vw SO22 56 A2
North Wallington PO16 23 E1
North Walls SO23 56 D2
North Way PO9 30 A4
North Weirs SO42 17 A3
Northam Rd SO14 51 F2
Northam St SO14 51 E1
Northampton La SO45 24 A5
Northanger Cl GU34 12 B2
Northarbour Rd PO6 20 A3
Northbourne Cl SO45 35 B6
Northbrook Rd,
Aldershot GU11 13 C3
Northbrook Rd,
Southampton SO14 51 F1
Northern Anchorage
SO19 51 H5
Northern Av SP10 14 B2
Northern Par PO6 20 B6
Northern Rd PO6 20 B5
Northerwood Av SO43 37 A5
Northerwood Cl SO52 45 B2
Northfield Cl,
Fleet GU52 26 D5
Northfield Cl,
Southampton SO32 15 A4
Northfield Rd,
Fleet GU52 26 D5
Northfield Rd,
Lymington SO41 42 F3
Northfield Rd,
Ringwood BH24 48 B2
Northgate Ho SO23 56 C2
Northlands Rd,
Eastleigh SO50 22 C3
Northlands Rd,
Romsey SO51 49 E4
Northmead GU14 25 A2
Northumberland Rd,
Bordon GU35 18 C5
Northumberland Rd,
Southampton SO14 51 F2
Northwood Rd PO6 20 B6
Northwood Sq PO16 23 C2
Norton Cl PO7 54 A3
Norton Dr PO16 23 B1
Norton Welch Cl SO52 45 C3
Norwich Pl PO13 38 B3
Norwich Rd PO6 20 A2
Nottingham Pl PO13 38 B3
Nouale La BH24 48 E3
Nursery Cl,
Emsworth PO10 31 H2
Nursery Cl, Hook RG27 32 A4
Nursery Fld GU33 40 B6
Nursery Gdns,
Romsey SO51 49 D3
Nursery Gdns,
Waterlooville PO8 21 A3
Nursery La PO13 38 A1
Nursery Rd,
Alresford SO24 43 D4
Nursery Rd, Alton GU34 12 C1
Nursery Rd,
Ringwood BH24 48 B4
Nursling Cres PO9 30 C1
Nutbeem Rd SO50 22 C5
Nutbourne GU9 13 A4
Nutburn Rd SO52 45 C2
Nutley Cl,
Bordon GU35 18 D5
Nutley Cl, Yateley GU46 57 D3
Nutwick Rd PO9 30 D2
Nutwood Way SO40 53 A1
Nyria Walk PO12 28 D4

Oak Bank SP10 14 B4
Oak Cl,
Basingstoke RG23 45 D6
Oak Cl, Lyndhurst SO43 37 B6
Oak Cl,
Southampton SO15 53 D4
Oak Cl, Tadley RG26 34 A3
Oak Ct GU14 25 D5
Oak Hanger Cl RG27 32 C5
Oak Hill SO24 43 D5
Oak Hill Rd GU35 33 E3
Oak La BH24 48 C2
Oak Lodge GU35 18 D4
Oak Park Dr PO9 30 C3
Oak Rd,
Farnborough GU14 25 B2
Oak Rd,
New Milton BH25 44 D1

Oak Rd,
Southampton SO32 15 D5
Oak St PO12 28 C4
Oak Tree Cl,
Bordon GU35 33 C3
Oak Tree Cl, Tadley RG26 34 E2
Oak Tree Dr,
Emsworth PO10 31 G1
Oak Tree Dr, Hook RG27 32 C4
Oak Tree Dr, Liss GU33 40 C4
Oak Tree Way SO50 22 D1
Oakdene GU34 12 B1
Oakfield Rd SO40 53 A4
Oakhanger Rd GU35 18 A2
Oakhill Cl SO53 22 A1
Oakhurst Dr PO7 54 C1
Oakhurst Gdns PO7 20 D1
Oakland Av GU9 13 A4
Oakland Rd RG28 55 B2
Oakland Ter RG27 32 C2
Oaklands, Hook RG27 32 B3
Oaklands,
Lymington SO41 41 E3
Oaklands, Yateley GU46 57 D2
Oaklands Av SO40 53 A4
Oaklands Cl SP6 27 E3
Oaklands Rd,
Havant PO9 30 C5
Oaklands Rd,
Petersfield GU31 46 B2
Oaklea Cl PO7 20 D1
Oakleigh Gdns SO51 49 D3
Oakley Dr GU51 26 C3
Oakley La RG23 45 C6
Oakley Pl, Fleet GU51 26 B2
Oakley Pl, Hook RG27 32 C2
Oakley Rd GU35 18 C2
Oakmeadow Cl PO10 31 H2
Oakmont Dr PO8 21 A6
Oakmount Av,
Eastleigh SO53 22 A2
Oakmount Av,
Southampton SO40 53 A4
Oakmount Rd SO53 22 A3
Oakridge Rd SO15 53 D4
Oaks Coppice PO8 21 B3
Oaktree Ct SO41 42 C3
Oaktree Rd GU35 18 C6
Oakwood Av BH25 44 D1
Oakwood Cl SO51 49 E1
Oakwood Ct BH25 44 C1
Oakwood Rd PO11 52 B4
Oast La GU11 13 C4
Oatlands SO51 49 C2
Oban Cl RG23 45 B5
O'Bee Gdns RG26 34 B1
Ober Rd SO42 17 B3
Oberfield Rd SO42 17 A2
Oberon Cl PO7 54 D2
Oberursel Way GU11 13 B1
Ocean Way SO14 51 F6
Ockenden Cl PO5 47 D3
Oconnell Rd SO50 22 B4
O'Connor Rd GU11 25 D6
Odette Gdns RG26 34 E2
Offa Ct SO51 49 C2
Ogle Rd SO14 50 D3
O'Gorman Av GU14 25 A3
Olave Cl PO13 38 C4
Old Acre Rd GU34 12 B3
Old Barn Cl BH24 48 D3
Old Basing Mall RG21 16 D2
Old Brickfield Rd GU11 13 C4
Old Brickyard Rd SP6 27 A2
Old Copse Rd PO9 30 B3
Old Down Rd SP10 14 A1
Old Farm Cl BH24 48 E1
Old Farm La PO13 38 A1
Old Farmhouse Mws
SO41 41 C1
Old Farm Walk SO41 41 C3
Old Gosport Rd PO16 23 C4
Old La GU11 13 B4
Old Manor Way PO6 20 D4
Old Mill Ho BH24 48 A4
Old Mill La GU31 46 F1
Old Milton Grn BH25 44 B4
Old Milton Rd BH25 44 B4
Old Odiham Rd GU34 12 B1
Old Orchards SO41 41 E4
Old Pumphouse Cl
GU51 26 D1
Old Rd, Gosport PO12 29 C5
Old Rd, Romsey SO51 49 C2
Old Rd,
Southampton SO14 51 F6
Old Reading Rd RG21 16 E2
Old Rectory Gdns GU14 25 C1
Old Redbridge Rd SO15 53 D3
Old River PO7 36 C5
Old School Cl,
Fleet GU51 26 B2
Old School Cl,
Hook RG27 32 C3
Old School Dr PO11 52 D5
Old School La GU46 57 C2

Old School Rd GU33 40 C5
Old Stacks Gdns BH24 48 D4
Old Star Pl*,
Havant St PO1 47 B2
Old Station App SO23 56 F3
Old Station Way GU35 18 A2
Old Timbers PO11 52 B4
Old Turnpike PO16 23 D1
Old Welmore GU46 57 E3
Old Winton Rd SP10 14 B4
Old Wymering La PO6 20 A3
Oldcorne Hollow GU46 57 A3
Oliver Rd SO41 41 B3
Oliver Rise GU34 12 C2
Olivia Cl PO7 54 D1
Omega Pk GU34 12 E3
Omni Bsns Centre
GU34 12 E3
Ontario Way GU30 39 B5
Open Flds GU35 33 A2
Orange Row PO10 31 H6
Orchard Cl,
Alresford SO24 43 D6
Orchard Cl,
Farnham GU9 13 C5
Orchard Cl,
Fawley SO45 24 C2
Orchard Cl,
Fordingbridge SP6 27 E2
Orchard Cl,
Hayling Island PO11 52 B5
Orchard Cl,
Lymington SO41 42 D2
Orchard Cl,
North Baddesley SO52 45 A1
Orchard Cl,
Ringwood BH24 48 B2
Orchard Cl, Totton SO40 53 A6
Orchard Cl,
Waterlooville PO8 21 C2
Orchard Flds GU51 26 A1
Orchard Gdns SP6 27 E4
Orchard Gro BH25 44 C4
Orchard La, Alton GU34 12 D2
Orchard La,
Romsey SO51 49 B3
Orchard La,
Southampton SO14 51 E5
Orchard Mead BH24 48 B2
Orchard Mt BH24 48 B3
Orchard Pl,
Southampton SO14 51 E6
Orchard Pl,
Whitchurch RG28 55 B3
Orchard Rd,
Farnham GU9 13 C5
Orchard Rd,
Havant PO9 30 B5
Orchard Rd,
Hayling Island PO11 52 C5
Orchard Way SO45 35 A4
Ordnance Ct PO6 20 D6
Ordnance Rd,
Aldershot GU11 13 D1
Ordnance Rd,
Gosport PO12 28 D4
Ordnance Row PO1 47 B2
Oriental Ter SO14 50 D5
Orion Cl PO13 38 A1
Orkney Rd PO6 20 C2
Ormsby Rd PO5 47 D4
Orsmond Cl PO7 54 B3
Orwell Rd GU31 46 B4
Osborn Rd PO16 23 C2
Osborn Rd South PO16 23 C3
Osborn Way RG27 32 B6
Osborne Cl, Alton GU34 12 A3
Osborne Cl,
Waterlooville PO7 54 D2
Osborne Ct,
Farnborough GU14 25 B6
Osborne Ct,
Lymington SO41 42 C3
Osborne Dr SO53 22 A2
Osborne Rd,
Andover SP10 14 A3
Osborne Rd, Fleet GU52 26 C4
Osborne Rd,
Lee-on-the-Solent
PO13 38 B4
Osborne Rd,
New Milton BH25 44 C2
Osborne Rd,
Petersfield GU31 46 C2
Osborne Rd,
Southampton SO40 53 B5
Osborne Rd,
Southsea PO5 47 D5
Osbourne Rd GU14 25 B5
Osier Rd GU31 46 A4
Osprey Dr PO11 52 D4
Osprey Gdns PO13 38 D4
Othello Dr PO7 54 C1
Ottawa Dr GU30 39 C5
Otterbourne Cres RG26 34 E4
Overbrook SO45 35 A4

Overbrook Way SO52 45 A1
Overdale Pl*, South Hurst GU35 18 C6
Overdale Walk GU35 18 C6
Overstrand Cres SO41 42 E4
Overton Cl GU11 13 D5
Ovington Rd SO50 22 C6
Owen Rd SO50 22 B4
Owslebury Gro PO9 30 B1
Oxburgh Cl SO50 22 B1
Oxdrove Way SO24 43 A1
Oxey Cl BH25 44 C4
Oxford Av SO14 51 E1
Oxford Cl PO16 23 A1
Oxford Mws SO14 51 E5
Oxford Rd GU14 25 B4
Oxford St SO14 51 E5
Oxlease Cl SO51 49 D1
Oyster Mws*, French St PO1 47 B4
Oyster St PO1 47 B4

Pack La RG23 45 C4
Paddington Ho RG21 16 C3
Paddock Ct RG27 32 B3
Paddock End PO7 36 C6
Paddock Gdns SO41 41 C1
Paddock Way, Alresford SO24 43 C6
Paddock Way, Liphook GU30 39 B3
Paddock Way, Petersfield GU31 46 A4
Padget Rd BH24 48 E1
Padnell Av PO8 21 A5
Padnell Pl PO8 21 B6
Padnell Rd PO8 21 A5
Padstow Pl SP6 27 D4
Padwick Av PO6 20 C3
Pages Bungalows RG21 16 E3
Pages Yd RG28 55 B3
Paget Rd PO12 29 A6
Paget St SO14 51 G4
Pagham Cl PO10 31 H5
Paimpol Pl SO51 49 B4
Painters Pightle RG27 32 A5
Pakenham Dr GU11 13 B1
Pallant Gdns PO16 23 F2
Palmer Dr SP10 14 D3
Palmers Rd PO10 31 H5
Palmers Rd Ind Est PO10 31 H5
Palmerston Av PO16 23 D2
Palmerston Rd, Hayling Island PO11 52 C3
Palmerston Rd, Southampton SO14 51 E3
Palmerston Rd, Southsea PO5 47 D5
Palmerston St SO51 49 B3
Palmyra Rd PO12 28 A1
Pamplyn Cl SO41 41 B2
Pan St PO1 47 D1
Pangbourne Av PO6 20 D4
Pannall Rd PO12 28 A1
Pantile Dr RG27 32 D5
Panton Cl PO10 31 G2
Paper Mill La GU34 12 D2
Paradise St PO1 47 D1
Parchment St SO23 56 D2
Parham Cl BH25 44 A1
Parham Dr SO50 22 B2
Parham Rd PO12 28 C2
Parish Rd GU14 25 B5
Park Av, Lymington SO41 41 C1
Park Av, Winchester SO23 56 E2
Park Cl, Basingstoke RG23 45 C5
Park Cl, Brockenhurst SO42 17 C2
Park Cl, Lymington SO41 42 E3
Park Cl, Southampton SO45 35 C3
Park Close Rd GU34 12 D1
Park Corner Rd RG27 32 C2
Park Cres PO10 31 F5
Park Ct SO41 42 D3
Park Gro PO6 20 C4
Park Hill GU52 26 B6
Park La, Fareham PO16 23 B1
Park La, Lymington SO41 42 D4
Park La, Portsmouth PO6 20 C3
Park La, Southampton SO15 50 C1
Park La, Waterlooville PO8 21 A6
Park Mt SO24 43 C4
Park Par PO9 30 A1
Park Pl GU52 26 B6
Park Rd, Aldershot GU11 13 D4
Park Rd, Farnborough GU14 25 D5
Park Rd, Fordingbridge SP6 27 E3
Park Rd, Gosport PO12 29 B5
Park Rd, Lymington SO41 41 C1
Park Rd, Milford on Sea SO41 42 E3
Park Rd, New Milton BH25 44 A4
Park Rd, Petersfield GU31 46 C3
Park Rd, Portsmouth PO1 47 B3
Park Rd, Southampton SO32 15 A5
Park Rd, Waterlooville PO7 36 B4
Park Rd North PO9 30 A4
Park Rd South PO9 30 A5
Park St, Bordon GU35 18 C4
Park St, Gosport PO12 28 B3
Park St, Southsea PO5 47 C3
Park Vw BH25 44 C2
Park Walk SO14 50 D2
Park Way PO9 30 A4
Parkers Cl BH24 48 E2
Parkers Pl RG21 16 D3
Parkfields GU46 57 D3
Parkland Dr BH25 44 A4
Parkland Gro GU9 13 B4
Parklands SO40 53 B3
Parklands Av PO8 21 A3
Parklands Bsns Pk PO7 36 B6
Parklands Cl PO12 28 B2
Parkside, Ringwood BH24 48 B4
Parkside, Southampton SO40 53 A6
Parkwood Centre PO7 54 A1
Parnell Rd SO50 22 C5
Parr Rd PO6 20 A3
Parsonage Barn La BH24 48 B3
Parsonage Cl, Fordingbridge SP6 27 E3
Parsonage Cl, Petersfield GU31 46 E1
Parsonage Park Dr SP6 27 E2
Parsonage Rd SO14 51 G1
Parsons Cl, Fleet GU52 26 B6
Parsons Cl, Portsmouth PO6 20 C6
Partridge Av GU46 57 B2
Partridge Rd, Brockenhurst SO42 17 C4
Partridge Rd, Southampton SO45 35 B5
Passfield Av SO50 22 B5
Passfield Cl SO50 22 B4
Passfield Mill Bsns Pk GU30 19 G5
Passfield Rd GU30 19 H6
Passfield Walk*, Exton Rd PO9 30 D1
Passingham Walk PO8 21 A4
Pasteur Rd PO6 20 B2
Pat Bear Cl SO15 53 D4
Paternoster Row SO23 56 D3
Patricks Cl GU33 40 D4
Patricks Copse Rd GU33 40 C4
Patten Av GU46 57 C3
Paul Cl GU11 13 A3
Pavilion Rd GU11 13 A2
Paxton Rd PO14 23 A3
Peabody Rd GU14 25 C5
Peacock La PO1 47 C4
Peakfield PO7 36 B5
Pealsham Gdns SP6 27 D2
Pear Tree Cl GU35 19 E2
Pear Tree Rd GU35 19 E2
Pearce Smith Ct BH25 44 A6
Pearces Pl RG20 37 B3
Pearmain Dr SO41 41 D4
Pearman Dr SP10 14 D3
Peartree Ct SO41 41 E3
Peartree Rd SO45 35 A4
Peatmoor Cl GU51 26 A1
Pebble Cl PO11 52 D5
Pebmarsh Rd PO6 20 A3
Peckham Av BH25 44 B2
Peddlars Gro GU46 57 E2
Pedlars Walk BH24 48 A3
Peel Cl SO51 49 F1
Peel Ct, Farnborough GU14 25 B6
Peel Ct, Hook RG27 32 B3
Peel Gdns RG20 37 A1
Peel Rd PO12 28 C3
Peel St SO14 51 G2
Pegasus Av SO41 36 C3
Pegasus Ct, Farnborough GU14 25 C5
Pegasus Ct, Whitchurch RG28 55 B2
Pegasus Rd GU14 25 A3
Pelham Cl GU35 18 C6
Pelham Rd, Gosport PO12 28 B3
Pelham Rd, Southsea PO5 47 D4
Pelham Ter PO10 31 H5
Pelican Mead BH24 48 E4
Pelton Rd RG21 16 A1
Pemberton Rd SO43 37 C5
Pembridge Rd SP6 27 F2
Pembroke Cl, Eastleigh SO50 22 B1
Pembroke Cl, Portsmouth PO1 47 C4
Pembroke Cl, Romsey SO51 49 B3
Pembroke Cl, Southampton SO40 53 B3
Pembroke Ct SP10 14 C3
Pembroke Par GU46 57 E2
Pembroke Rd PO1 47 B4
Pembury Pl GU12 13 D2
Pembury Rd PO9 30 C5
Pen Cl SP10 14 D3
Pendleton Gdns SO45 24 A4
Penfords Pad SO32 15 D6
Peninsula Rd SO22 56 A4
Peninsula Sq SO23 56 B3
Penn Cl BH25 44 A4
Penner Rd PO9 30 A6
Pennington Cl SO41 41 B4
Pennington Oval SO41 41 A3
Penns Rd GU31 46 B2
Penns Wood GU14 25 C4
Penny Hedge BH25 44 C5
Penny St PO1 47 B4
Pennys Cl SP6 27 E2
Pennys Cres SP6 27 E2
Pennys Hatch RG20 37 C2
Pennys La SP6 27 E2
Penrhyn Cl, Aldershot GU12 13 C3
Penrhyn Cl, Eastleigh SO50 22 B2
Penrith Rd RG21 16 B4
Penryn Dr GU35 33 F3
Pentere Rd PO8 21 A2
Penwood Gdns*, Stockbridge Cl PO9 30 D1
Penwood Grn*, Minley Ct PO9 30 D1
Peper Harow PO8 21 B2
Pepys Cl PO12 29 B7
Percy Cl SO45 35 A1
Percy Rd PO12 28 C4
Perins Cl SO24 43 B6
Periwinkle Cl GU35 19 F2
Peronne Cl PO6 20 C6
Peronne Rd PO6 20 B6
Perowne St GU11 13 B1
Perry Way GU35 33 B4
Pervin Rd PO6 20 C3
Pesthouse La RG28 55 B2
Peterborough Rd PO6 20 A2
Peterscroft Av SO40 15 A3
Petersfield Bsns Pk GU31 46 A3
Petersfield By-Pass GU31 46 A4
Petersfield Rd, Bordon GU35 18 B6
Petersfield Rd, Havant PO9 30 A3
Petersfield Rd, Winchester SO23 56 F4
Petrie Rd PO13 38 C4
Petty Cl SO51 49 D4
Petworth Gdns SO50 22 C1
Peverel Ct GU30 39 B3
Phillips Cres GU35 33 B3
Phoenix Ct, Aldershot GU11 13 C2
Phoenix Ct, Newbury RG20 37 B2
Phoenix Park Ter RG21 16 C1
Picket Cl SP6 27 E3
Pickford St GU11 13 C2
Picton Rd SP10 14 A6
Pier Rd PO1 47 C5
Pier St PO13 38 B5
Pigeon House La PO7 20 A1
Pikes Hill SO43 37 B4
Pikes Hill Av SO43 37 B4
Pilgrim Park Homes Caravan Pk BH24 48 D2
Pilgrim Pl SO41 41 D3
Pilgrims Cl BH25 44 D1
Pilgrims Gate SO22 56 A1
Pilgrims Way, Andover SP10 14 C1
Pilgrims Way, Bordon GU35 33 A3
Pine Cl, Ashurst SO40 15 B1
Pine Cl, Dibden Purlieu SO45 35 A5
Pine Cl, North Baddesley SO52 45 A2
Pine Cotts GU33 40 C1
Pine Ct PO10 31 G2
Pine Gro, Fleet GU52 26 D5
Pine Gro, Havant PO9 30 C5
Pine Rd, Romsey SO51 49 F4
Pine Rd, Southampton SO32 15 D5
Pine View Cl GU9 13 B6
Pine Vw GU35 33 E2
Pine Walk GU33 40 C2
Pinehill Rd GU35 18 D4
Pinehurst RG26 34 D3
Pinehurst Av GU14 25 A3
Pinehurst Cotts GU14 25 A3
Pines Rd GU51 26 A1
Pinetree Gdns PO8 21 B6
Pinewood Cl, Romsey SO51 49 E1
Pinewood Cl, Sandhurst GU47 57 F1
Pinewood Cl, Tadley RG26 34 A2
Pinewood Cres SO45 35 C5
Pinewood Dr SO45 35 C5
Pinewood Hill GU51 26 B1
Pinewood Rd SO41 36 A2
Pinks La RG26 34 B1
Pipers Ash BH24 48 E2
Pipers Patch GU14 25 A1
Pipit Cl, Gosport PO12 28 B1
Pipit Cl, Waterlooville PO8 21 A2
Pippin Cl SO41 41 E3
Pipsons Cl GU46 57 D2
Pirbright Rd GU14 25 B3
Pirelli St SO14 50 C3
Pitreavie Rd PO6 20 C5
Pitts La SP10 14 A5
Plantation Rd RG26 34 B1
Plantation Way GU35 18 A6
Platform Rd SO14 51 E6
Player Ct SP6 27 F2
Players Cres SO40 53 A6
Pleasance Way BH25 44 B2
Pleasant Hill RG26 34 D2
Pless Rd SO41 42 B3
Plevna Pl GU34 12 C2
Plough Rd GU46 57 E2
Plover Dr SO41 42 F4
Plovers Rd PO8 21 B2
Plovers Way GU34 12 D1
Plumpton Way GU34 12 C4
Plymouth St PO5 47 D3
Polkerris Way GU52 26 D6
Polygon Ct SO15 50 C1
Pond Cft GU46 57 E2
Pond Cl BH25 44 B1
Pond Piece PO7 36 B5
Pond Rd, Bordon GU35 33 D4
Pond Rd, Farnborough GU14 25 A3
Pond View Cl GU51 26 D1
Pondside La SO32 15 B5
Pondtail Rd GU51 26 D3
Pook La PO9 30 C6
Pool Rd RG27 32 B2
Popes Hill RG20 37 A2
Popes La SO40 53 A4
Poplar Cl, Tadley RG26 34 A2
Poplar Cl, Waterlooville PO8 21 C6
Poplar Cres BH24 48 D3
Poplar Gro PO11 52 C3
Poplar Way, Ringwood BH24 48 D3
Poplar Way, Southampton SO52 45 B1
Porlock Rd SO16 53 D2
Portchester Sq RG21 16 D2
Porters La SO14 50 D6
Portersbridge St SO51 49 B3
Portland Cl GU31 46 E1
Portland Gro SP10 14 B3
Portland Rd, Southsea PO5 47 D5
Portland Rd, Waterlooville PO7 54 A2
Portland Sq GU33 40 C5
Portland St, Fareham PO16 23 D3
Portland St, Portsmouth PO1 47 C2
Portland St, Southampton SO14 50 D3
Portland Ter SO14 50 D2
Portsdown Hill Rd PO6 20 A1
Portsmouth Rd, Lee-on-the-Solent PO13 38 C6
Portsmouth Rd, Liphook GU30
Portsmouth Rd, Portsmouth PO6
Portsmouth Rd, Waterlooville PO8
Portswood Rd PO6
Portway RG26
Potash Ter PO9
Potley Hill Rd GU46
Potters Fld GU33
Potters Ind Pk GU52
Potters Walk RG21
Poulner Hill BH24
Poulner Pk BH24
Pound Cl, Bordon GU35
Pound Cl, Ringwood BH24
Pound Gate GU34
Pound Hill SO24
Pound La SO40
Pound Lea PO11
Pound Mdw RG28
Pound Rd, Aldershot GU12
Pound Rd, Lymington SO41
Pound Tree Rd SO14
Poveys Mead RG20
Powell Cres SO40
Powis Cl BH25
Powlett Rd SO41
Poyner Cl PO16
Poynings Pl PO1
Poynters Cl SP10
Prestwood Cl BH25
Preymead Ind Est GU9
Priestlands SO51
Priestlands La SO41
Priestlands Pl SO41
Priestlands Rd SO41
Primrose Dr RG27
Primrose Walk GU46
Primrose Way SO51
Primula Rd GU35
Prince Alfred St PO12
Prince George St PO1
Prince Georges St PO9
Prince of Wales Cl PO7
Prince of Wales Rd PO12
Princes Bldgs SO23
Princes Cl, Bordon GU35
Princes Cl, Southampton SO32
Princes Cres SO43
Princes Ct SO14
Princes Dr PO7
Princes Rd, Petersfield GU31
Princes Rd, Romsey SO51
Princes Way GU11
Princess Ct SO23
Princess Dr GU34
Princess Gdns PO8
Princess Rd SO40
Printers Row SO23
Priors Cl RG20
Priors Keep GU52
Priors Rd RG26
Priory Cl SO32
Priory Gdns SO23
Priory Rd SO50
Priory St GU14
Privet Rd GU35
Prochurch Rd PO8
Proctor Dr SO52
Promenade, Lee-on-the-Solent PO13
Promenade, Lee-on-the-Solent PO13
Propeller Rd GU14
Prospect La PO9
Prospect Pl SO45
Prospect Pl*, Mill La GU34
Prospect Rd SO24
Provost St SP6
Puddleslosh La SP6
Pulens Cres GU31
Pulens La GU31
Pullman Way BH24
Pump La PO8
Purbeck St PO1
Purbrook Rd RG26
Purbrook Way PO9
Pye St PO1
Pyle Cl PO8
Pylewell Rd SO45
Pyrford Mws SO41

'ay PO8 21 A2
.a GU46 57 E3
Rd SO23 56 F4
ws PO12 28 C4
, Fareham PO16 23 D3
,
gton SO41 41 E2
Cl GU30 39 C5
Annes Walk
16 D3
Elizabeth Av
41 C2
Elizabeth Dr
13 B1
Katherine Rd
41 E2
St,
orth PO10 31 H6
St,
gton SO41 41 C2
St,
outh PO1 47 B2
ictoria Ct GU14 25 A1
Av SP10 14 A3
Cl,
rough GU14 25 A6
Cl,
-the-Solent
38 C4
Cl,
y SO51 49 D3
Cl,
mpton SO45 35 C4
Cres,
ea PO5 47 D4
Cres,
oville PO8 21 C1
Ct GU14 25 B5
Gate Rd GU14 25 A6
Gdns SP6 27 E2
Gro PO5 47 D5
Par,
stoke RG21 16 C3
Par,
rst SO43 37 C5
Par,
oville PO7 54 B2
Pl PO5 47 D4
Rd, Alton GU34 12 B3
Rd,
stoke RG21 16 A3
Rd,
n PO16 23 C3
Rd,
t PO12 28 C3
Rd,
-the-Solent
38 C6
Rd,
rst SO43 37 D5
Rd,
y RG20 37 C3
Rd,
eld GU31 46 A2
Rd,
outh PO1 47 B1
Rd,
rch RG28 55 C4
Rd,
ot GU11 13 A2
Rd,
ough GU14 25 B5
Rd, Fleet GU52 26 C4
Ride SO52 45 A2
er SO14 51 E5
Way,
od BH24 48 C3
Way,
mpton SO14 51 E5
Way,
ea PO5 47 D4
head GU14 25 A2
ay BH25 44 A2
ee Way RG27 32 C5
s GU14 25 B4
BH24 48 B3
se Vw SO43 37 C4
P10 14 C3
e Rd GU34 12 B3
SO45 35 B3
d PO10 31 H3
Rd SO14 51 G1
Rd PO16 23 E1
t PO5 47 D3
GU14 25 A4
Rd GU14 25 A5
GU12 13 D3
O11 52 D4
otts SO15 53 D4
GU33 40 C5
l,
ton BH25 44 B2
l,
od BH24 48 E2
SO51 49 D1

Ramilles Pk GU11 25 C6
Ramley Rd SO41 41 A2
Rampart Gdns PO6 20 B6
Rampart Row PO12 29 E5
Ramparts Ind Est PO6 20 C6
Rampton Rd RG28 55 C4
Rams Walk GU31 46 C3
Ramsdell Cl RG26 34 E4
Ramsey Ct BH25 44 B2
Ramsey Rd PO11 52 C4
Ramshill GU31 46 D2
Ranfurly Gdns SO45 35 A5
Rapallo Cl GU14 25 B2
Rareridge La SO32 15 D4
Ratcliffe Rd SO45 35 B5
Raven Cl GU46 57 B3
Raven Rd, Hook RG27 32 B6
Raven Rd,
Southampton SO14 51 F1
Raven Sq SO50 22 A5
Ravens Way SO41 42 D4
Ravenscourt Rd SO41 41 C3
Ravenscroft RG27 32 C5
Rawlings Rd RG27 32 B6
Rayleigh Rd RG21 16 B3
Raynes Rd PO13 38 D6
Reading Rd,
Farnborough GU14 25 B5
Reading Rd, Hook RG27 32 B4
Reading Rd,
Yateley GU46 57 A1
Reading Rd North GU51 26 A2
Reading Rd South GU51 26 A3
Readon Cl GU31 46 D2
Record Rd PO10 31 F5
Recreation Rd SP10 14 C2
Rectory Cl,
Gosport PO12 29 A6
Rectory Cl, Tadley RG26 34 F4
Rectory La GU30 39 C1
Rectory Rd,
Basingstoke RG23 45 A5
Rectory Rd,
Farnborough GU14 25 B1
Rectory Rd, Havant PO9 30 B5
Rectory Rd, Hook RG27 32 B6
Red La GU35 33 D1
Red Lion La RG21 16 D3
Redan Gdns GU12 13 D2
Redan Rd GU12 13 D2
Redbridge Causeway
SO15 53 C4
Redbridge Dr SP10 14 A4
Redbridge Flyover
SO15 53 D3
Redbridge La SO16 53 D2
Redbridge Twrs SO16 53 D3
Rede Ct GU14 25 B4
Redhouse Mws
GU30 39 B5
Redlands La,
Emsworth PO10 31 H2
Redlands La,
Fareham PO14 23 A4
Redlynch Cl PO9 30 C2
Redon Way SP10 14 A1
Redshank Rd PO8 21 B1
Redvers Buller Rd GU11 25 B6
Redvers Cl SO41 41 D3
Redwood Cl,
Lymington SO41 41 C1
Redwood Cl,
Ringwood BH24 48 C3
Redwood Gro PO9 30 C1
Redwoods Way GU52 26 C6
Reedmace Cl PO7 54 C3
Reeds Pl PO12 28 B3
Reeds Rd PO12 28 B1
Reeves Rd GU12 13 D2
Regal Cl PO6 20 C3
Regency Gdns PO7 54 A3
Regency Pl BH24 48 B2
Regent Cl GU51 26 C3
Regent Mws GU31 46 A2
Regent Pl PO5 47 C4
Regent St, Fleet GU51 26 C3
Regent St,
Southampton SO14 50 D3
Regents Ct PO9 30 B6
Relay Rd PO7 54 A1
Renouf Cl SO41 41 B3
Reservoir La GU31 46 C1
Rest A Wyle Av PO11 52 C2
Retail Village,
Harbour Par SO15 50 C3
Reubens Cres RG26 34 E3
Reynards Cl RG26 34 D2
Reynolds Ct,
Andover SP10 14 A1
Reynolds Ct,
Romsey SO51 49 D4
Rhinefield Cl SO42 17 B3
Rhinefield Rd SO42 17 A3
Rhyme Hall Mws SO45 24 D2
Ribble Cl SO53 22 A1
Ribble Ct SP10 14 D1

Richard Moss Ho SO23 56 D2
Richards Cl SO45 24 B3
Richmond Cl,
Bordon GU35 18 C5
Richmond Cl,
Fleet GU52 26 B5
Richmond Cl,
Hayling Island PO11 52 A3
Richmond Ct SO41 42 D4
Richmond Dr PO11 52 A3
Richmond La SO51 49 D1
Richmond Pl,
Portsmouth PO1 47 C2
Richmond Pl,
Southsea PO5 47 D5
Richmond Rd,
Gosport PO12 28 A4
Richmond Rd,
Lee-on-the-Solent
PO13 38 B4
Richmond St SO14 51 F5
Riders Grn PO9 30 A1
Riders La PO9 30 A1
Ridgeway Cl SO53 22 A1
Ridgeway La SO41 41 C4
Ridgeway Walk SO53 22 A1
Ridley Cl GU52 26 A4
Rimes La RG26 34 B4
Rimington Gdns SO51 49 E1
Rimmers Ct*,
Broad St PO1 47 B4
Ringwood By-Pass
BH24 48 A3
Ringwood Dr SO52 45 A1
Ringwood Rd SO40 53 A4
Ringwood Trading Est
BH24 48 C4
Ritchie Cl PO11 52 C4
Ritson Way PO9 30 B4
Rival Moor Rd GU31 46 F3
River Ct SO41 41 E2
River Gdns SO41 42 E3
River Rd GU46 57 B1
River Way,
Andover SP10 14 C1
River Way, Havant PO9 30 B3
Riverdale Av PO7 54 C2
Riverdale Cl SP6 27 E2
Rivermead Cl SO51 49 A3
Rivermede GU35 19 E3
Rivers Cl GU14 25 C5
Riversdale Gdns PO9 30 B4
Riverside BH24 48 A4
Riverside Av PO16 23 F1
Riverside Cl GU33 40 B5
Riverside Gdns SO51 49 A4
Riverside Mws PO17 54 C5
Riverside Pl SP6 27 F3
Riverside Rd GU30 19 H5
Riverside Ter*,
Spring Gdns PO10 31 H5
Riverside Walk SO23 56 E4
Riverway Ind Est
GU34 12 E2
Robert Mack Ct*,
Britain St PO1 47 C2
Robert Whitworth Dr
SO51 49 C2
Roberts Cl PO17 54 B5
Roberts Rd, Hythe SO45 35 A2
Roberts Rd,
Southampton SO15 50 A1
Roberts Rd, Totton SO40 53 A6
Robertson Rd SO24 43 C5
Robin Gro BH25 44 B2
Robinia Cl PO7 54 C3
Robins Grove Cres
GU46 57 B2
Robinson Way GU35 18 D4
Rochester Gro GU51 26 B3
Rochester St SO14 51 G2
Rochford Rd,
Basingstoke RG21 16 A3
Rochford Rd,
Portsmouth PO6 20 A3
Rock Gdns GU11 13 A2
Rockville Dr PO7 54 A3
Roding Cl RG21 16 F2
Rodmel Ct GU14 25 D4
Rodney Way PO8 21 B2
Roebuck Cl,
New Milton BH25 44 D2
Roebuck Cl,
Portsmouth PO6 20 B4
Rogers Cl PO12 28 B2
Rogers Ct*,
Draymans Way GU34 12 C2
Rokes Pl GU46 57 A3
Roland Cl PO8 21 C2
Roman Grn PO7 36 A5
Roman Quay SP6 27 E4
Roman Rd SO45 35 A6
Roman Row SO32 15 C5
Roman St SO14 50 D4
Romsey By-Pass SO51 49 A4
Romsey Cl SO50 22 C3

Romsey Ind Est SO51 49 B2
Romsey Rd,
Eastleigh SO50 22 C3
Romsey Rd,
Lyndhurst SO43 37 C4
Romsey Rd,
Winchester SO22 56 A3
Rookcliff Way SO41 42 C3
Rookes Cl PO8 21 C2
Rookes La SO41 41 C4
Rookes Mws GU31 46 D2
Rookswood Cl RG27 32 C5
Rookwood Vw PO7 36 B4
Ropley Cl RG26 34 D3
Ropley Rd PO9 30 C1
Rosary Gdns GU46 57 D2
Rose Cl SO45 35 B5
Rose Hill PO8 21 A3
Rose Hodson Ct RG20 37 A1
Rose Rd SO40 53 B5
Rose Walk GU51 26 B1
Rosebank Cl RG26 34 E2
Rosebay Gdns RG27 32 D4
Rosebery Av,
Portsmouth PO6 20 C4
Rosebery Av,
Southampton SO45 35 C5
Rosebery Cres SO50 22 D1
Rosebery Rd SO24 43 C5
Rosedale GU12 13 D2
Rosedale Av SO51 49 D3
Rosedene Gdns GU51 26 A1
Roselands PO8 21 A3
Rosemary Dr RG26 34 E4
Rosemary La PO1 47 B2
Rosemary Walk PO13 38 D4
Rosemary Way PO8 21 B4
Rosewarne Ct SO23 56 C1
Rosewood Gdns BH25 44 A1
Rosewood Rd GU35 19 F2
Ross Rd BH24 48 E1
Ross Way PO13 38 C4
Rosslyn Cl SO52 45 B2
Rossmore Gdns GU11 13 A3
Rothbury Pk BH25 44 D2
Rother Cl GU31 46 F2
Rother Ho GU33 40 B5
Rotherbank Farm La
GU33 40 C3
Rotherwick Ct GU14 25 B5
Rotherwick Rd RG26 34 E4
Rothesay Rd PO12 28 A1
Round Cl GU46 57 F3
Round Hill SP6 27 E3
Round Way PO7 54 C1
Roundmead Rd RG21 16 A3
Rounton Rd GU52 26 C5
Rowan Av PO8 21 B6
Rowan Cl,
Lee-on-the-Solent
PO13 38 D5
Rowan Cl,
Romsey SO51 49 F4
Rowan Cl, Tadley RG26 34 F3
Rowan Dale GU52 26 A6
Rowan Rd, Havant PO9 30 D2
Rowan Rd, Tadley RG26 34 F3
Rowan Tree Cl GU33 40 C5
Rowans Pk SO41 41 C3
Rowanside Cl GU35 33 E4
Rowhill Av GU11 13 B3
Rowhill Cres GU11 13 B3
Rowhills Cl GU9 13 A4
Rowlands Av PO7 54 B1
Rowlands Castle Rd
PO8 21 D2
Rownhams La SO52 45 A1
Rownhams Rd SO52 45 B3
Rowse Cl SO51 49 C2
Roxburghe Cl GU35 18 D5
Royal Clarence Yd PO12 28 D3
Royal Cres SO14 51 F5
Royal Oak Cl GU46 57 E2
Royal Oak Pass SO23 56 C3
Royal Way PO7 54 C2
Royle Ct PO9 30 D1
Royston Av SO50 22 C2
Royston Pl BH25 44 C5
Rubens Cl BH25 44 C1
Rufford Cl,
Eastleigh SO50 22 C1
Rufford Cl, Fleet GU52 26 B5
Rufus Ct SO43 37 C6
Rumbridge Gdns SO40 53 B5
Rumbridge St SO40 53 B5
Rushes Fm GU31 46 B2
Rushes Rd GU31 46 B2
Rushfield Rd GU33 40 B5
Rushington Av SO40 53 A5
Rushington La SO40 53 A6
Rushmoor Cl GU52 26 B4
Rushmoor Ct GU14 25 B6
Ruskin Rd SO50 22 C2
Ruskin Way PO8 21 A4
Russell Cl PO13 38 C4
Russell Ct BH25 44 C2

Russell Pl PO16 23 B3
Russell Rd, Havant PO9 30 B3
Russell Rd,
Lee-on-the-Solent
PO13 38 C5
Russell St,
Gosport PO12 28 A3
Russell St,
Southampton SO14 51 E4
Russell Way GU31 46 D4
Russet Cl SO24 43 C5
Russett Cl SO41 41 E3
Russett Rd GU34 12 D2
Russetts Dr GU51 26 B3
Rustic Glen GU52 26 A6
Rutland Cl GU11 13 C1
Rydal Cl GU35 18 D2
Rydal Dr GU52 26 A6
Rydal Rd PO12 28 A1
Ryde Gdns GU46 57 B2
Ryde Pl PO13 38 D6
Ryde Ter SO14 51 G5
Rye Dale SO40 15 B1
Rye Paddock La SO45 24 D1
Ryebeck Rd GU52 26 B5
Ryecroft PO9 30 D4
Ryefield Cl GU31 46 F3
Ryelaw Rd GU52 26 B6
Ryves Av GU46 57 A3

Sabre Ct GU11 13 A2
Sackville St PO5 47 D3
Sadlers La SO45 35 B5
Sainsbury Cl SP10 14 A5
St Albans Rd,
Havant PO9 30 C1
St Albans Rd,
Southampton SO14 51 F1
St Andrews Cl SO52 45 A1
St Andrews Rd,
Bordon GU35 18 A5
St Andrews Rd,
Gosport PO12 28 B4
St Andrews Rd,
Hayling Island PO11 52 D5
St Andrews Rd,
Southampton SO14 51 E1
St Annes Cl SP10 14 A4
St Annes Gdns SO41 41 C3
St Anns Cres PO12 28 A3
St Anns Rd PO8 21 C1
St Barbe Cl SO51 49 D4
St Benedicts Cl GU11 13 B3
St Blaize Rd SO51 49 E2
St Bonnet Dr SO32 15 C5
St Catherines Rd SO50 22 C1
St Christophers Cl
SO52 45 B3
St Clement St SO23 56 C3
St Clements Cl SO51 49 B2
St Clements Yd SO23 56 C3
St Colmans Av PO6 20 C3
St Cross Rd SO23 56 C4
St Davids Cl GU9 13 A5
St Edwards Rd,
Gosport PO12 28 B4
St Edwards Rd,
Southsea PO5 47 D4
St Faiths Cl PO12 28 A3
St Francis Cl SO45 24 A6
St Francis Pl PO9 30 A2
St Francis Rd,
Gosport PO12 29 C7
St Francis Rd,
Southampton SO45 24 A6
St Georges Av PO9 30 D4
St Georges Bsns Centre
PO1 47 B2
St Georges Cl GU9 13 C6
St Georges Cres SP6 27 E2
St Georges Rd,
Cosham PO6 20 C3
St Georges Rd,
Fordingbridge SP6 27 E2
St Georges Rd,
Portsmouth PO1 47 B3
St George's Rd,
Aldershot GU12 13 C3
St George's Rd,
Badshot Lea GU9 13 C6
St Georges Rd East
GU12 13 D2
St Georges Sq,
Portsmouth PO1 47 B2
St Georges Sq,
Southampton SO32 15 C5
St Georges St,
Southampton SO14 51 E4
St Georges St,
Winchester SO23 56 C2
St Georges Walk PO7 54 A2
St Georges Way PO1 47 C2
St Giles Cl SO23 56 F4
St Giles Hill SO23 56 F3
St James Ct GU51 26 A3
St James La SO22 56 A3

St James Rd, Emsworth PO10 31 G5
St James Rd, Fleet GU51 26 A3
St James Ter SO22 56 B3
St James Villas SO22 56 B4
St James's Rd PO5 47 D3
St James's St PO1 47 C2
St Johns Cl, Gosport PO12 28 B3
St Johns Cl, Hayling Island PO11 52 B5
St Johns Cl, Hook RG27 32 C5
St Johns Gdns SO51 49 B2
St Johns Piece RG23 45 D6
St Johns Rd, Andover SP10 14 C2
St Johns Rd, Basingstoke RG23 45 D4
St Johns Rd, Eastleigh SO50 22 D2
St Johns Rd, Portsmouth PO6 20 C3
St Johns St, Southampton SO45 35 C2
St Johns St, Winchester SO23 56 F3
St Johns Walk RG21 16 D2
St Joseph's Rd GU12 13 C3
St Judes Cl PO5 47 D4
St Lawrence Rd, Alton GU34 12 C2
St Lawrence Rd, Eastleigh SO50 22 D2
St Lawrence Rd, Southampton SO14 51 F5
St Leonards Av PO11 52 C4
St Lucia Pk GU35 18 D2
St Lukes Rd PO12 28 A2
St Margarets Rd PO11 52 C4
St Marks Cl, Farnborough GU14 25 B5
St Marks Cl, Gosport PO12 29 A6
St Marks Rd, Gosport PO12 29 A7
St Marks Rd, Lymington SO41 41 A2
St Martins Cl SO23 56 F2
St Mary Gro SO41 36 C3
St Mary St SO14 51 F2
St Marys SO51 49 B4
St Marys Av PO12 29 A6
St Marys Bldgs SO14 51 F3
St Marys Cl GU34 12 C3
St Marys Ct RG21 16 E3
St Marys Pl SO14 51 E3
St Marys Rd, Hayling Island PO11 52 B4
St Marys Rd, Liss GU33 40 B4
St Marys Rd, Newbury RG20 37 B2
St Marys Rd, Southampton SO14 51 E1
St Matthews Cl SO14 51 F2
St Matthews Rd PO6 20 C3
St Michaels Cl, Fleet GU51 26 D3
St Michaels Cl, Southampton SO45 24 A4
St Michaels Gdns SO23 56 C4
St Michaels Rd, Portsmouth PO1 47 C3
St Michaels Rd, Southampton SO40 53 A3
St Michaels Rd, Winchester SO23 56 C4
St Michael's Rd GU12 13 C3
St Michaels Sq SO14 50 D5
St Michaels St SO14 50 D5
St Nicholas Cl GU51 26 A2
St Nicholas Row PO17 54 C5
St Nicholas St PO1 47 C4
St Pauls Hill SO22 56 B1
St Pauls Rd PO5 47 C3
St Pauls Sq PO5 47 C3
St Peter St SO23 56 D2
St Peters Cl RG26 34 E4
St Peters Gdns GU46 57 D2
St Peters Pk GU11 13 A3
St Peters Rd, Petersfield GU31 46 C3
St Peters Rd, Southampton SO14 51 F2
St Peters Sq PO10 31 H6
St Peters St SO32 15 C5
St Philips Ct GU51 26 C1
St Swithun Cl SO32 15 B5
St Swithun St SO23 56 C4
St Swithuns Cl SO51 49 F2
St Swithuns Ter SO23 56 C4
St Swithuns Villas SO23 56 C4
St Thomas Pass SO23 56 C3
St Thomas Pk SO41 41 C2
St Thomas St, Lymington SO41 41 D2
St Thomas St, Winchester SO23 56 C4
St Thomas's Ct*, St Thomas's St PO1 47 B4
St Thomas's St PO1 47 B4
St Valerie Rd PO12 29 B5
St Vincent Cres PO8 21 B2
St Vincent Rd PO12 28 B2
St Vincent St PO5 47 D3
Salerno Cl GU11 13 B1
Salesian Vw GU14 25 D5
Salisbury Cl, Alton GU34 12 D4
Salisbury Cl, Eastleigh SO50 22 D3
Salisbury Ct SO50 22 D3
Salisbury Rd, Alresford SO24 43 C5
Salisbury Rd, Andover SP10 14 A4
Salisbury Rd, Farnborough GU14 25 B2
Salisbury Rd, Fordingbridge SP6 27 F3
Salisbury Rd, Portsmouth PO6 20 C4
Salisbury Rd, Ringwood BH24 48 B2
Salisbury Rd, Southampton SO40 53 A3
Salisbury Road Arc SO40 53 A4
Salisbury St, Fordingbridge SP6 27 F3
Salisbury St, Southampton SO15 50 D1
Salisbury Ter PO13 38 C5
Salterns La, Hayling Island PO11 52 D4
Salterns La, Southampton SO45 24 C1
Saltmarsh La PO11 52 A2
Saltmarsh Rd SO14 51 F5
Saltram Rd GU14 25 D3
Salvia Cl PO7 54 C3
Samber Cl SO41 41 B2
Sampson Rd PO1 47 B1
San Diego Rd PO12 28 B2
Sanderlings BH24 48 E4
Sandford Cl RG20 37 C2
Sandford Ct GU11 13 A2
Sandford Rd, Aldershot GU11 13 A2
Sandford Rd, Tadley RG26 34 C2
Sandhill La PO13 38 D3
Sandhurst Rd, Southampton SO15 50 B1
Sandhurst Rd, Yateley GU46 57 E2
Sandilands Way SO45 35 C5
Sandle Copse SP6 27 B3
Sandleheath Rd SP6 27 A2
Sandmartin Cl BH25 44 A6
Sandown Cl GU34 12 D4
Sandown Cres GU11 13 C4
Sandown Rd PO6 20 B4
Sandpiper Cl PO8 21 B1
Sandringham Cl GU34 12 A3
Sandringham Rd GU31 46 C2
Sandy Cl GU31 46 F3
Sandy La, Hook RG27 32 C3
Sandy La, Lyndhurst SO43 37 B6
Sandy La, Southampton SO52 45 D1
Sandy La, Southampton SO52 45 D2
Saor Mws SP10 14 A2
Sapphire Ridge PO7 54 D2
Saracen Cl SO41 41 B4
Sarah Way GU14 25 A2
Sarisbury Cl RG26 34 D3
Sarum Hill RG21 16 B3
Sarum Rd RG26 34 C2
Saunders Gdns RG26 34 E3
Savernake Cl SO51 49 E2
Savile Cres GU35 18 D4
Savoy Cl SP10 14 B4
Saxon Mws GU34 12 C2
Saxon Rd, Blackfield SO45 24 A4
Saxon Rd, Southampton SO15 50 A2
Saxon Walk SO53 22 A1
Saxon Way SO51 49 E3
Saxony Way GU46 57 C4
School Cl GU52 26 D3
School La, Emsworth PO10 31 G6
School La, Liss GU33 40 C5
School La, Lymington SO41 41 D2
School La, Milford on Sea SO41 42 E2
School La, Ringwood BH24 48 B3
School La, Waterlooville PO7 36 A4
School La, Yateley GU46 57 B3
School Rd, Bordon GU35 18 C2
School Rd, Fareham PO17 54 C5
School Rd, Fawley SO45 24 C2
School Rd, Havant PO9 30 A5
School Rd, Hythe SO45 35 B2
School Rd, Romsey SO51 49 F1
School Rd, Totton SO40 53 B5
Schooners Cl PO13 38 C4
Scots Ct RG27 32 D4
Scott Rd, Cosham PO6 20 C6
Scott Rd, Eastleigh SO50 22 B4
Scott Rd, Portsmouth PO1 47 B1
Scullards La SO14 50 D3
Scures Rd RG27 32 A5
Sea Crest Rd PO13 38 D5
Sea Front PO11 52 A4
Sea Front Est PO11 52 D5
Sea Grove Av PO11 52 C5
Sea La PO13 38 A2
Sea Mill Gdns*, Kent St PO1 47 C2
Sea Rd, Lymington SO41 42 E4
Sea Rd, New Milton BH25 44 A5
Seafield Cl BH25 44 B5
Seafield Rd BH25 44 A5
Seafields PO10 31 G6
Seagers Ct PO1 47 B4
Seagull La PO10 31 H5
Seahorse Walk PO12 28 D4
Seal Ho RG21 16 D2
Seal Rd RG21 16 D3
Sealark Rise PO12 28 C1
Seamead PO13 38 A2
Searing Way RG26 34 D2
Searles Cl SO24 43 D5
Searles La RG27 32 D4
Seathrift Cl PO13 38 C4
Seaton Cl SO41 41 D1
Seaview Ter PO10 31 H6
Seaward Av BH25 44 A5
Seaward Rd SO45 35 C3
Seaward Twr PO12 28 E4
Seaway BH25 44 D5
Seawinds SO41 42 B3
Sebastian Gro PO7 54 D1
Sebastopol Rd GU11 13 C1
Second Av, Havant PO9 30 C4
Second Av, Portsmouth PO6 20 B3
Second Marine Av BH25 44 C6
Second St SO45 24 B2
Sedgeley Gro PO12 28 A1
Selangor Av PO10 31 E5
Selborne Av GU11 13 D5
Selborne Cl GU31 46 D1
Selborne Dr SO50 22 C2
Selborne Rd PO9 30 A5
Selborne Way GU35 18 A5
Selbourne Walk*, Ashurst RG26 34 D3
Selsdon Av SO51 49 E2
Selsmore Rd PO11 52 C4
Selwyn Dr GU46 57 B2
Selwyn Gdns SO50 22 C2
Senlac Rd SO51 49 E3
Sentinel Cl PO7 54 D1
Serpentine Rd, Fareham PO16 23 C1
Serpentine Rd, Southsea PO5 47 D5
Service Rd PO6 20 A3
Seton Dr RG27 32 A6
Sevenoaks Rd PO6 20 B3
Seventh St SO45 24 A1
Severn Ct SP10 14 D1
Severn Gdns RG23 45 C6
Seville Cres SP10 14 C2
Seward Rise SO51 49 F2
Seymoor Ct GU51 26 B1
Seymour Cl SO53 22 A1
Seymour La SO52 45 B2
Seymour Rd, Bordon GU35 33 E3
Seymour Rd, Lee-on-the-Solent PO13 38 D6
Seymour Rd, Ringwood BH24 48 C1
Shaftesbury Ct, Bordon GU35 18 C5
Shaftesbury Ct, Farnborough GU14 25 B5
Shaftesbury Rd, Gosport PO12 28 C4
Shaftesbury Rd, Southsea PO5 47 D5
Shaftesbury St SP6 27 E4
Shaggs Mdw SO43 37 C6
Shakespeare Bsns Pk SO50 22 D3
Shakespeare Rd SO50 22 B2
Shalbourne Rd PO12 28 A1
Shamrock Cl PO12 28 D4
Shamrock Way SO45 35 B1
Shannon Ct SP10 14 D1
Sharpley Cl SP6 27 D2
Sharps Rd PO9 30 C1
Sharvells Rd SO41 42 C2
Shaw La RG26 34 B4
Shaw Pightle RG27 32 A5
Shaw Rd BH24 48 E1
Shawcross Ind Pk PO6 20 C6
Shawfield Rd PO9 30 C5
Shear Hill GU31 46 E1
Shearing Cres SP10 14 D3
Sheep Fair SP10 14 C3
Sheep St GU31 46 C3
Sheepwash Rd, Waterlooville PO8 21 C5
Sheepwash Rd, Waterlooville PO8 21 D2
Sheet Link GU31 46 E1
Sheldons La RG27 32 B5
Sheldons Rd RG27 32 B5
Sheldrake Gdns SO41 36 C2
Shelley Cl GU51 26 B3
Shelley Walk GU46 57 B4
Shelley Way SO41 42 E3
Shenstone Ct BH25 44 B3
Shepherds Down SO24 43 C6
Shepherds Row SP10 14 C3
Shepherds Spring La SP10 14 B2
Shepherds Way GU30 39 C5
Sheppard Cl, Waterlooville PO8 21 A2
Sheppard Cl, Whitchurch RG28 55 B3
Sherborne Ct SO50 22 C1
Sherborne Rd RG21 16 B1
Sherbourne Rd GU14 25 C5
Sherfield Av PO9 30 B1
Sheridan Cl GU11 13 C3
Sheridan Cres RG26 34 B2
Sheridan Ho SO23 56 C2
Sheringham Rd PO6 20 A2
Sherringham Cl SO45 24 D2
Sherwin Walk PO12 29 A6
Sherwood Cl GU33 40 C2
Sherwood Rd PO12 28 A4
Shetland Cl PO6 20 C2
Shinglebank Dr SO41 42 D3
Ship Leopard St PO1 47 B2
Shipley Cl GU34 12 D1
Shipley Ct GU30 39 B4
Shire Ct GU11 13 A2
Shires Way GU46 57 D1
Shirley Rd SO15 50 A1
Shoblands Way SO45 35 C5
Shoot La PO13 38 D3
Shore Cl SO41 42 E4
Shore Cres SO32 15 C5
Shore La SO32 15 C5
Shore Rd SO45 35 C2
Shorefield Cres SO41 42 C2
Shorefield Rd SO41 42 A1
Shorefield Way SO41 42 C2
Short Hill SO51 49 F1
Short Row PO1 47 B1
Short St GU11 13 B1
Shotterfield Ter GU33 40 C4
Shrubbs Av SO41 41 D1
Shrubbs Hill Gdns SO43 37 C6
Shrubbs Hill Rd SO43 37 B5
Shyshack La RG26 34 B1
Sian Cl GU52 26 C5
Sidmouth Rd SP10 14 D3
Silchester Rd RG26 34 E1
Silkweavers Rd SP10 14 C2
Silver Birch Cl, Fleet GU52 26 A6
Silver Birch Cl, Liss GU33 40 C4
Silver Glades GU46 57 C4
Silver Hill SO23 56 E3
Silver Park Cl GU52 26 C5
Silver St, Lymington SO41 36 A1
Silver St, Lyndhurst SO43 37 A5
Silver St, Southsea PO5 47 C4
Silverdale, Fleet GU52 26 B4
Silverdale, New Milton BH25 44 C5
Silverdale Rd RG26 34 D2
Silvers End SO45 35 B5
Silversands Gdns PO11
Silverthorne Way PO7
Silvertrees PO10
Silvester Rd PO8
Simmons Walk RG21
Simnel St SO14
Simpson Rd PO6
Sir Christopher Cl SO45
Sir Georges Rd SO15
Siskin Cl SO32
Siskin Gro PO7
Six Oaks Rd SO52
Sixth Av PO6
Skipper Way PO13
Sky End La SO41
Skylark Rise RG28
Skylark Way PO13
Slade Cl SO41
Slade Ct PO1
Slades Hill SO45
Slindon Gdns PO9
Slindon St PO1
Slingsby Cl PO1
Smallfield Dr RG27
Smallwood Dr RG26
Smeeton Rd PO13
Smith Cl SO45
Smith St PO12
Smithe Cl SO50
Smiths Fld SO51
Snowberry Cres PO9
Soake Rd PO7
Soberton Rd PO9
Solartron Rd GU14
Solbys Rd RG21
Solent Av SO41
Solent Cl, Eastleigh SO53
Solent Cl, Lymington SO41
Solent Ct SO41
Solent Dr, Hayling Island PO11
Solent Dr, New Milton BH25
Solent Dr, Southampton SO45
Solent Pines SO41
Solent Rd, Havant PO9
Solent Rd, Hythe SO45
Solent Rd, Southampton SO15
Solent Way SO41
Somborne Dr PO9
Somerley Vw BH24
Somers Rd PO5
Somerset Av GU35
Somerset Rd GU14
Somervell Cl PO12
Somervell Dr PO16
Somerville Cres GU46
Somerville Rd BH24
Sonnet Way PO7
Soper Gro RG21
Sorrel Cl, Romsey SO5
Sorrel Cl, Waterlooville PO7
South Atlantic Dr GU11
South Av, New Milton BH25
South Av, Portsmouth PO6
South Av, Southampton SO45
South Cl, Alresford SO24
South Cl, Havant PO9
South Cl, Romsey SO5
South Cross St PO12
South End Rd SP10
South Front, Romsey SO51
South Front, Southampton SO14
South Gro SO41
South Hurst GU35
South Lawns Walk BH25
South Normandy PO1
South Pl PO13
South Rd, Alresford SO24
South Rd, Hayling Island PO11
South Rd, Liphook GU30
South Rd, Newbury RG20
South St, Andover SP
South St, Eastleigh SO50
South St, Emsworth PO10
South St, Farnborough GU14
South St, Gosport PO

ıt, Havant PO9 30 B5
ıt,
gton SO41 41 B3
t,
ampton SO45 35 B4
t, Southsea PO5 47 D4
er PO1 47 B2
iew Cl PO8 21 A5
iew Gdns SP10 14 C4
w SO22 56 A2
Veirs SO42 17 A4
Western Ho SO14 51 F5
npton Rd,
gh SO50 22 C6
npton Rd,
m PO16 23 C2
npton Rd,
gbridge SP6 27 F4
npton Rd,
gton SO41 41 C1
npton Rd,
urst SO43 37 D5
npton Rd,
outh PO6 20 A3
npton Rd,
ood BH24 48 B3
npton Rd,
y SO51 49 C4
npton Rd,
npton SO45 35 A2
npton Row*,
: PO1 47 B2
npton St GU14 25 A6
ourne Rd SO41 41 B3
ook Cl PO9 30 B6
ook Rd,
PO9 30 B6
ook Rd,
mpton SO15 50 B2
Dr GU51 26 C2
wn Rd,
outh PO6 20 C3
wn Rd,
RG26 34 D2
d Rd RG21 16 B3
n Haye RG27 32 B3
n La BH25 44 A4
n Oaks BH25 44 B4
n Rd,
stoke RG21 16 C4
n Rd,
GU35 18 C1
n Rd,
ton SO41 41 C2
n Rd,
mpton SO15 50 B3
nhay PO7 36 B5
ld BH24 48 B4
ld Mws BH24 48 B4
lds Cl SO32 15 C5
te St SO23 56 C4
te Villas SO23 56 C4
nds SO41 41 B4
gh Gro PO11 52 B3
gh Rd,
rth PO10 31 G2
gh Rd,
PO9 30 C5
ead Rd GU11 13 C3
a St PO5 47 D4
a Ter PO5 47 C4
w Rd GU35 33 D3
w Rise GU34 12 B1
ark Cl GU46 57 C2
ys PO13 38 B1
ck Hill Rd PO6 20 A1
ck Rd,
n PO17 54 C5
ck Rd,
ooville PO7 36 A5
n Av PO12 28 C1
n Ct GU51 26 A2
e Ho SO23 56 C2
d Cl SO22 56 A4
d Rd SO22 56 A4
Ct PO13 38 D3
Cl, Fleet GU52 26 D5
Cl,
Island PO11 52 C4
Dr PO13 38 D5
Rd,
h SO50 22 B5
Rd,
rth PO10 31 F2
Rd,
lton BH25 44 C2
s Ct GU35 18 C6
Cl GU34 12 D1
SP10 14 D1
: SO22 56 B1
: PO1 47 D1
Hill SO40 53 A6
Way SO40 53 A6
RG26 34 F3
BH25 44 C5
Cl PO9 30 D3

Spindle Warren PO9 30 D3
Spindlewood Cl BH25 44 B4
Spinnaker Cl PO11 52 B3
Spinney Dale SO45 35 C5
Spinney Gdns SO45 35 C5
Spitalfields Rd GU34 12 C2
Spitalhatch GU34 12 D2
Spithead Av PO12 29 C7
Spittlefields BH24 48 D3
Spokane Cl GU11 13 B3
Spring Ct PO13 38 C5
Spring Garden La PO12 28 C3
Spring Gdns,
Alresford SO24 43 B6
Spring Gdns,
Emsworth PO10 31 H6
Spring Gdns,
Portsmouth PO1 47 D2
Spring Gdns,
Southampton SO52 45 B2
Spring Pl SO51 49 A3
Spring Rd,
Lymington SO41 41 F3
Spring Rd,
Southampton SO45 35 C3
Spring St PO1 47 D1
Spring Vale PO8 21 B4
Spring Way SO24 43 B6
Spring Woods GU52 26 A4
Springbank Ct BH24 48 D3
Springfield RG23 45 D5
Springfield Av RG27 32 B2
Springfield Cl,
Fareham PO17 54 C5
Springfield Cl,
Lymington SO41 41 F3
Springfield La GU51 26 A2
Springfield Way PO13 38 A1
Springholm Cl GU9 13 C6
Springwood Av PO7 54 C3
Springwood Ct BH24 48 D3
Spruce Av,
Bordon GU35 18 A4
Spruce Av,
Waterlooville PO7 54 C3
Spruce Walk PO13 38 D4
Spur Rd,
Portsmouth PO6 20 B3
Spur Rd,
Waterlooville PO7 54 B2
Spurs Ct GU11 13 A2
Squarefield Gdns RG27 32 C4
Squirrels Walk SO45 35 A5
Stable Cl RG27 32 A5
Stable La*,
Folly La GU31 46 C3
Stable Rd GU35 18 C1
Stable Vw GU46 57 D1
Stafford Rd GU31 46 C1
Staffwise Bsns Centre
PO6 20 B4
Stagshorn Rd PO8 21 C1
Stakes Hill Rd PO7 54 B2
Stallard Cl PO10 31 G5
Stallards La BH24 48 A3
Stamford Av PO11 52 A4
Stamshaw Prom PO6 20 A6
Stanbridge Rd PO9 30 C2
Standford Ct PO9 30 D1
Standford Hill GU35 19 F5
Standford La GU35 19 G5
Standford St SO14 51 F4
Stanfield RG26 34 D2
Stanhope Rd PO1 47 D2
Stanley La PO5 47 D5
Stanley Rd,
Emsworth PO10 31 H6
Stanley Rd,
Lymington SO41 41 F4
Stanley St PO5 47 D5
Stannington Cl BH25 44 C3
Stannington Cres SO40 53 A3
Stannington Way SO40 53 B3
Stanstead Rd SO50 22 B2
Stanton Dr GU51 26 A3
Stanton Rd GU31 46 B2
Staple Gdns SO23 56 C2
Staple Ho SO23 56 C2
Stapleford Cl SO51 49 E1
Star La BH24 48 A3
Starling Sq SO50 22 A5
Station App,
Alresford SO24 43 D4
Station App,
Andover SP10 14 A2
Station App,
Basingstoke RG21 16 C1
Station App,
Farnborough GU14 25 A1
Station App,
Portsmouth PO1 47 B2
Station App,
Whitchurch RG28 55 B1
Station Cl PO17 54 C5
Station Hill,
Eastleigh SO50 22 D4

Station Hill,
Winchester SO23 56 C1
Station Mall RG21 16 D2
Station Rd,
Aldershot GU11 13 C2
Station Rd,
Alresford SO24 43 D4
Station Rd, Alton GU34 12 D2
Station Rd,
Basingstoke RG23 45 A5
Station Rd,
Bishops Waltham SO32 15 B5
Station Rd,
Bordon GU35 18 B2
Station Rd,
Fareham PO17 54 C5
Station Rd,
Farnborough GU14 25 A1
Station Rd,
Fordingbridge SP6 27 C3
Station Rd,
Hayling Island PO11 52 A3
Station Rd, Hook RG27 32 B5
Station Rd,
Liphook GU30 39 B5
Station Rd, Liss GU33 40 B4
Station Rd,
New Milton BH25 44 C2
Station Rd,
Petersfield GU31 46 C2
Station Rd,
Romsey SO51 49 B3
Station Rd, Totton SO15 53 D4
Station Rd,
Whitchurch RG28 55 B1
Station Rd,
Winchester SO23 56 B2
Station Rd North SO40 53 C4
Station Rd South SO40 53 C4
Station St,
Lymington SO41 41 E2
Station St,
Portsmouth PO1 47 D2
Staunton Av PO11 52 A4
Stead Cl PO11 52 D4
Steel St PO5 47 C4
Steele Cl SO53 22 A3
Steeple Dr GU34 12 B2
Stem La BH25 44 A1
Step Ter SO22 56 A2
Stephen Cl PO8 21 B6
Stephen Martin Gdns
SP6 27 D3
Stephens Rd RG26 34 F3
Stephenson Cl PO12 29 A6
Stevens Hill GU46 57 E3
Stiles Dr SP10 14 D3
Stillions Cl GU34 12 D3
Stilwell Cl GU46 57 E2
Stirling Av PO7 54 C2
Stirling Cl,
New Milton BH25 44 D2
Stirling Cl,
Southampton SO40 53 B3
Stirling Cres SO40 53 B3
Stirling Walk SO51 49 B3
Stockbridge Cl PO9 30 D1
Stockbridge Rd SO22 56 A1
Stockbridge Way GU46 57 D4
Stockheath La PO9 30 A3
Stockheath Rd PO9 30 A1
Stockheath Way PO9 30 B2
Stockton Av GU51 26 B1
Stockton Pk GU51 26 B1
Stockwood Way GU9 13 B4
Stodham La GU33 40 A6
Stoke Gdns PO12 28 C4
Stoke Ho RG26 34 D2
Stoke Rd PO12 28 B4
Stone La PO12 29 B5
Stone Sq PO9 30 B2
Stone St PO5 47 D4
Stonechat Cl GU31 46 F3
Stonechat Rd PO8 21 A2
Stonedene Cl GU35 33 E4
Stoneham Cl GU31 46 A2
Stoneham La SO50 22 A6
Stoneham Pk GU31 46 A2
Stonehill Pk GU35 33 E4
Stonehill Rd GU35 33 E4
Stonehills SO45 24 D2
Stonehouse Rd GU30 39 D3
Stoneleigh Av SO41 36 A1
Stonemasons Ct SO23 56 D2
Stoney Cl GU46 57 D4
Stony La PO1 47 B1
Stookes Way GU46 57 B4
Stopples La SO41 36 A1
Stour Cl GU31 46 B4
Stour Rd RG23 45 C6
Stourhead Cl GU14 25 C1
Stovold's Way GU11 13 B3
Stragwyne Cl SO52 45 A1
Stratfield Av RG26 34 E4
Stratfield Ct RG26 34 F3
Stratfield Pl BH25 44 A2

Stratford Ct GU14 25 B2
Stratford Pl,
Eastleigh SO50 22 D3
Stratford Pl,
Lymington SO41 41 C1
Stratford Rd PO7 54 C1
Strathfield Rd SP10 14 A6
Strathmore Rd PO12 28 C4
Streamside GU51 26 B3
Street End SO52 45 C1
Strides La BH24 48 A3
Strokins Rd RG20 37 B1
Strongs Cl SO51 49 E2
Stroudwood Rd PO9 30 B2
Stubbington Av GU35 18 C5
Stubbington La PO13 38 A2
Stubbs Ct SP10 14 A1
Stuckton Rd SP6 27 F4
Studland Dr SO41 42 C3
Studland Rd PO13 38 C5
Stukeley Rd RG21 16 A4
Sudbury Rd PO6 20 A2
Suffolk Rd SP10 14 A4
Sullivan Cl GU14 25 A1
Sultan Rd PO10 31 H5
Summerhill Rd PO8 21 A5
Summerlands Walk*,
Bramshaw Ct PO9 30 D1
Sun Hill Cres SO24 43 D6
Sun La SO24 43 D6
Sun St PO1 47 C2
Sunbeam Way PO12 29 B5
Sunbury Cl GU35 18 D4
Sundridge Cl PO6 20 B3
Sunningdale SO45 35 A4
Sunny Walk PO1 47 B2
Sunny Way SO40 53 A4
Sunnyfield Rd BH25 44 B5
Sunnyheath PO9 30 A2
Sunnyside,
Fleet GU51 26 A1
Sunnyside,
Newbury RG20 37 A3
Sunnyside Rd GU35 33 E4
Sunset Av SO40 53 A3
Sunset Rd SO40 53 A4
Sunshine Av PO11 52 D5
Suntrap Gdns PO11 52 D5
Surbiton Rd SO50 22 D1
Surrey St PO1 47 D2
Sussex Gdns GU31 46 C3
Sussex Pl PO5 47 D4
Sussex Rd,
Petersfield GU31 46 D4
Sussex Rd,
Southampton SO14 50 D2
Sussex Rd,
Southsea PO5 47 D4
Sussex St SO23 56 C2
Sussex Ter PO5 47 D4
Sutherland Cl,
Bordon GU35 18 C5
Sutherland Cl,
Romsey SO51 49 E1
Sutherland Ct SP10 14 A1
Sutton Gdns SO23 56 D2
Sutton Pl SO42 17 D3
Suttonfield GU35 18 B6
Swains Cl RG26 34 E3
Swains Rd RG26 34 E3
Swallow Cl,
Havant PO9 30 D3
Swallow Cl,
Yateley GU46 57 B2
Swallow Ct PO13 38 C3
Swallow Dr SO41 42 F4
Swallow Sq SO50 22 A5
Swan Cl PO10 31 H6
Swan La SO23 56 C1
Swan Mead BH24 48 E4
Swan St,
Newbury RG20 37 A3
Swan St,
Petersfield GU31 46 B3
Swanage Rd PO13 38 C4
Swanley Cl SO50 22 C2
Swann Mws RG27 32 C2
Swans Walk PO11 52 D4
Swanwick Walk RG26 34 D3
Swarraton Rd PO9 30 B2
Sway Ct PO9 30 D1
Sway Rd SO42 17 C6
Swedish Houses RG26 34 F4
Swift Cl, Lee-on-the-Solent
PO13 38 D3
Swift Cl,
Waterlooville PO8 21 B1
Swiss Rd PO7 54 A2
Sycamore Cl,
Lymington SO41 42 D2
Sycamore Cl,
Romsey SO51 49 F4
Sycamore Cl,
Southampton SO52 45 B1
Sycamore Dr PO11 52 B3
Sycamore Pk GU34 12 D2

Sycamore Rd,
Bishops Waltham
SO32 15 D5
Sycamore Rd,
Farnborough GU14 25 B3
Sycamore Rd,
Hythe SO45 35 A3
Sycamore Rd,
Lymington SO41 36 A1
Sydmanton Cl SO51 49 D4
Sydney Rd,
Bordon GU35 18 D4
Sydney Rd,
Gosport PO12 28 B4
Syers Cl GU33 40 B4
Syers Rd GU33 40 C4
Sylvan Cl SO41 36 C3
Sylvan Dr SO52 45 A3
Sylvan Way GU52 26 A6
Sylvaner Ct RG21 16 C1
Symes Rd SO51 49 D3
Symonds St SO23 56 C4
Syon Pl GU14 25 C2

Tadburn Cl,
Eastleigh SO53 22 A1
Tadburn Cl,
Romsey SO51 49 D3
Tadburn Grn SO51 49 B4
Tadburn Rd SO51 49 D3
Tadfield Cres SO51 49 D3
Tadfield Rd SO51 49 D3
Tadley Common Rd
RG26 34 F1
Tadley Hill RG26 34 F3
Tagdell La PO8 21 A1
Talavera Pk GU11 13 C1
Talgarth Dr GU14 25 C3
Tamar Down PO7 54 C2
Tamar Dr RG23 45 D5
Tamarisk Cl PO13 38 A2
Tanfield La PO17 54 B6
Tanfield Pk PO17 54 B5
Tangier Ct GU11 13 A2
Tangier La SO32 15 A5
Tangley Walk*,
Bramshaw Ct PO9 30 D1
Tanhouse La GU34 12 B2
Tanker Rd GU14 25 A5
Tankerton Cl PO6 20 A3
Tanner St SO23 56 E3
Tanners La PO7 36 C4
Tanners Rd SO52 45 C3
Tanners Way RG23 45 C5
Tansy Cl PO7 54 C3
Tarberry Cres PO8 21 C1
Tate Rd SO15 53 D4
Tates Rd SO45 35 C4
Tattenham Rd SO42 17 C4
Tavistock Cl SO51 49 E1
Tavistock Gdns PO9 30 D5
Taylors Cl GU35 19 E2
Taylors La GU35 19 E2
Teal Cl,
Hayling Island PO11 52 D4
Teal Cl,
Waterlooville PO8 21 B1
Teazle Cl GU31 46 F4
Tegdown GU31 46 E2
Telconia Cl GU35 33 E4
Tempest Av PO7 54 C2
Temple Rd GU33 40 C2
Temple St PO1 47 D1
Tench Way SO51 49 B2
Tennyson Cl SO32 15 D5
Tennyson Gdns PO16 23 A2
Tennyson Rd,
Eastleigh SO50 22 B5
Tennyson Rd,
Lee-on-the-Solent
PO13 38 B3
Terminus Ter SO14 51 F5
Tern Cl SO45 35 D5
Tesimond Dr GU46 57 A3
Test Cl GU31 46 B4
Test Ct SP10 14 D1
Test La SO16 53 C1
Test Mws RG28 55 B3
Test Rd RG28 55 B3
Test Valley Bsns Centre
SO16 53 C1
Test Valley Bsns Pk
SO52 45 C1
Testcombe Rd PO12 29 A5
Testwood La SO40 53 A3
Testwood Pl SO40 53 B3
Tewkesbury Av PO12 28 A1
The Abbey SO51 49 A3
The Alders GU9 13 C6
The Aloes GU51 26 C3
The Anchorage PO12 28 C4
The Arcade,
Aldershot GU11 13 C1
The Arcade, Liss GU33 40 B4
The Avenue,
Alresford SO24 43 B5

The Avenue, Fareham PO14 23 A3
The Avenue, Gosport PO12 29 A6
The Avenue, Liphook GU30 39 A4
The Avenue, Petersfield GU31 46 C3
The Avenue, Southampton SO32 15 A5
The Bartons SP6 27 E3
The Birches Cl SO52 45 A1
The Boltons SO41 42 D4
The Boreen GU35 33 E3
The Borough GU31 46 B3
The Bourne GU52 26 B5
The Briars GU52 26 C5
The Bris BH24 48 A3
The Broadway SO23 56 E3
The Brook SO24 43 C1
The Bucklers SO41 42 B2
The Burrows RG26 34 C1
The Butts GU34 12 B4
The Byfrons GU14 25 B3
The Cascades Shopping Centre PO1 47 D1
The Causeway GU31 46 B4
The Cedars GU51 26 C3
The Chantry Centre SP10 14 B3
The Circle PO17 54 B4
The Cloisters, Lymington SO41 41 C3
The Cloisters, Ringwood BH24 48 E4
The Cloisters, Romsey SO51 49 B2
The Close, Liphook GU30 39 B6
The Close, New Milton BH25 44 C5
The Close, Portsmouth PO6 20 D3
The Close, Ringwood BH24 48 B3
The Close, Winchester SO23 56 D4
The Conservatory SO23 56 F3
The Cooperage GU34 12 B3
The Coppice, Brockenhurst SO42 17 A3
The Coppice, Waterlooville PO8 21 A2
The Copse, Eastleigh SO53 22 B1
The Copse, Romsey SO51 49 F1
The Covert SO51 49 E4
The Crescent, Eastleigh SO50 22 C3
The Crescent, Farnborough GU14 25 B2
The Crescent, Romsey SO51 49 D2
The Crescent, Yateley GU46 57 D2
The Croft GU46 57 D2
The Crossways PO12 28 B3
The Custards SO43 37 C4
The Danes RG21 16 E3
The Dean SO24 43 C3
The Dell, Newbury RG20 37 B2
The Dell, Yateley GU46 57 C3
The Drive, Basingstoke RG23 45 C6
The Drive, Fareham PO16 23 A2
The Drive, Havant PO9 30 B3
The Drive, Southampton SO40 53 A6
The Droke PO6 20 C3
The Elms SP10 14 A3
The Fairway, Bordon GU35 18 A6
The Fairway, New Milton BH25 44 C5
The Firs GU30 39 B5
The Fishermans PO10 31 H6
The Forest Shopping Centre GU35 18 D4
The Forum PO9 30 A4
The Fowey SO45 24 A3
The Furlong BH24 48 A3
The Gables RG28 55 D3
The Gallop GU46 57 D1
The Gardens PO9 30 D5
The Garth, Alton GU34 12 D2
The Garth, Farnborough GU14 25 C2
The George Yd SO24 43 D4
The Gillies PO16 23 A4
The Glade PO7 54 C1
The Glebe, Basingstoke RG21 16 C3
The Glebe, Lee-on-the-Solent PO13 38 A1
The Green, Farnham GU9 13 C6
The Green, Liss GU33 40 B4
The Green, Lymington SO41 42 E3
The Green, Romsey SO51 49 F1
The Green, Tadley RG26 34 F4
The Green, Waterlooville PO7 36 B4
The Green, Whitchurch RG28 55 C3
The Greenway PO10 31 G2
The Grove, Aldershot GU11 13 C2
The Grove, Farnborough GU14 25 C4
The Grove, Hook RG27 32 B3
The Grove, Liphook GU30 39 B3
The Hanger GU35 33 A1
The Hard PO1 47 B2
The Harrage SO51 49 C3
The Hassocks PO7 54 D2
The Haven, Eastleigh SO50 22 D1
The Haven, Gosport PO12 29 B6
The Hawthorns, Southampton SO32 15 A4
The Hawthorns, Tadley RG26 34 A2
The Heath PO7 36 C5
The Heights PO16 23 F1
The Hollow RG20 37 A2
The Horsefair SO51 49 B3
The Hundred SO51 49 B3
The Kerridge Ind Est GU34 12 D2
The Knowlings RG28 55 C4
The Lane, Gosport PO12 29 A7
The Lane, Southampton SO45 24 D2
The Lane, Tadley RG26 34 E3
The Laurels, Farnham GU9 13 A4
The Laurels, Fleet GU51 26 B2
The Liberty PO7 36 B6
The Limes PO9 30 B6
The Lines RG20 37 B1
The Link, Waterlooville PO7 54 C1
The Link, Yateley GU46 57 C2
The Links GU35 18 A6
The Lydgate SO41 42 B3
The Lynch RG28 55 C3
The Mall SP10 14 B3
The Mallards PO9 30 A6
The Maltings, Fareham PO16 23 F1
The Maltings, Liphook GU30 39 C4
The Maltings, Petersfield GU31 46 C3
The Marlands Shopping Centre SO14 50 D2
The Marsh SO45 35 B2
The Martells BH25 44 C5
The Mary Rose St PO1 47 D2
The Mead, Farnborough GU14 25 A2
The Mead, Liphook GU30 39 B3
The Mead, Liss GU33 40 C4
The Mead, Petersfield GU31 46 B3
The Mead, Southampton SO45 35 A4
The Meadow, Romsey SO51 49 C1
The Meadow, Waterlooville PO7 36 B5
The Meadows SO43 37 C6
The Meads SO51 49 A4
The Mews, Gosport PO12 28 E4
The Mews, Havant PO9 30 A2
The Mews, Petersfield GU31 46 D2
The Mount, Bordon GU35 33 C2
The Mount, Ringwood BH24 48 E2
The Nook SO50 22 D2
The Oaks, Tadley RG26 34 D3
The Oaks, Yateley GU46 57 D4
The Oakwood Centre PO9 30 D2
The Old Flour Mill PO10 31 H6
The Old Forge RG26 34 A2
The Old Rd PO6 20 B5
The Old Vineries SP6 27 C3
The Orchard, Hook RG27 32 B4
The Orchard, Lymington SO41 42 E3
The Orchard, Portsmouth PO6 20 C4
The Orchard, Waterlooville PO7 36 B5
The Oval GU33 40 C4
The Paddock, Bordon GU35 33 A3
The Paddock, Brockenhurst SO42 17 C3
The Paddock, Gosport PO12 29 A5
The Paddock, Hook RG27 32 C1
The Paddock, Newbury RG20 37 A2
The Paddocks SO45 24 C2
The Pallant PO9 30 B4
The Pantiles SP6 27 C3
The Parade, New Milton BH25 44 B4
The Parade, Portsmouth PO1 47 B1
The Parade, Yateley GU46 57 E2
The Parchment PO9 30 B5
The Pastures PO7 36 B5
The Pentagon SO45 24 B3
The Pines SP10 14 A2
The Polygon SO15 50 C1
The Precinct, Gosport PO12 28 E4
The Precinct, Waterlooville PO7 54 B2
The Precinct Poll PO11 52 C4
The Priory SO32 15 B5
The Promenade SO45 35 C2
The Purrocks GU31 46 C1
The Quadrangle SO50 22 C2
The Queens Mall PO1 47 D3
The Recess SO50 22 D2
The Redan PO12 29 C7
The Retreat, Eastleigh SO50 22 D2
The Retreat, Southsea PO5 47 D4
The Ridgeway GU34 12 C4
The Ridings GU33 40 D5
The Rise SO42 17 C3
The Rookery, Emsworth PO10 31 H5
The Rookery, Whitchurch RG28 55 B2
The Rose Est RG27 32 C6
The Rosery PO12 29 B7
The Roundabouts GU33 40 C4
The Sanderlings PO11 52 C5
The Sands GU35 18 A5
The Seagulls PO13 38 D6
The Sett GU46 57 B3
The Shipyard Ind Est SO45 35 C2
The Sidings GU11 13 D1
The Smithy PO7 36 B5
The Soke SO24 43 D3
The Solent PO13 38 A4
The Spain GU31 46 C3
The Spinney, Denmead PO7 36 B6
The Spinney, Hook RG27 32 B5
The Spinney, Waterlooville PO8 21 A2
The Spinney, Yateley GU46 57 C2
The Spring PO7 36 C6
The Spur PO17 54 B4
The Square, Fareham PO17 54 C5
The Square, Liphook GU30 39 B4
The Square, Lymington SO41 41 B3
The Square, Petersfield GU31 46 C3
The Square, Southampton SO45 24 D2
The Square, Winchester SO23 56 D3
The Swan Centre SO50 22 D4
The Sweep BH24 48 B3
The Sycamores GU14 25 C3
The Tanneries Ind Est PO9 30 A5
The Thicket SO51 49 E4
The Tins SO41 41 D2
The Tithe PO7 36 B5
The Tyleshades SO51 49 D4
The Vale, Basingstoke RG23 45 C5
The Vale, Southampton SO45 35 A4
The Vale, Southsea PO5 47 D5
The Verne GU52 26 B6
The Vikings SO51 49 E3
The Vinery BH25 44 D2
The Vineyards SO52 45 C2
The Walk SO22 56 B3
The Warren, Aldershot GU11 13 B2
The Warren, Tadley RG26 34 D3
The Watermeadows SP10 14 A5
The Weir RG28 55 B4
The Westering SO51 49 E2
The Wicket SO45 35 A4
The Willows, New Milton BH25 44 D5
The Willows, Waterlooville PO7 36 B5
The Woodlands GU35 18 C6
The Wrekin GU14 25 D4
The Yews PO8 21 D1
Third Av, Havant PO9 30 C4
Third Av, Portsmouth PO6 20 B3
Third St SO45 24 B1
Thirlmere SO50 22 B4
Thirlmere Cl GU35 18 C1
Thirlmere Cres GU52 26 A6
Thistle Down PO8 21 B4
Thomas Rd SO52 45 B2
Thoresby Ct BH25 44 A2
Thorn Cl, Eastleigh SO50 22 C1
Thorn Cl, Petersfield GU31 46 F4
Thornbrake Rd PO12 29 C5
Thornbury Av SO45 24 A5
Thorneley Rd RG20 37 B2
Thorness Cl SO16 53 D2
Thorngate Way PO12 28 D4
Thornhill Cl SO45 24 A3
Thornhill Rd SO45 24 A3
Thorpe Gdns GU34 12 A2
Three Acre Cl BH25 44 A4
Three Acre Dr BH25 44 A4
Three Acres PO7 36 C6
Three Minister Ho SO23 56 C2
Three Tun Cl PO1 47 B2
Threefield La SO14 51 E5
Throgmorton Rd GU46 57 A3
Tichborne Down SO24 43 C6
Tichborne Rd SO50 22 C6
Tidworth Rd PO9 30 A1
Tiffany Cl SO41 36 B1
Tilburys Cl GU35 18 C4
Tilebarn La SO42 17 C6
Tilford Rd PO8 21 A2
Tilmore Gdns GU31 46 C1
Tilmore Rd GU31 46 C1
Tilney Cl GU34 12 B2
Timberlake Rd RG21 16 B2
Timbermill Ct SP6 27 E4
Tindal Cl GU46 57 D2
Tintern Gro SO15 50 B1
Tintern Rd PO12 28 A4
Tiptree Cl SO50 22 C1
Titchfield Cl RG26 34 E4
Titchfield La PO17 54 A5
Tithe Barn SO41 41 D1
Titus Gdns PO7 54 D1
Toby St PO1 47 D1
Tobys Gdns GU31 46 C3
Tockington Ct GU46 57 D2
Toledo Gro SP10 14 D2
Tollgate Cl RG23 45 C4
Tolpuddle Way GU46 57 F3
Tomlins Cl RG26 34 D4
Tonbridge St PO5 47 D5
Tonnant Cl PO13 38 A1
Toomer Cl SO45 24 B3
Top La BH24 48 B3
Topaz Gro PO7 54 D1
Tor Way GU31 46 D3
Torberry Dr GU31 46 E3
Tormead SO45 35 A4
Tornay Gro SO52 45 A2
Toronto Pl PO12 28 B3
Torquay Av PO12 28 A1
Torrington Cl GU35 19 F1
Totland Ct SO41 42 C3
Totland Rd PO6 20 B3
Totnes Cl SO50 22 B1
Tottenhale Cl SO52 45 B3
Tournerbury La PO11 52 C3
Tower Cl GU30 39 B3
Tower Ct SO23 56 C1
Tower Hill Ct RG20 37 A2
Tower Rd, Liphook GU30 39 B3
Tower Rd, Winchester SO23 56 C2
Tower St, Alton GU34 12 B3
Tower St, Emsworth PO10
Tower St, Portsmouth PO1
Tower St, Winchester SO23
Town Hall Ct RG28
Town Hall Rd PO9
Town La GU31
Town Mill La RG28
Town Mill Rd SP10
Town Quay SO14
Townsend Cl RG21
Toynbee Cl SO50
Toynbee Rd SO50
Trafalgar Ho SO23
Trafalgar Pl SO41
Trafalgar Sq PO12
Trafalgar St SO23
Trafalgar Way SO45
Tranmere Cl SO41
Transort Rd GU14
Trebourba Dr PO12
Tredenham Cl GU14
Treeside Av SO40
Treeside Dr GU9
Trefoil Cl, Hook RG27
Trefoil Cl, Waterlooville PO7
Tregaron Av PO6
Tregolls Dr GU14
Trenchard Pk GU35
Trent Ct SP10
Trent Way PO13
Tribe Rd PO12
Tricorn Centre PO1
Trinity Cl PO12
Trinity Ct SO40
Trinity Gdns PO16
Trinity Grn PO12
Trinity Rd SO14
Trinity St PO16
Trinity Ter SO23
Trosnant Rd PO9
Trust Cl RG27
Tudor Av PO10
Tudor Cl PO11
Tudor Cres PO6
Tudor Ct RG26
Tudor Dr GU46
Tulls La GU35
Tunbridge Cres GU30
Tunbridge La GU30
Tunns Ct SO23
Tunstall Rd PO6
Tunworth Ct PO9
Tunworth Mws RG26
Turbary Gdns RG26
Turk St GU34
Turner Ct SP10
Turners Farm Cres SO41
Turnpike Way RG23
Turnstone End GU46
Tutland Rd SO52
Twittens Way PO9
Twoways Ct GU35
Twyford Dr PO13
Twyford Rd SO50
Tylers Cl SO41
Tylston Mdw GU30
Tyne Ct SP10
Tyseley Rd PO5

Ubsdell Cl BH25
Ullswater SO50
Ullswater Cl GU35
Ullswater Gro SO24
Undershore SO41
Undershore Rd SO41
Unicorn Rd PO1
Union La RG20
Union Rd PO9
Union St, Aldershot GU11
Union St, Andover SP1
Union St, Fareham PO16
Union St, Farnborough GU14
Union St, Portsmouth PO1
Union St, Winchester SO23
Union Ter GU11
Uplands Av BH25
Uplands Cres PO16
Upper Arundel St PO1
Upper Bere Wood PO7
Upper Brook St SO23
Upper Bugle St SO14
Upper Cres Rd SO52
Upper Elms Rd GU11
Upper Farm Rd RG23
Upper Grove Rd GU34
Upper Heyshott GU31

High St SO23 56 B2
House Ct PO17 54 B5
Mt GU33 40 B6
Mullins La SO45 35 A4
Piece PO7 36 D5
St Michaels Gro
23 A4
St Michael's Rd
13 C3
St GU51 26 B2
Wardown GU31 46 E2
Weybourne La
13 A4
Wharf PO16 23 D4
Cl GU14 25 C2
Gdns PO12 28 B2
La SO41 36 A1
o PO12 28 A2
a Way SP10 14 C2
ne Ct PO7 54 D1
Pk PO10 31 G5
Cl SO45 24 A4
Side GU30 39 B2
lene SO45 35 B5
ade Cl RG27 32 B6
ard Rd PO12 28 C1
Rd GU35 18 D4
ll Rd RG27 32 A5
Cl PO12 28 A2
ans GU34 12 D3
ll Way GU31 46 B3
Way PO6 20 B4
Ct SO16 53 D2
d Cl GU52 26 C4
d Rd GU52 26 B4
da Ct SO45 35 B1
Cl PO7 54 D1
Ter GU12 13 D2
Ct PO6 20 D6
a Cres PO8 21 B4
Valk GU11 13 C4
Cl GU35 33 B3
Cl PO12 28 A3
Rd PO12 28 A3
Cl SP10 14 A3
d RG27 32 C5
BH25 44 B2
e Gdns SO41 36 B3
e Hill,
GU34 12 C2
e Hill,
RG27 32 C3
e La,
gton SO41 36 B2
e La,
GU46 57 C1
e Rd,
GU34 12 B4
e Rd,
GU46 57 B1
Av PO11 52 B4
Ct,
er SP10 14 A3
Ct, Fleet GU51 26 B2
Gdns,
GU51 26 A2
Gdns,
gbridge SP6 27 C4
Gdns,
ood BH24 48 C4
Pl,
rt PO12 29 B5
Pl,
gton SO41 41 D3
Pl,
y SO51 49 B3
Rd,
hot GU11 13 C2
Rd, Alton GU34 12 C2
Rd,
gh SO50 22 D1
Rd,
orth PO10 31 F5
Rd,
rough GU14 25 A2
Rd, Fleet GU51 26 A2
Rd,
gbridge SP6 27 C3
Rd,
ton SO41 42 C3
Rd,
outh PO1 47 B1
Rd,
mpton SO32 15 B5
Rd,
oville PO7 54 A2
Rd,
ster SO23 56 C1
Sq PO13 38 B4
St,
stoke RG21 16 C4
St,
t PO12 28 C3
St,
mpton SO14 51 G2

Victory Av PO8 21 A2
Victory Rd PO1 47 B2
Victory Roundabout RG21 16 B2
Vigo La GU46 57 C4
Vigo Rd SP10 14 C3
Viking Cl SO45 24 B5
Villa Gdns PO7 54 B1
Village Rd PO12 29 A6
Village St GU31 46 F1
Village Way GU46 57 D2
Villiers Rd, Southampton SO45 35 A6
Villiers Rd, Southsea PO5 47 D5
Vimoutiers Ct SP6 27 E3
Vincent Cl BH25 44 B2
Vincent Rd BH25 44 B2
Vincents Walk SO14 50 D3
Vine St GU11 13 B2
Vinegar Hill SO41 42 D3
Viney Av SO51 49 E2
Viney Rd SO41 41 E4
Vinson Rd GU33 40 D5
Virginia Gdns GU14 25 B3
Vitre Gdns SO41 41 D4
Vivian Cl GU52 26 C5
Vyne Cl GU34 12 B1
Vyne Rd RG21 16 C1
Vyse La SO14 50 D5

Wade Ct Rd PO9 30 C6
Wade La PO9 30 B6
Wagon La RG27 32 C4
Wagtail Dr BH25 44 A2
Wagtail Rd PO8 21 B2
Wainsford Cl SO41 41 A3
Wainsford Ct SO41 41 A3
Wainsford Rd SO41 41 A3
Wakefords Way PO9 30 D1
Walberton Av PO6 20 C3
Walden Gdns PO8 21 B1
Wales St SO23 56 F2
Walkers La North SO45 24 A4
Walkers La South SO45 24 A6
Wallace Way GU11 13 A1
Walldown Rd GU35 18 C6
Walled Mdw SP10 14 C3
Wallington Hill PO16 23 E2
Wallington Shore Rd PO16 23 E1
Wallington Way PO16 23 D1
Wallrock Walk PO10 31 G2
Walnut Cl, Aldershot GU11 13 C4
Walnut Cl, Alton GU34 12 C1
Walnut Cl, New Milton BH25 44 B2
Walnut Cl, Yateley GU46 57 D4
Walnut Tree Cl PO11 52 B4
Walpole Gdns RG27 32 C2
Walpole Rd PO12 28 D4
Walsingham Cl PO6 20 A2
Waltham St PO5 47 D3
Walton Cl, Fleet GU51 26 A3
Walton Cl, Gosport PO12 28 A4
Walton Rd PO12 28 A4
Walworth Rd SP10 14 D1
Wanstead Cl BH24 48 D1
Warbler Cl PO8 21 A1
Warblington Av PO9 30 D5
Warblington Cl RG26 34 E4
Warblington Rd PO10 31 F6
Warblington St PO1 47 B3
Ward Cl SP10 14 A1
Ward Cres PO10 31 H3
Ward Ct PO11 52 A5
Wardens Cl, Hayling Island PO11 52 B2
Wardens Cl, Waterlooville PO7 54 B2
Warfield Av PO7 54 B2
Warfield Cres PO7 54 B2
Warnford Cl PO12 28 A4
Warren Av SO53 22 A1
Warren Cl, Bordon GU35 18 A4
Warren Cl, Eastleigh SO53 22 A1
Warren Cl, Fleet GU52 26 C4
Warren Gdns SO51 49 E1
Warren Pk SO41 42 A1
Warren Rd GU33 40 C2
Warrington Mws GU11 13 A3
Warrys Cl SO45 35 B6
Warwick Av BH25 44 D1
Warwick Cl, Aldershot GU11 13 D3
Warwick Cl, Whitchurch RG28 55 B3
Warwick Cres PO5 47 D3
Warwick Rd SO40 53 A3
Warwick Way PO17 54 C5
Wash Brook RG27 32 B4
Washbrook Rd PO6 20 A2

Washford Cl GU35 19 E3
Washford La, Bordon GU35 19 E2
Washford La, Bordon GU35 19 E3
Washington Rd PO10 31 G5
Water Cl SO23 56 E4
Water La, Alton GU34 12 E4
Water La, Andover SP11 14 A6
Water La, Dibden Purlieu SO45 35 A4
Water La, Southampton SO15 50 C1
Water La, Totton SO40 53 A4
Water La, Winchester SO23 56 F2
Watercress Ct GU34 12 D2
Watercress Mdw SO24 43 B6
Waterford Cl SO41 41 E3
Waterford La SO41 41 E3
Waterford Rd BH25 44 D1
Watergate PO12 28 E4
Waterloo Ct SP10 14 B3
Waterloo Rd, Aldershot GU12 13 D2
Waterloo Rd, Gosport PO12 29 C7
Waterloo Rd, Havant PO9 30 B4
Waterloo Rd, Lymington SO41 41 E1
Waterloo Rd, Southampton SO15 50 A1
Waterloo St PO5 47 D3
Waterloo Ter SO15 50 D1
Waterloo Way BH24 48 C4
Waterman Cl GU35 19 E4
Watermans La SO45 35 A6
Watermills Cl SP10 14 A5
Waters Green Ct SO42 17 D3
Waters Grn SO42 17 D2
Watersedge Gdns PO10 31 G6
Watership Dr BH24 48 E4
Waterside SO45 35 B1
Waterside Cl, Bordon GU35 19 E3
Waterside Cl, Ringwood BH24 48 C1
Waterside Ct GU34 12 D2
Waterside Gdns PO16 23 F2
Waterside Rd SO51 49 C1
Watery La SP10 14 C1
Wavendon Av BH25 44 A5
Waveney Cl PO13 38 C4
Waverley Av GU51 26 B1
Waverley Cl, Fordingbridge SP6 27 E2
Waverley Cl, Romsey SO51 49 E1
Waverley Rd, Farnborough GU14 25 C2
Waverley Rd, Fordingbridge SP6 27 E2
Waverley Rd, New Milton BH25 44 C3
Waverley Rd, Southampton SO15 50 A2
Wayfarers Walk, Alresford SO24 43 A3
Wayfarers Walk, Waterlooville PO7 36 B4
Waynflete Cl SO32 15 B5
Wayside Cl SO41 42 D2
Wayte St PO6 20 B3
Weapon Rd GU14 25 A4
Weatherby Gdns RG27 32 C2
Weavers Cl SP10 14 C3
Weavers Grn PO9 31 E3
Webb Cl PO11 52 C5
Webb La PO11 52 C5
Webbs Fm Cl RG28 55 B4
Weevil La PO12 28 D2
Welch Rd PO12 28 A2
Weldon Cl GU52 26 C6
Well Cl BH25 44 A3
Wellands Rd SO43 37 C5
Wellesley Cl PO7 54 B3
Wellesley Ct SP10 14 B5
Wellesley Gate GU11 13 C2
Wellesley Rd, Aldershot GU11 13 A1
Wellesley Rd, Andover SP10 14 A5
Wellington Av, Aldershot GU11 13 A1
Wellington Av, Bordon GU35 18 C5
Wellington Av, Fleet GU51 26 C1
Wellington Centre GU11 13 C1
Wellington Cl PO8 21 D2
Wellington Cres RG26 34 A2
Wellington Ct BH25 44 C1
Wellington Gdns GU11 13 B2
Wellington Rd SP10 14 A2

Wellington Retail Pk PO7 54 A1
Wellington St, Aldershot GU11 13 C1
Wellington St, Southsea PO5 47 D3
Wellington Way PO7 54 B2
Wellmans Mdw RG20 37 A1
Wells La RG28 55 B4
Wells Pl SO50 22 D4
Wells Rd SO50 22 D4
Welton Ct RG21 16 B2
Wembley Gro PO6 20 D5
Wendover Cl BH25 44 A4
Wendover Rd PO9 30 A4
Wensley Gdns PO10 31 H3
Wentworth Cl, Farnham GU9 13 A5
Wentworth Cl, Yateley GU46 57 D3
Wentworth Dr PO8 21 B1
Wentworth Gdns GU34 12 B2
Wesermarsch Rd PO8 21 A4
Wesley Walk RG21 16 D2
Wessex Av BH25 44 C3
Wessex Cl SO45 24 A5
Wessex Est BH24 48 D2
Wessex Gate Ind Est PO8 21 C2
Wessex Gdns, Andover SP10 14 A2
Wessex Gdns, Romsey SO51 49 E3
Wessex Rd BH24 48 D2
West Bay Rd SO15 50 A3
West Cl SO41 41 A3
West Common SO45 24 A6
West End Cl SO22 56 A2
West End Ter SO22 56 A2
West Fryerne GU46 57 D1
West Green Rd RG27 32 A2
West Grn GU46 57 B2
West Hayes SO41 41 E2
West Hill Dr SO45 35 A2
West La, Hayling Island PO11 52 A3
West La, Southampton SO52 45 A1
West Marlands Rd SO14 50 D2
West Park Rd SO15 50 C2
West Quay Rd SO15 50 A2
West Quay Retail Pk SO15 50 C3
West Quay Shopping Area SO14 50 C3
West Rd, Emsworth PO10 31 F6
West Rd, Lymington SO41 42 B2
West Rd, Southampton SO14 51 E6
West St, Alresford SO24 43 D4
West St, Andover SP10 14 B3
West St, Emsworth PO10 31 H5
West St, Fareham PO16 23 A3
West St, Fordingbridge SP6 27 E4
West St, Havant PO9 30 A4
West St, Hythe SO45 35 A2
West St, Portsmouth PO1 47 B4
West St, Ringwood BH24 48 A3
West St, Southampton SO14 50 D4
West St, Tadley RG26 34 F2
West Station Rd GU11 13 C2
West Street Cl RG26 34 F2
West View Rd GU35 33 E3
West Vw GU35 18 A6
West Way SO41 41 B4
Westborn Rd PO16 23 C2
Westbourne Av PO10 31 H4
Westbourne Cl PO10 31 H4
Westbourne Rd PO10 31 H2
Westbroke Gdns SO51 49 C1
Westbrook Cl RG23 45 C6
Westbrooke Cl, Andover SP10 14 B3
Westbrooke Cl, Waterlooville PO8 21 B2
Westbrooke Rd GU34 12 B3
Westbury Cl BH25 44 C4
Westbury Rd BH24 48 D3
Westcliff Cl PO13 38 C3
Westcliff Walk SO45 35 B1
Westerham Cl PO6 20 B3
Western Av, Andover SP10 14 A2
Western Av, Emsworth PO10 31 F5
Western Esp, Southampton SO14 50 C2

Western Esp, Southampton SO14 50 D5
Western Par, Emsworth PO10 31 F6
Western Par, Southsea PO5 47 C4
Western Rd, Aldershot GU11 13 A2
Western Rd, Andover SP10 14 A3
Western Rd, Bordon GU35 18 C1
Western Rd, Fareham PO16 23 C3
Western Rd, Havant PO9 30 A4
Western Rd, Liss GU33 40 B4
Western Rd, Lymington SO41 41 C2
Western Rd, Portsmouth PO6 20 A4
Western Rd, Winchester SO22 56 A1
Western Ter SO14 51 F4
Western Way PO16 23 A3
Westfield Av, Fareham PO16 23 A4
Westfield Av, Hayling Island PO11 52 B4
Westfield Cl RG26 34 F3
Westfield Oaks PO11 52 B4
Westfield Rd, Gosport PO12 28 A4
Westfield Rd, Lymington SO41 41 F3
Westfield Rd, Southampton SO40 53 A4
Westgate PO13 38 A1
Westgate St SO14 50 D5
Westgrove SP6 27 E3
Westgrove Gdns PO10 31 G5
Westland Gdns PO12 29 A5
Westmarch Bsns Centre SP10 14 C1
Westmead GU14 25 A2
Westmead Cl PO11 52 A4
Westminster Cl GU51 26 B1
Westminster Ct BH25 44 B6
Westminster Ho RG21 16 C3
Westminster Rd SO41 42 B3
Westmoreland Ct SO41 36 A2
Westmorland Way SO53 22 B1
Weston Rd, Eastleigh SO50 22 C3
Weston Rd, Petersfield GU31 46 D3
Westover Rd, Fleet GU51 26 C2
Westover Rd, Lymington SO41 42 D3
Westover Rd, Southampton SO16 53 D3
Westwood Cl PO10 31 H3
Westwood Ct SO40 53 A1
Westwood Rd SO43 37 B4
Wetherby Gdns GU14 25 B5
Wetherdown GU31 46 D3
Wey Lodge Cl GU30 39 D3
Weybourne Rd GU9 13 A5
Weybridge Mead GU46 57 E2
Weyhill Cl RG26 34 E4
Weyhill Rd SP10 14 A3
Weyland Cl GU30 39 B3
Weywood Cl GU9 13 B5
Weywood La GU9 13 A4
Wharf Hill SO23 56 F4
Whartons Cl SO40 15 C1
Wheatcroft Rd PO13 38 C4
Wheatley Rd GU11 13 B1
Wheatsheaf Ct GU35 33 B2
Wheeler Cl, Gosport PO12 28 B2
Wheeler Cl, Whitchurch RG28 55 C4
Wheelers Hill RG27 32 C5
Wheelers Walk SO45 24 A5
Whin Holt GU52 26 B4
Whinchat Cl RG27 32 B2
Whippingham Cl PO6 20 A3
Whitaker Cres SO41 41 B3
Whitby Cl GU14 25 D4
Whitby Ct SO41 42 C3
Whitby Rd SO41 42 B3
Whitchurch By-Pass RG28 55 A3
White Barn Cres SO41 36 C2
White Hart Alley*, White Hart Rd PO1 47 B4
White Hart La RG21 16 E4
White Hart Rd, Gosport PO12 29 B5
White Hart Rd, Portsmouth PO1 47 B4
White Heather Ct SO45 35 B1
White Ho Gdns GU31 46 B1

White Horse La PO7 36 D4
White Horses BH25 44 A6
White House Gdns GU46 57 D2
White Knights BH25 44 B6
White Ladies Cl PO9 30 C5
White Lion Courtyard BH24 48 A3
White Lion Walk PO12 28 D3
White Lion Way GU46 57 D2
White Swan Rd PO1 47 C2
Whitebeam Cl PO8 21 C3
Whitebeam Way SO52 45 B1
Whitecroft SO45 35 B4
Whitedown GU34 12 B3
Whitedown La GU34 12 A3
Whitedown Rd RG26 34 C2
Whitefield Rd BH25 44 B2
Whitehart Flds BH24 48 D2
Whitehaven PO8 21 D2
Whitehill Pk GU35 18 D6
Whitehill Rd GU35 19 E6
Whitemoor Rd SO42 17 A3
Whitenap Cl SO51 49 E4
Whitenap La SO51 49 E4
Whites Cl RG27 32 A5
Whites La SO45 24 D2
Whites Pl PO12 28 B3
Whites Rd GU14 25 D5
Whitethorn Rd PO11 52 D4
Whitewater Rise, Hook RG27 32 D4
Whitewater Rise, Southampton SO45 35 A5
Whitley Rd GU46 57 D4
Whitsbury Rd SP6 27 D1
Whitstable Rd PO6 20 A3
Whittington Cl, Emsworth PO10 31 G5
Whittington Cl, Southampton SO45 35 A4
Whitworth Cl PO12 28 A4
Whitworth Rd PO12 28 A4
Whyteways SO50 22 C2
Wick 1 Ind Est BH25 44 A2
Wick 2 Ind Est BH25 44 A2
Wick Cl BH25 44 A3
Wick Dr BH25 44 A3
Wickham Cft PO17 54 B5
Wickham Cl, Alton GU34 12 A4
Wickham Cl, Fleet GU52 26 A5
Wickham Cl, Tadley RG26 34 E2
Wickham Ct GU52 26 A5
Wickham Pl GU52 26 A5
Wickham Rd, Fareham PO16 23 D1
Wickham Rd, Fleet GU52 26 A5
Wickham St PO1 47 B2
Wickor Cl PO10 31 H3
Wickor Way PO10 31 H3
Widbury Rd SO41 41 B4
Wide Lane Cl SO42 17 C3
Widgeon Cl PO12 28 B1
Widgeons GU34 12 C1
Widley Court Dr PO6 20 C4
Widley Rd PO6 20 C3
Widley Walk PO7 20 C1
Wigmore Rd RG26 34 B2
Wilberforce Rd, Gosport PO12 29 C7
Wilberforce Rd, Southsea PO5 47 D4
Wild Herons RG27 32 D5
Wildground La SO45 35 B6
Wildwood Dr RG26 34 A2
Wildwood Gdns GU46 57 C4
Will Hall La GU34 12 A3
Willems Av GU11 13 A1
William Cl PO13 38 A1
William Farthing Cl GU11 13 B2
William Price Gdns PO16 23 C1
William Rd SO41 41 D1
William St SO14 51 H1
William Way GU34 12 D1
Williams Ind Pk BH25 44 A2
Williams Way GU51 26 D2
Willis Av SO52 45 C2
Willis Rd, Gosport PO12 28 D4
Willis Rd, Portsmouth PO1 47 D2
Willments Ind Est SO19 51 H5
Willoughby Cl GU34 12 A2
Willow Av SP6 27 E2
Willow Cl, Bordon GU35 18 D4
Willow Cl, Camberley GU16 25 D2
Willow Cl, Havant PO9 30 C5
Willow Cl, Liphook GU30 39 C4
Willow Ct GU34 12 B3
Willow Gdns, Liphook GU30 39 C5
Willow Gdns, Southampton SO52 45 B1
Willow Gro SP10 14 A4
Willow Pl PO12 28 B3
Willow Rd, Liss GU33 40 C5
Willow Rd, Southampton SO32 15 D5
Willow Rd, Tadley RG26 34 E3
Willow Tree Av PO8 21 B6
Willow Walk BH25 44 C6
Willow Wood Rd PO11 52 C4
Willowdene Cl BH25 44 D2
Willowford GU46 57 D2
Wills Way SO51 49 D4
Wilmer Rd SO50 22 C5
Wilmott La PO12 28 A3
Wilsom Cl GU34 12 D2
Wilsom Rd GU34 12 D2
Wilson St SO14 51 G2
Wilsons Rd GU35 33 E3
Wilton Ct GU14 25 C2
Wilton Dr PO8 21 B3
Wilton Gdns BH25 44 A2
Wilton Pl PO5 47 D5
Wiltshire St PO5 47 C3
Wilverley Av PO9 30 C2
Wilverley Cl SO41 41 A4
Wilverley Pl SO45 24 A4
Wilverley Rd SO42 17 C3
Wincanton Cl GU34 12 D4
Winchcombe Cl GU51 26 B2
Winchcombe Rd RG21 16 A4
Winchester Gdns SP10 14 B5
Winchester Rd, Alresford SO24 43 A6
Winchester Rd, Andover SP10 14 B5
Winchester Rd, Basingstoke RG21 16 B4
Winchester Rd, Fareham PO17 54 B4
Winchester Rd, Newbury RG20 37 A3
Winchester Rd, Petersfield GU31 46 A2
Winchester Rd, Romsey SO51 49 C3
Winchester Rd, Southampton SO32 15 A4
Winchester Rd, Whitchurch RG28 55 B5
Winchester St, Andover SP10 14 B3
Winchester St, Basingstoke RG21 16 C4
Winchester St, Farnborough GU14 25 B6
Winchfield Gdns RG26 34 E4
Windermere Gdns, Alresford SO24 43 D6
Windermere Gdns, Southampton SO40 53 A4
Windermere Rd GU35 18 C1
Windfield Dr SO51 49 E2
Windmill Cl SO41 42 D3
Windmill Copse SO45 35 A5
Windmill Dr GU35 33 D2
Windmill Fld PO7 36 D5
Windmill Hill GU34 12 D3
Windmill La GU34 12 E4
Windmill Rd GU12 13 D2
Windrush Gdns PO7 54 A3
Windrush Way SO45 35 B4
Windsor Cl, Alton GU34 12 A3
Windsor Cl, Lymington SO41 36 A1
Windsor Ct GU51 26 C2
Windsor Ho SO23 56 E2
Windsor La PO5 47 D3
Windsor Pk GU34 12 C4
Windsor Rd, Alresford SO24 43 B5
Windsor Rd, Andover SP10 14 A3
Windsor Rd, Bordon GU35 19 E2
Windsor Rd, Farnborough GU14 25 C4
Windsor Rd, Gosport PO12 28 A4
Windsor Rd, Petersfield GU31 46 C2
Windsor Rd, Portsmouth PO6 20 C4
Windsor Ter SO14 50 D2
Windsor Walk GU35 19 E2
Windsor Way GU11 13 C2
Winfield Way PO10 31 H2
Wingate Ct GU11 13 B1
Wingrove Rd SO40 15 B1
Winifred Rd PO7 54 B1
Winkfield Row PO8 21 B3
Winkle St SO14 50 D6
Winkworth La RG7 34 E1
Winnipeg Cl GU30 39 B5
Winscombe Av PO8 21 A6
Winsor Rd SO40 53 B5
Winston Churchill Av PO1 47 D3
Winston Cl, Eastleigh SO50 22 C2
Winston Cl, Hayling Island PO11 52 A4
Winston Ct BH25 44 B4
Winston Way BH24 48 C2
Winstone Cres SO52 45 B3
Winterbourne Rd SO51 49 E1
Winterhill Rd PO6 20 A3
Winterthur Way RG21 16 C2
Winton Chase SP10 14 D3
Winton Cl SO41 41 F3
Winton Cres GU46 57 D3
Winton Rd, Aldershot GU11 13 B3
Winton Rd, Petersfield GU31 46 C2
Winton Sq RG21 16 C4
Winton St SO14 51 E2
Wisbech Way SO41 36 B3
Wises Alley PO12 28 E4
Wistaria La GU46 57 C3
Wisteria Dr GU35 18 C4
Wisteria Gdns PO9 30 D2
Witan Ct RG28 55 A2
Witchampton Cl PO9 30 C1
Wither Rise RG23 45 C4
Witherslack Cl GU35 33 E4
Withy Cl SO51 49 C2
Wittcomb Ter GU35 18 C6
Witton Hill SO24 43 C5
Woburn Av GU14 25 C1
Woburn Ct PO13 38 C6
Wolseley Rd GU11 13 C2
Wolsey Way SO41 42 E3
Wolversdene Cl SP10 14 D4
Wolversdene Gdns SP10 14 D4
Wolversdene Rd SP10 14 C3
Wolverton Rd, Havant PO9 30 A1
Wolverton Rd, Southampton SO14 51 F2
Wolverton Rd, Tadley RG26 34 A3
Wolvesey Ter SO23 56 F4
Wood La, Fleet GU51 26 D2
Wood La, Lymington SO41 42 D3
Wood Lawn Cl BH25 44 B4
Wood Rd SO40 15 B2
Woodbourne GU9 13 A4
Woodbourne Cl, Liss GU33 40 C4
Woodbourne Cl, Yateley GU46 57 D3
Woodbury Av, Havant PO9 30 B6
Woodbury Av, Petersfield GU31 46 B1
Woodcock La SO41 36 C2
Woodcott Ho RG26 34 D2
Woodcroft La PO8 21 A3
Woodend GU14 25 B3
Woodford Cl BH24 48 D3
Woodland Rise GU52 26 A6
Woodland Way SO41 42 C3
Woodlands, Fareham PO16 23 F2
Woodlands, Fleet GU51 26 B1
Woodlands Av, Emsworth PO10 31 G3
Woodlands Av, Farnham GU9 13 A4
Woodlands Cl SO45 35 A6
Woodlands Ct, Alton GU34 12 A4
Woodlands Ct, Southampton SO45 35 A6
Woodlands Gdns SO51 49 E2
Woodlands La, Hayling Island PO11 52 A2
Woodlands La, Liss GU33 40 D6
Woodlands Rd, Brockenhurst SO42 17 C5
Woodlands Rd, New Milton BH25 44 A6
Woodlands Rd, Southampton SO40 15 A3
Woodlands Rd, Tadley RG26 34 A2
Woodlands Way, Andover SP10 14 C3
Woodlands Way, Havant PO9 30 B2
Woodlands Way, Southampton SO52 45 A2
Woodleigh GU51 26 B3
Woodleigh Cl PO9 31 E2
Woodley Gdns SO41 41 C1
Woodley La SO51 49 D2
Woodley Rd PO12 29 C5
Woodpath PO5 47 D4
Woodpecker Cl, Bordon GU35 18 C5
Woodpecker Cl, Havant PO9 30 D4
Woodpecker Way SO50 22 A5
Woodrow PO7 36 B5
Woodruffe Walk PO10 31 G2
Woodsedge PO7 54 D3
Woodside Av, Eastleigh SO50 22 B3
Woodside Av, Lymington SO41 41 D4
Woodside Cl, Bordon GU35 18 D4
Woodside Cl, Lymington SO41 41 E4
Woodside Cres GU35 18 C4
Woodside Gdns SO40 15 B1
Woodside La SO41 41 D4
Woodside Pk GU35 18 C4
Woodside Rd, Eastleigh SO50 22 A2
Woodside Rd, Farnham GU9 13 A4
Woodside Rd, Southampton SO52 45 B2
Woodstock Av PO8 21 A3
Woodstock La BH24 48 B3
Woodstock Rd PO12 29 C5
Woodvale Gdns BH25 44 D1
Woodville Dr PO1 47 C4
Woodville Rd SO45 24 C2
Wool Gro SP10 14 D3
Woolmer La GU30 39 C1
Woolmer St PO10 31 F2
Woolmer Trading Est GU35 18 C4
Woolmer Way GU35 18 C5
Woolner Av, Petersfield GU31 46 C2
Woolner Av, Portsmouth PO6 20 D3
Wooteys Way GU34 12 C1
Wootton Rd PO13 38 D6
Wootton St PO6 20 B4
Worcester Pl SO41 41 E3
Wordsworth Av GU46 57 B3
Wordsworth Cl SO32 15 D5
Worsley Rd PO5 47 D4
Worthy Ct PO9 30 C1
Worthy La SO23 56 C1
Worthy Rd BH25 44 B2
Worting Rd RG21 16 A3
Wote St RG21 16 D3
Wraysbury Park Dr PO10 31 G1
Wren Cl, Alton GU34 12 D1
Wren Cl, New Milton BH25 44 A3
Wren Cl, Ringwood BH24 48 E4
Wren Cl, Yateley GU46 57 B2
Wren Rd SO50 22 A5
Wyborn Cl PO11 52 C5
Wychwood Dr SO45 24 A6
Wye Ct SP10 14 D1
Wykeham Fld PO17 54 C6
Wykeham Pl SO41 41 D3
Wykwood GU30 39 C4
Wyld Green La GU33
Wymering Ct GU14
Wymering La PO6
Wymering Manor Cl PO6
Wyndham Cl, Waterlooville PO8
Wyndham Cl, Yateley GU46
Wyndham Mws PO1
Wyndham Pl SO15
Wyndham St GU12
Wynne Gdns GU52
Wynyards Gap SO52
Wyvern Cl SO53

Yaldhurst La SO41
Yapton St PO1
Yarborough Rd PO5
Yarrell Mead SO41
Yateley Rd GU46
Yelverton Av SO45
Yeoman Ind Pk SO16
Yeoman Pk SO16
Yeomans La GU30
Yeomans Pl GU35
Yeomans Way SO40
Yeovil Cl GU14
Yeovil Rd GU14
Yerville Gdns SO41
Yetminster Rd GU14
Yew Cl RG20
Yew Tree Av PO8
Yew Tree Cl RG23
Yew Tree Gdns PO7
Yew Tree Pl GU33
Yoells Cres PO8
Yoells La PO8
Yonge Cl SO50
York Av BH25
York Bldgs SO14
York Cl, Bordon GU35
York Cl, Petersfield GU31
York Cl, Southampton SO14
York Cl, Totton SO40
York Cres GU11
York Mws GU34
York Pl, New Milton BH25
York Pl, Portsmouth PO1
York Rd, Aldershot GU11
York Rd, Eastleigh SO50
York Rd, Farnborough GU14
York St PO1
York Ter PO6
York Walk SO14
Yorke St PO5
Yorkwood GU33
Youngs Rd GU34

Zetland Rd PO12

Edition 104 L